MAJOR-GENERAL SIR AMYATT HULL, K.C.B.

[Frontispiece

THE 56th DIVISION

THE
FIFTY SIXTH
DIVISION

1st London Territorial Division

1914 – 1918

By
MAJOR C.H. DUDLEY WARD,
D.S.O., M.C.

With a Foreword by
GENERAL LORD HORNE OF STIRKOKE,
G.C.B., K.C.M.G.

PUBLISHED BY
THE NAVAL & MILITARY PRESS

Printed and bound by Antony Rowe Ltd, Eastbourne

TO THE MEMORY

OF

MAJOR-GENERAL
SIR CHARLES PATRICK AMYATT HULL,
K.C.B.

Born July 3rd, 1865
Died July 24th, 1920

FOREWORD

WHEN day broke on the 28th March, 1918, the 56th
London Territorial Division was in position on the
southern portion of the Vimy Ridge. At nightfall
the division still held its ground, having beaten back
three separate assaults delivered in great strength
by picked German troops specially trained in the
attack and inspired with confidence resulting from
the successes of the previous week. Truly a great
achievement, and important as great, for the Vimy
Ridge covered the city of Arras and the coalfields
of Béthune.

Important as this success was held to be at the
time, a time of great strain upon the forces of the
Empire, it was not till later on, when Ludendorff
took us into his confidence, that we learned its full
significance. Ludendorff gives us to understand that
the failure of the German effort of 28th March
constituted the turning-point of the 1918 campaign.
That evening Ludendorff recognised the beginning of
the end ; the German nation lost heart ; the *moral*
of the German Army deteriorated rapidly.

I have selected the above—one of the many achieve-
ments of the 56th London Territorial Division—to
illustrate the stage of efficiency to which the troops
of our Territorial Army had attained in war.

I saw much of our Territorial troops in France :

I had seen something of them in pre-war days, and I recall an absence of appreciation of the devotion of those whose patriotic enthusiasm put life into the great organisation evolved from the brain of a statesman to whom history will give the credit hitherto unworthily begrudged to Lord Haldane.

I take this opportunity of paying my tribute of respect and admiration to the Territorial Army as a whole, and the 56th London Division in particular.

This note would not be complete without reference to that fine soldier, the late Major-Gen. Sir Amyatt Hull, whose professional qualities and personal charm gained the respect and affection of all ranks, and who imbued with his own unconquerable spirit the officers and men of the division which he commanded so long, and of which he was so justly proud.

HORNE OF STIRKOKE,
General.

CONTENTS

FOREWORD BY GENERAL LORD HORNE OF STIRKOKE, G.C.B., K.C.M.G.

CHAPTER I

FORMATION AND THE ATTACK ON THE GOMMECOURT SALIENT

CHAPTER II

THE SOMME

CHAPTER III

LAVENTIE-RICHBOURG

CHAPTER IV

THE BATTLES OF ARRAS, 1917

CHAPTER V

YPRES

CHAPTER VI

CAMBRAI

CHAPTER VII

THE GERMAN OFFENSIVE

CHAPTER VIII

THE ADVANCE TO VICTORY

CHAPTER IX

THE ARMISTICE

Special thanks are due to Messrs. Hutchinson & Co., publishers of *My War Memories* 1914–1918, by Gen. Ludendorff, and *General Headquarters* 1914–1916, *and Its Critical Decisions*, by Gen. von Falkenhayn ; also to Messrs. Cassell & Co., publishers of *Out of My Life*, by Field-Marshal von Hindenburg, for permission to print extracts from these works.

LIST OF ILLUSTRATIONS

MAPS

THE FIFTY-SIXTH DIVISION

CHAPTER I

FORMATION AND THE ATTACK ON THE GOMMECOURT SALIENT

AFTER the declaration of war, when the first news of the Expeditionary Force began to trickle across the Channel, the people of England were told that troops were marching to the lilting tune with the Cockney refrain :

Good-bye, Piccadilly,
Farewell, Leicester Square,
It's a long, long way to Tipperary,
But my heart's right there.

Within a few months territorial battalions were marching in France and singing the same absurd song. But the London, the Cockney spirit, impudent, noisy, but good-tempered and friendly, always wide awake, observant, and ready for a scrap, above all never down-hearted, led the way from the very beginning of the war. It is with the light-hearted crowd of Piccadilly and Leicester Square that we are concerned, for the whole of London some time or other passes through those thoroughfares.

.   .   .   .

There is something peculiarly fascinating in following the fortunes of London troops, particularly Territorial troops.

For some reason there has been a tendency of late years to look down on the men of London, to dismiss them as weaklings, as men of poor physique, with maybe smart tongues and clothes, but without the necessary stamina for hardy soldiers. It would be difficult to say on what ground such an opinion was based. At least it has no historical foundation. The Trained Bands of London have a very definite place in the history of England.

Although it is not the oldest corps, the Artillery Company of London, formed to train men in the use of the long bow, cross bow, and hand gun, dates back to the time of Henry VIII. Westminster and the County of Middlesex were ever to the fore in raising Volunteers as distinct from the Militia, though the distinction was not always too clear. St. George's, Hanover Square—Pimlico—Inns of Court—Bloomsbury—St. James's are names to be found in every record of effort to meet a national danger. Enfield, Tottenham, Stoke Newington, Chelsea, Kensington, Chiswick, Battersea, Clapham, Clerkenwell, Deptford, Hungerford, Islington, Lambeth, and Wandsworth have all raised companies for the defence of England in former times of stress.

There is no need to labour the point. Every student of the history of the British Army knows what the Service owes to London. The Londoner has always proved himself a valiant soldier, and has not withheld from enlistment.

What England owes to the Territorial is above computation. As the descendant of the old Volunteer he was enrolled to serve in England alone. But when war with the Central Powers was declared he did not hesitate—his response was immediate and unanimous. Territorials landed in France in 1914, and continued to arrive in that country in a steady stream as they could be spared from Great Britain.

When the 56th Division was assembled in France during the first days of February 1916, it was not, therefore, a new unit, looking about with wondering eyes at new scenes, and standing, as it were, on the tiptoes of expectation as it paused on the outskirts of the great adventure. The twelve battalions of infantry were veterans.[1]

On the 5th February Major-Gen. C. P. A. Hull, to whom command of the new division was given, arrived at Hallencourt, between Abbeville and Amiens, where his staff was to meet.

Lieut.-Col. J. E. S. Brind .	G.S.O.1.
Major A. E. G. Bayley .	G.S.O.2.
Capt. T. W. Bullock . .	G.S.O.3.
Bt. Lieut.-Col. H. W. Grubb	A.A. and Q.M.G.
Capt. W. M. Sutton . .	D.A.A.G.
Major F. J. Lemon . .	D.A.Q.M.G.
Lieut. H. C. B. Way . .	A.D.C.

The presence of these officers, however, did not constitute a division. Brigade commanders and their staffs arrived—Brig.-Gen. F. H. Burnell-Nugent, 167th Brigade, Brig.-Gen. G. G. Loch, 168th Brigade, Brig.-Gen. E. S. Coke, 169th Brigade—and we find a wail of despair going up from the 169th Brigade: " No rations, fuel, or stationery yet available "— " No divisional organisation exists " (this on the 8th), and a wealth of meaning in this note written on the 18th : " The Brigade Interpreter (who should have

[1] Appendix A.

been available at first) arrived at last. Rain whole day." Could anything be more tragic ?

Our sympathies are entirely with the staff on these occasions, for though the situation cannot be described as chaotic, it is bewildering. Troops were arriving from all directions and at all times of the day ; the machinery was not in running order, and its creaking wheels, which occasionally stopped, necessitated the most careful watching and a great deal of work. When an organisation is being made, no one can say " that is not my job," for it seems as though all jobs are his for the time being. The Interpreter would have been most useful if only to arrange the billeting—and what is a staff officer without stationery ?

The Brigades were as follows :

The 167th Infantry Brigade ; commanded by Brig.-Gen. F. H. Burnell-Nugent, with Capt. G. Blewitt as his Brigade Major and Capt. O. H. Tidbury as Staff Captain. The battalions of this brigade were the 1/1st London Regt., the 1/3rd London Regt., the 1/8th Middlesex Regt., and the 1/7th Middlesex Regt.

The 168th Infantry Brigade ; commanded by Brig.-Gen. G. G. Loch, with Capt. P. Neame, V.C., as his Brigade Major, and Major L. L. Wheatley as Staff Captain. The battalions of this brigade were the 1/4th London Regt., the 1/12th London Regt. (Rangers), the 1/13th London Regt. (Kensingtons), and the 1/14th London Regt. (London Scottish).

The 169th Infantry Brigade ; commanded by Brig.-Gen. E. S. Coke, with Capt. L. A. Newnham as his Brigade Major, and Capt. E. R. Broadbent as Staff Captain. The battalions were the 1/2nd London Regt. (Royal Fusiliers), the 1/5th London Regt.

(London Rifle Brigade), the 1/9th London Regt. (Queen Victoria's Rifles), and the 1/16th London Regt. (Queen's Westminster Rifles).

It is not easy to keep the brigade groupings in mind at this stage—arrangements were recast and designations were changed. The 1/1st (London) Bde. R.F.A., the 2/1st (London) Field Coy. R.E., the 2/1st (London) Field Ambulance were posted to the 167th Brigade. The 1/2nd London Bde. R.F.A., the 2/2nd London Field Coy. R.E., and the 2/2nd London Field Ambulance were posted to the 168th Brigade. The 1/3rd London Bde. R.F.A. and the 2/3rd London Field Ambulance to the 169th Brigade. But we find that subsequent changes result in—

the 1/1st London Bde. R.F.A. becoming 280th Bde. R.F.A ;

the 1/2nd London Bde. R.F.A. becoming 281st Bde. R.F.A. ;

the 1/3rd London Bde. R.F.A. becoming 282nd Bde. R.F.A. ;

and a newly-formed 18-pounder brigade, the 283rd Bde. R.F.A. Also the two field companies of the Royal Engineers become known as the 512th and 513th Field Companies, and were joined by the 416th Edinburgh Field Coy., which was posted to the 169th Infantry Brigade.

And the Royal Army Service Corps, which appears at first as numbers 1, 2, 3, and 4 Companies, become the 213th, with the 214th, 215th, and 216th posted to the three infantry brigades in numerical order.

The Stokes trench mortar batteries were numbered 167th, 168th, and 169th ; the medium trench mortar batteries as X, Y, and Z. They were posted in numerical or alphabetical order to the infantry brigades. There was also a heavy trench mortar battery designated V Battery, which was formed in May 1916.

The pioneer battalion was the 1/5th Battalion Cheshire Regt. The veterinary unit was the 1/1st London Mobile Veterinary Section.

These were the bits of machinery forming the 56th Division.

The first divisional conference was held on the 11th February, when most of the officers attending had their first introduction to Gen. Hull. He was a tall, good-looking man with an abrupt manner, but of singular charm. It did not take him long to win the complete confidence of his division.

In the midst of the work of getting the machine properly fitted together, there were the usual rumours and warning orders which came to nothing. The first information Gen. Hull received was that the VI Corps, of which his division formed a part, would relieve the XVII French Corps and would move to the area Domart-en-Ponthieu. The move took place on the 27th February, in the midst of a heavy fall of snow, which made the roads very heavy for transport. And a further move was made on the 12th March to the Doullens area, between that town and St. Pol.

Whenever units were behind the line they trained. It did not matter how long the individual soldier had been in France and Belgium, he was never excused as a " fully trained soldier." Even instructors were sent from time to time to receive fresh instruction at Divisional, Corps, or Army schools. And so, during the period of assembly, the units of the 56th Division trained. Some were attached for ten days or a fortnight to the 14th Division for work in a " forward position " round about Dainville—infantry, artillery, engineers, and field ambulance took their turn at this work ; others carried on the routine of exercise on the training-grounds in the neighbourhood of their billets. The Commander-in-Chief, Sir Douglas Haig, visited the divisional area and the school at Givenchy on the 30th March.

In studying the adventures of a division, whether it is holding the line or whether it is in a reserve area, one must always visualise a great deal more than the twelve battalions of infantry which make or repel the final charge in any engagement. A division occupies and works over a large area, and depends, of course, on a base of supplies. When a person is told of the front taken up by a division, he will look at the map and measure off the width of the front line. " There," he says, " is the division " ! But the division covers quite a big area in depth as well. Not only do the billets of troops not actually employed in the front line go back a long way in successive stages, but the wagons and lorries of the Royal Army Service Corps work back many miles. The narrowest measurement of a divisional area is usually the front line.

Perhaps the following list, showing the dispositions of the division in billets during March, will give those with no experience some idea of what is meant by the word " division " :

Divisional Headquarters	Le Cauroy
Divisional Artillery Headquarters . . .	Le Cauroy
Divisional R.E. Headquarters . . .	Le Cauroy
5th Cheshire Regt.	Grand Rullecourt
B Squadron King Edward's Horse . .	Grand Rullecourt
Divisional Cyclists' Coy.	Grand Rullecourt

8   ATTACK ON GOMMECOURT SALIENT

1/4th London Howitzer Bde. . . .	Wamlin and Rozière
Divisional Ammunition Column . . .	Etrée-Wamin
Headquarters Divisional Train . . .	Bruilly
No. 1 Coy. Divisional Train . . .	Wamin
56th Sanitary Section	Le Cauroy
Mobile Veterinary Section	Bruilly
Salvage Company	Le Cauroy
R.E. Ordnance Dump	Le Cauroy
Divisional Canteen and Shops . . .	Le Cauroy
Divisional Schools	Givenchy-le-Noble

167TH INFANTRY BRIGADE

Brigade Headquarters	Rebreuve
167/1st and X56th	
Trench Mortar Batteries	Rebreuve
1/1st London Regt.	Ivergny
1/3rd London Regt.	Cannettemont
1/7th Middlesex Regt.	Beaudricourt
1/8th Middlesex Regt.	Rebreuviette
1/1st London Bde. R.F.A.	Rebreuve
2/1st London Field Coy. R.E. . . .	Honval
No. 2 Coy. Train	Rebreuviette
2/1st London Field Ambulance . . .	Ivergny

168TH INFANTRY BRIGADE

Brigade Headquarters	Manin
168/1st Trench Mortar Battery . . .	Magnicourt
Y56th Trench Mortar Battery . . .	Berlencourt
1/4th London Regt.	Beaufort
1/12th London Regt.	Ambrines
1/13th London Regt.	Lignereuil
1/14th London Regt.	Villers-sire-Simon
1/2nd London Bde. R.F.A.	Berlencourt
2/2nd London Field Coy. R.E. . . .	Sars-les-Bois
No. 3 Coy. Train	Denier
5th Entrenching Battalion	Blavincourt
2/2nd London Field Ambulance . . .	Liencourt

169TH INFANTRY BRIGADE

Brigade Headquarters	Houvin-Houvigneul
169/1st and Z56th Trench Mortar Batteries .	Houvin-Houvigneul
1/2nd London Regt.	Séricourt
1/5th London Regt.	Magnicourt
1/9th London Regt.	Houvigneul

1/16th London Regt.	Moncheaux
1/3rd London Bde. R.F.A.	Bouret-sur-Canche
No. 4 Coy. Train	Houvin-Houvigneul
2/3rd London Field Ambulance . . .	Houvin-Houvigneul
Divisional Supply Column	Liencourt
Divisional Ammunition Sub-Park . . .	Avesnes-le-Comte

All these units contribute to an advance. Some
designation, such as " shops," may strike the ear as
strange, an unlikely unit to help much in an advance ;
but a man cannot march without boots, a gun can
neither shoot nor advance with a broken spring, a
motor lorry will not bring up a single tin of " bully
beef " if its axle breaks, and all these things are put
right by men who are labelled " shops." Even the
Divisional Canteen plays its part, and has on occasions
pushed well forward to refresh wearied troops.

We say these units contribute to an advance !
They contribute to every action, to every move—
they are the division.

As a further measure, which will give the importance
of the unit rather than the size of it, the maximum
British effort was 99 infantry, 6 cavalry, and 4
yeomanry divisions (the latter were more often
infantry than cavalry).

The work of perfecting the organisation went on
through the months of February, March, and April.
The problem of how to create from nothing had
sometimes to be faced as the Army usually faces such
conundrums—by cutting a bit from something else
which did exist. Capt. Newnham notes in the
169th Brigade diary under date 17th April : " Brigade
Machine Gun Coy. formed. Capt. J. R. Pyper,
4th London, to command, and Capt. J. B. Baber,
Queen's Westminsters, second in command. Company
formed from existing personnel in battalions, each

battalion finding a section, and some from Headquarters. No M.G.C. gunners available, as per War
Office letter. Already weak battalions lose good men
and reinforcements will have to come from them as
well."

The health of the division was good except for an
outbreak of measles in the 169th Brigade.

On the 3rd May the 167th Brigade moved to
Souastre, under the VII Corps, and the rest of the
division followed on the 6th May, Divisional Headquarters being established at Hénu.

On the 9th May the C.R.A., Brig.-Gen. R. J. C.
Elkington, took over artillery positions from the
C.R.A. 14th Division on the Hébuterne front.

.   .   .   .

Three months had elapsed since the division had
commenced to assemble at Hallencourt. Troops
were well rested and trained, and were now to be
launched in the big operations of 1916. It would be
as well at this point to note the general situation, as
from now on the 56th Division took a prominent part
in the severe fighting which commenced on 1st July.

We will give the German point of view as expressed
by Gen. von Falkenhayn and published in his war
book [1] :

"France has been weakened almost to the limits of
endurance, both in a military and economic sense—
the latter by the permanent loss of the coalfields in
the north-east of the country. The Russian armies
have not been completely overthrown, but their
offensive powers have been so shattered that she can

[1] *General Headquarters, 1914-1916, and its Critical Decisions—*
Gen. von Falkenhayn.

never revive in anything like her old strength. The
armies of Serbia can be considered as destroyed.
Italy has no doubt realised that she cannot reckon on
the realisation of her brigand's ambitions within
measurable time, and would therefore probably be
only too glad to be able to liquidate her adventure in
any way that would save her face.

If no deductions can be drawn from these facts, the
reasons are to be sought in many circumstances . . .
the chief among them cannot be passed over, for it is
the enormous hold which England still has on her
allies."

He then goes on to discuss what can be done to
break the will of England. He says that the history
of the English wars against the Netherlands, Spain,
France, and Napoleon is being repeated. That
England is " obviously staking everything on a war
of exhaustion." He puts the winter of 1917 as the
latest date when a food crisis and " the social and
political crisis that always follow them, among the
members of our alliance," will occur, and asks, or
rather states, that England must be shown that her
venture has no prospects. But " in this case, of
course, as in most others involving higher strategic
decisions, it is very much easier to say what has to
be done than to find out how it can and must be
done."

How can one inflict a decisive defeat on England on
land ? Invasion is impossible—the German Navy
is convinced of that.

"As far as our own Continent of Europe is concerned,
we are sure of our troops, and are working with known
factors. For that reason we must rule out enterprises
in the East, where England can only be struck at

indirectly. Victories at Salonica, the Suez Canal, or
in Mesopotamia can only help us in so far as they
intensify the doubts about England's invulnerability
which have already been aroused among the Mediter-
ranean peoples and in the Mohammedan world.
Defeats in the East could do us palpable harm among
our allies. We can in no case expect to do anything
of decisive effect on the course of the war, as the pro-
tagonists of an Alexander march to India or Egypt, or
an overwhelming blow at Salonica, are always hoping.
Our allies have not the necessary means at their
disposal. We are not in a position to supply them,
owing to the bad communications, and England,
which has known how to swallow the humiliations of
Antwerp and Gallipoli, will survive defeats in those
distant theatres also.

When we turn from them to the European theatre,
where England can be struck on land, we cannot close
our eyes to the fact that we are faced with an extraordinarily difficult problem."

It would seem that England was giving poor von
Falkenhayn a lot of trouble. After looking vainly
in the East for a vulnerable point in her armour, he is
forced to turn his eyes to the West. And in the West
he does not like the look of the British Army. He
cannot collect more than twenty-five or twenty-six
divisions to attack with, and they are not nearly
enough !

" Attempts at a mass break-through, even with an
extreme accumulation of men and material, cannot be
regarded as holding out prospects of success against
a well-armed enemy whose *moral* is sound and who is
not seriously inferior in numbers. The defender has
usually succeeded in closing the gaps. The salients
thus made, enormously exposed to the effects of

flanking fire, threaten to become a mere slaughter-house. The technical difficulties of directing and supplying the masses bottled up in them are so great as to seem practically insurmountable."

He sweeps aside the idea of attacking the English Army with a final complaint that, even if he drove it completely from the Continent, "England may be trusted not to give up even then," and France would not have been very seriously damaged, so that a second operation would have to be taken against her. It would be impossible to get sufficient men.

England's allies are called her "tools," and the only thing to do is to smash up the "tools." But no weapon is to be discarded, and so unrestricted submarine warfare must be undertaken against this arch-enemy.

" If the definite promises of the Naval Authorities that the unrestricted submarine war must force England to yield in the course of the year 1916 are realised, we must face the fact that the United States may take up a hostile attitude. She cannot intervene decisively in the war in time to enable her to make England fight on when that country sees the spectre of hunger and many another famine rise up before her island. There is only one shadow on this encouraging picture of the future. We have to assume that the Naval Authorities are not making a mistake."

As for the "tools," Italy is ruled out as a possible one to be broken as she is not of much account in Falkenhayn's opinion, and he thinks there will soon be internal troubles. Russia is also ruled out because he does not see any gain in the capture of

Petrograd or Moscow, and there are also "internal troubles." There is France left.

"As I have already insisted, the strain on France has almost reached the breaking-point—though it is certainly borne with the most remarkable devotion. If we succeed in opening the eyes of her people to the fact that in a military sense they have nothing more to hope for, that breaking-point would be reached and England's best sword knocked out of her hand. . . . Within our reach behind the French sector of the Western Front there are objectives for the retention of which the French Staff would be compelled to throw in every man they have. If they do so the forces of France will bleed to death. . . . The objectives of which I am speaking now are Belfort and Verdun."

Altogether this document, which was prepared for the Kaiser and must have been read by that potentate with mixed feelings, was not the work of an optimist. It reads more like despair, as though Falkenhayn was saying, " I can still fight, I can still hurt, but I am bound to go down in the end " ! One cannot see any very shrewd reasoning in it, for he not only underrated the valour of the French (as the Germans always did), but he was placed in very serious difficulties by the successful attack of Brussiloff on the Austrians in June, so that he also undervalued the strength of Russia. For this misfortune, however, the Germans blame the Austrians, condemning them for their offensive against the Italians in May, which was undertaken against German advice and made the Brussiloff adventure possible. But this document shows the policy and plans of Germany for the year 1916—the great German effort on Verdun, which was to bleed France to death, dominates all other events. The attack was launched on the 21st February and coincides with the formation of the 56th Division, and the subsequent movements of the division were connected with the wide-spreading influence of the Verdun battle.

In his dispatch dated the 29th May, Sir Douglas Haig sums up the early situation very briefly. Since the 19th December, 1915,

" the only offensive effort made by the enemy on a great scale was directed against our French Allies near Verdun. The fighting in that area has been prolonged and severe. The results have been worthy of the highest traditions of the French Army and of great service to the cause of the Allies. The efforts made by the enemy have cost him heavy losses both in men and in prestige, and he has made these sacrifices without gaining any advantage to counterbalance them.

During the struggle my troops have been in readiness to co-operate as they might be needed, but the only assistance asked for by our Allies was of an indirect nature—viz., the relief of the French troops on a portion of their defensive front. This relief I was glad to be able to afford."

On the other hand, plans for a Franco-British offensive had been fully discussed by Sir Douglas Haig and Marshal Joffre and complete agreement arrived at. Vast preparations were in progress. Sir Douglas Haig desired to postpone the attack as long as possible, because both the British Army and the supply of ammunition were growing steadily, and time would enable the newer troops to complete their training. But though the original plans had no connection with Verdun, they were bound to influence and be influenced by the great German attack.

It may be said that the Entente Powers were not looking for a speedy termination of the war, but were bent on inflicting heavy blows on Germany and her allies, while Germany was seeking, by a concentration on France at Verdun, to gain a decision in the West. Falkenhayn's advice was being followed, although the unrestricted submarine warfare was postponed for the time being.

The plan for the British offensive was that the main attack should be delivered by the Fourth Army, under Sir Henry Rawlinson, on a front stretching from Maricourt, on the right, to Serre, on the left; while farther north the Third Army, under Sir E. H. H. Allenby, would make an attack on both sides of the Gommecourt salient.

For an offensive on this scale enormous preparations were necessary. There was no end to the amount of stores to be accumulated, from ammunition to horseshoes. In the forward trench system many miles of trenches had to be dug—assault trenches, assembly trenches, communication trenches, trenches for telephone wires—dugouts had to be constructed for sheltering troops, for dressing-stations, for storing food, water, and engineering material, not forgetting ammunition. We are bound to admit, however, that in those days, although much work was done on dugouts, the infantry saw precious little of them. Mining they saw, indeed, but dugouts were rare.

Then there were dumps to be made at convenient points, and many miles of railway line, both standard and narrow gauge, to bring the stores within reach of the fighting troops. Roads had to be constructed, and in some places causeways had to be built over marshy valleys. Wells were sunk, over a hundred pumping stations were installed, and a hundred and twenty miles of water-mains laid.

The whole country behind this vast front was teeming with men and horses, with wagons and motor lorries. At night it was as though an army of gigantic ants were at work, stretched out in long lines, building and excavating, marching in solemn silent processions with grim, determined purpose in the slowness of their gait, and bowed down under loads of material. They passed and repassed in never-ending streams ; the roads were congested with motor and wagon traffic ; paths across the open country could be traced by the shadowy silhouettes of men in single file. And the horizon flickered with the flash of guns as with summer lightning, while shells passed overhead with a long-drawn, ghostly wail, or fell with a sharp swish and a crash. The line, that maze of foul mud-filled ditches constructed in a belt of shell-pounded and festering earth, was indicated at night by floating starlights rising irregularly as sparks, bursting into brilliancy, and remaining for a moment, suspended in the blackness of the sky like arc lamps, then dying once more to so many sparks before they fell to the ground.

Sometimes the nights would be quiet—that is to say, quiet except for occasional crashes at intervals of several minutes—although the constant flickering on the horizon would never cease ; at others they would be " lively," one might almost say there would be a sensation of hustle, so swift would be the wailing passage and so continuous the crash of bursting shells. This might last all through the night as an organised " shoot," or would come suddenly, without warning, a swift artillery attack on roads, working parties, or billets—what was afterwards known as "harassing fire" though it was in a more intense form—and shifting from one point to another, from front line to roads, from roads to billets, from billets to some spot where troops were suspected to be working. Or there would be a raid with an angry concentration of artillery from both sides.

And night after night the preparation for the "Big Push" went on.

.   .   .   .   .   .

The 56th Division, now trained and "shaken together," arrived in the Hébuterne sector, on the right of the Gommecourt salient and towards the left of the front under preparation for the British effort. The 167th Brigade took over the front-line system held by the 145th Brigade, 48th Division, on the 4th May. The 168th Brigade marched from their billets in the Doullens area on the 6th, and the 169th Brigade followed on the 7th May. Divisional Headquarters were established at Hénu.

First blood was drawn for the division by the 167th Brigade on the 18th May. A German patrol attempted to bomb a sap held by the 3rd London Regt., and was beaten off with the loss of one officer and one N.C.O. killed. These proved to be of the 169th Infantry Regt., 52nd Division, one of the divisions of the XIV German Corps and a normal identification.

The system of holding the line was one of "grouping." On the 22nd May Brig.-Gen. Coke, 169th Brigade, was in command of the line, which was held by two battalions of the 169th Brigade and two battalions of the 168th Brigade. In support was Brig.-Gen. Nugent, with his headquarters at

Souastre, having under his command his own four battalions and one of the 169th Brigade. Brig.-Gen. Loch, 168th Brigade, with his headquarters at Grenas, had two of his own battalions and one of the 169th Brigade.

Plans were now in preparation for a very remarkable achievement.

We have seen that the scheme for the big British offensive included an attack on the Gommecourt salient. This was to be undertaken by the Third Army, and the task fell to the VII Corps (Gen. Snow), holding the front in question. For the moment we will confine ourselves to the point that the 56th Division was to be one of the attacking divisions.

When Gen. Hull was informed of what he was expected to do, he was at once confronted with an obvious difficulty—the front line of his sector was some seven hundred yards away from the enemy! It was not impossible to shorten this distance, but, with one exception, the several ways of doing it must result in heavy casualties; the enemy would be bound to see what was afoot, and would try by every means in his power to prevent and to hinder its execution, and render it as costly as he could. It would also be a lengthy business unless it was boldly tackled. Gen. Hull decided on the boldest of all courses.

He traced out a new line which was, on an average, four hundred yards in advance of the old one. This meant working, in some spots, within two hundred and fifty yards of the enemy. *And he decided to dig it in one night!* It meant that at least three thousand yards of trench must be constructed in a few hours, a task of appalling magnitude; and it must be remembered that every effort was always made to limit the number of men in any working party required for No Man's Land. When he announced his intentions there was something like consternation at Corps Headquarters.

The task was allotted to Brig.-Gen. Nugent and the 167th Brigade. He had at his disposal, over and above the five battalions of his " group," one company of the 5th Cheshire Regt. with a half of the 2/2nd London Field Coy. R.E.

So that the men might know the lie of the land, the 167th Brigade was sent on ahead of the rest of the division and straight into the line, which it held for a fortnight. The Engineers, the company officers of battalions concerned, and the brigade staff made most careful reconnaissance, patrolling every night, noting landmarks, getting acquainted with that silent, eerie tract separating the two lines of combatants. Conversations throughout the day were punctuated with references to " the strong point," " the lonely tree," the " May bush," " the Z hedge," " the head of Sap 4," as landmarks became familiar. Sometimes German patrols were met, sometimes imagined.

It was decided to divide the whole front into four sections—A, B, C, and D. The only difficulty was the junction between B and C, but this was eventually marked by a heap of white stones—a small heap.

Four days before the date fixed for the operation, the brigade was relieved, and during the following days the whole of the arrangements were rehearsed— with the exception of the actual digging—first by day and then by night.

Meanwhile the artillery were warned that nothing was to be done by them to rouse the enemy while the work was being carried out, but that all batteries must be manned and ready for instant action. All known machine-gun emplacements were carefully registered, and arrangements were made with the Brigadier-General commanding the Corps heavy artillery to register on all German batteries whose zone of fire included the area of the work. Two of the Divisional 4·5 howitzers were to assist in the counter-battery work.

Although the trench was dug in one night, the whole operation required three nights to complete. On the first night, the 25–26th May, covering parties crept out and took up positions in advance of the selected line. Then engineers followed, quiet and certain in all that they did, and marked out the line with string and pegs. On the left they got to work speedily : the pegs were about nine inches long and made from small round stakes from which the bark had not been removed ; the string was ordinary jute twine which had been prepared with loops at the proper intervals to mark the angle of bays and traverses. They were undisturbed, and C and D sections were marked out.

But in A and B sections the night was one of excursions and alarms. First of all there was great difficulty in getting the covering party through our own wire, which suggests an unfortunate oversight ; and then German patrols were encountered. The latter occurrence was a contingency which had always been reckoned with. A game of hide and seek ensued, but meanwhile time passed. There was no question of clearing No Man's Land when other parties were working on the left, and so the marking had to be abandoned. It did not, however, cause any serious inconvenience.

The next night each battalion marched from billets

fully armed for digging. Ten per cent. carried picks, and the remainder carried shovels which had been carefully sharpened. Each man had three sandbags, one being wrapped round the shovel or pick to prevent noise, and between them they also carried a quantity of white tape.

In the line ten exits had been made by cutting through our wire and constructing steps out of the trench—trench ladders had also been provided by the engineers in case the steps should be impassable through rain. White boards were hung on the wire to mark these gaps for the withdrawal.

The communication trenches to be used by the working battalions were left quite clear by the troops holding the line, and, at the appointed time, the head of each battalion was at the selected entrance and advanced in the following order : covering parties, taping parties, working parties.

The covering parties, consisting of sixty officers and men in six groups, had orders to use rifle fire as sparingly as possible, but to make full use of the bayonet if enemy patrols were encountered.

When the covering parties had been given time to get out, the two other groups of parties followed at short intervals. And half an hour after the digging parties had left the trench, wiring and carrying parties, about a hundred men to each battalion, went out. There were three thousand men in No Man's Land !

The boldness of Gen. Hull's enterprise was amply justified. By 2.30 a.m. the trench had been made and was held by posts, found from the covering parties, reinforced with Lewis guns ; they had rations, water, and shovels to improve their positions, and were in telephonic communication with the old trench, and all the working parties had filed away as silently as they had come.

During the ensuing day the Royal Flying Corps successfully prevented any enemy aeroplanes from approaching our lines, but our airmen photographed the new line themselves, and at noon Gen. Hull was able to see from a photograph what work had been done.

On the night of 27–28th the same number of men were out working again, improving the front-line trench and wire, digging support lines and two other communication trenches. The new work had been pegged out the previous night by the engineers.

The 56th Division had then started its career with the astounding feat of having in the space of forty-eight hours constructed and wired a new system of trenches, comprising 2,900 yards of fire trench and 1,500 yards of communication trenches, in No Man's Land and within 250 yards of the enemy. Casualties were 8 killed and 55 wounded. A little luck had waited on audacity, but the success of the whole operation was undoubtedly due to the intelligence and keenness of the men. They had nothing much to help them. Gen. Hull had, indeed, ordered two or three wagons, loaded with empty shell-cases and biscuit tins, to drive up and down the roads in rear of his lines, and the artillery fired an occasional round from a howitzer as a means of distracting the attention of the enemy, but it only required one foolish man to lose his head and disaster would have descended on the whole brigade.

It is interesting to note the dress. The covering parties were in full fighting kit and carried one day's ration ; the taping, digging, and wiring men had no equipment, but carried a rifle, loaded with ten rounds, and one bandolier ; the wire-carrying party had no arms or equipment.

The first stage was over. There was, however, still an enormous lot of work to be done—the trenches had to be improved, deepened, revetted, emplacements had to be made for machine guns and trench mortars, stores for ammunition of all sorts had to be constructed, cables had to be buried—it is but a repetition of what was going on everywhere on that front.

.   .   .   .   .   .

Gen. Hull and his G.S.O.1, Lieut.-Col. J. E. S. Brind, an artilleryman, were considering the problem of attack.   The main features of it are noted by Gen. Hull as follows :

(a) The village of Hébuterne, which affords concealment from view to within a short distance of our present line and good observation of the German positions between Gommecourt and the spur north of the sunken road (K17a and b) on the right of the divisional front.

(b) The valleys west of Hébuterne, which afford good artillery positions and cover from view, except from the trees in Gommecourt Park.

(c) The spur running eastward from Hébuterne just north of the Hébuterne-Puisieux Road, which defilades the area, north of the spur, from the German trenches, south of the spur.

(d) Gommecourt Park and village, which, to a certain extent, dominate the ground to the south.

(e) The spur running from E29c (north-east of Gommecourt) through K5a and b to the Rossignol Wood along the southern portion of which spur runs the German fourth line.

This spur commands the eastern edge of Gommecourt, dominates the German trench system south-east and south of Gommecourt, and affords concealment, both for battery positions in the valley to the east and for a covered means of approach for a counter-attack against the captors of Gommecourt.

(f) The valley south-east of Nameless Farm, in which runs the Puisieux-Gommecourt Road, a line of approach covered from view from our present line.

It was once asked after a severe action for the capture of some rising ground, " What is the use of turning Fritz off a hill ? There is always another hill behind it." Which was true enough. But it is as well to remember that the high ground to the left as far as Blairville, held at this date by the Germans, was in 1918 in our hands, and it enabled Sir Douglas Haig to turn the whole of the old Somme position.

Of the German line Gen. Hull says :

" The German position south-east of Gommecourt Park and village consists of three lines of trenches, of which the first is heavily wired, the second lightly wired, the third does not appear to be wired at all unless there is sunken wire on the road. All three lines are visible from our present position except the second and third lines behind the strong point K11c and d. The northern flank of this system of trenches rests on the southern edge of Gommecourt Park, the trenches along which are organised to fire south. The southern flank of the system rests on the strong point K11c.

In rear of this system is another consisting of two lines of trenches running from the south-east corner of Gommecourt along the ridge in 5Ka, b, and c, to Rossignol Wood. The front trench of this system is heavily wired and visible."

In a most interesting paper on the proposed attack Gen. Hull says :

" The object of the VII Corps attack will be to establish itself on the line 16 Poplars–Nameless Farm–Little Z–Tree at E23a12.

The 46th Division will attack from the north and the question was discussed :

    (a) Should we endeavour to secure a footing on the ridge E29c–K5a in the initial assault, or

    (b) Should the 56th Division first secure the German third line from the south-east corner of Gommecourt Wood and then, under Corps direction, launch a second attack to secure the ridge ?

Whichever solution the Corps Commander considers it wisest to adopt, there is one point which I wish to urge : that no advance through the village or park of Gommecourt should be attempted until the ridge E29c–K5a is secured.

The clearing of the village and wood is bound to be a costly enterprise if the enemy makes any attempt to fight it out. It is to be hoped that the heavy bombardment will very seriously affect the *moral* of the garrison of the village and park, and I consider that the knowledge that they were cut off from escape and from reinforcements might have so great an effect on the German troops as to make them surrender and so save us valuable troops for further operations.

I was, and still am, in favour of the first solution, i.e. to secure the Quadrilateral in the first assault. The reasons which have been urged against this course are:

    (a) That at Loos no success was achieved after a certain limited distance had been carried.

    (b) That in the event of either the 46th or the 56th Divisions failing to achieve their objective, the detachment of the other would be in an extremely isolated position.

I have carefully considered both these arguments, and do not think there is any reason to alter my opinion.

At Loos the 47th Division was the only division to which a definite objective was given. Its rôle was to form a defensive flank on the right of the IV Corps. Its left flank advanced nearly 2,500 yards behind the German front line without serious loss or difficulty. In the present case I am proposing an advance, at one point on each divisional front, of only 800 yards, in the case of the 56th Division, and less in the case of the 46th Division. In the present case, too, we have the additional advantage of much heavier artillery, more ammunition, and a salient to attack.

As regards the second argument, that in the event of one or other attack failing the detachment of the other division would be isolated :

In the event of my reaching my objective in K5a, and the 46th Division failing to reach E29c, I should consider it my duty to put in troops (if necessary from my reserve brigade) to help the 46th Division.

Troops at K5a would be within 500 yards of the unit at the south-eastern edge of Gommecourt, and in direct communication by visual signalling with my present trench system, so that they can hardly be considered isolated, and the risk, if any, is, I consider, worth running in order to isolate completely the enemy troops in Gommecourt Park and village.

I do not like the idea of delay and a second attack to capture the Quadrilateral in K5a. The second attack would have to be launched from our front line trenches, as I do not consider it would be feasible to organise and launch an attack from the newly-captured trenches. Any delay would enable the enemy to put his barrage in front of our front-line system, as if there is a weak point in our organisation, it is in the number of counter-batteries available to deal with the enemy guns. If we delay we lose the advantage surprise would give us."

While these problems were being discussed, Sir Douglas Haig had decided to hurry on his preparations. We have seen that his desire was to delay as much as possible and perfect his machine, also that every day meant to him added strength. But meanwhile the Entente Powers were being pressed in another direction. The Austrians had attacked the Italians with great initial success. By the end of May the situation on that front was so serious that the Russian offensive was opened in the early days of June in order to relieve the pressure.

The Germans accuse the Austrians of having drained their front in Galicia of artillery for their Italian offensive, and also of holding the line with troops of poor quality. However that may be, Gen. Brussiloff's army, " after a relatively short artillery preparation . . . got up from their trenches and simply marched forward." Falkenhayn has a delightful observation on the whole business : " A ' reconnaissance ' like Brussiloff's was only possible, of course, if the General had decisive reason for holding a low opinion of his enemy's power of resistance. And on this point he made no miscalculation."

The immediate effect of the Russian success was the transfer of three divisions from the Western Front, and later more followed ; but the Germans were still very strong in numbers, and there was no slacking off of their efforts on Verdun. They were able to help the Austrians to check the Russian advance and eventually to repulse it, but, on the other hand, the Italian counter-attack met with success and drove the Austrians back.

Sir Douglas Haig says that

"The heroic defence of our French Allies had already

gained many weeks of inestimable value and had caused the enemy very heavy losses ; but the strain continued to increase. In view, therefore, of the situation in the various theatres of war, it was eventually agreed between Gen. Joffre and myself that the combined French and British offensive should not be postponed beyond the end of June. The object of that offensive was threefold :

(1) To relieve the pressure on Verdun.
(2) To assist our Allies in the other theatres of war by stopping any further transfer of German troops from the Western Front.
(3) To wear down the strength of the forces opposed to us."

We begin to see now the dominating influence of Verdun. In any case the offensive could not have been postponed much longer, and if it was an alteration of plan forced by the enemy, it was not to be compared with the abandonment by the Germans of their offensive—which Falkenhayn says he had prepared against the British with the object of forestalling the Entente blow on the Western Front—due to the uncomfortable situation of the Austrians.

Probably, however, the date did influence the approaching action of the 56th Division. The new front line was still a long way from the enemy. The Queen's Westminster Rifles succeeded in advancing a small sector of the line by a hundred yards and, had there been time, the whole division would have crept closer before jumping on the enemy.

The weather, too, was very bad.

In due course Gen. Hull issued his preliminary instructions, from which it will be seen that the decision to attempt the capture of the Quadrilateral in one operation had been taken :

" The attack of the 56th Division will be carried out by the 168th and 169th Brigades, whose tasks will be as follows :

(a) The objective of the 168th Brigade will be to capture the German line from Fair Trench, about K11d13, along Farm, Fame and Elbe, Felon, to a point in Fell fifty yards north-west of the trench junction at K5c52, and to establish itself in three strong points :

(1) About Farmyard, Farmer, Farm.
(2) About Elbe, between Et and Felon.
(3) About cross-trenches of Fell and Felon with Epte.

168th Brigade will be responsible for the construction of a fire trench facing south-east to connect the right flank of the captured line to our present line in W47.

(b) The task of the 169th Brigade will be carried out in three phases. The object of the 169th Brigade in the first phase will be to capture the line of German trenches from the left of the 168th Brigade along Fall, Fellow, the Cemetery, Eck, the Maze, Eel, and Fir, and to establish strong points :

(1) From Feud through Ems to the Cemetery inclusive.
(2) About the Maze.
(3) About the south-east corner of Gommecourt Park.

The second phase of the 169th Brigade attack will take place immediately after the first phase.

The objective of the second phase is the Quadrilateral of the trenches in the south-east portion of K5a. The artillery lifts will be timed on the assumption that the infantry will reach Ems (between Etch and Fillet) twenty-five minutes after zero ; and Exe (between Etch and Fillet) twenty-seven minutes after zero time.

The third phase will take place directly after the Quadrilateral is captured, and will consist of the securing of the cross-trenches at K5a78 (where Indus crosses Fill and Fillet) and joining hands with the 46th Division along Fill. Fillet will be consolidated facing east.

The following will be carried on the man :

    200 rounds S.A.A. ;
    Waterproof sheet ;
    Haversack ;
    Iron ration and current day's ration ;
    Two to three sand-bags ;
    Two tube helmets ;
    Proportion of wire-cutters, bill-hooks, tools."

The instructions for the 167th Brigade are practically embodied in the following paragraphs :

" One company 167th Brigade will be placed at the disposal of the Brigadier-General commanding 169th Brigade, to hold sectors Y49 and Y50.

Seven officers and 200 men of the 167th Brigade will be detailed for the control of smoke, and will be under the orders of the Divisional Gas Officer. Approximately 1,200 men will be required for work under the C.R.E. on communication trenches across No Man's Land and for carrying parties."

Practice attacks, based on these instructions, were carried out by the brigades in reserve.

We have written of the constructive preparations which were going on all along the line of proposed attack. These preparations were continued until the last moment. But meanwhile another element was introduced—that of destructive preparation. It is scarcely necessary to point out that neither form of preparation could be concealed from the enemy. The Germans knew as well as we did where we would attack.

The Gommecourt sector to be attacked was held
by the German 169th and 170th Regiments, with
about 1½ battalions on the front line, 1 battalion in
support, 2 battalions in reserve in Bucquoy, and
2 companies at Ablainzeville. Their artillery consisted of 5 batteries of heavy artillery and 12 batteries
of field artillery. These batteries were divided into
three groups at Quesnoy Farm, on the left of the
British position, Biez Wood and Puisieux. There
was a further group of guns near Adinfer Wood which
could assist in the defence.

The 56th Divisional Artillery, together with the
heavy VII Corps guns, had now to prepare for the
infantry assault by smashing up not only the wire
and trench system, but billets and gun positions
behind the German lines as well. As regards
villages, most attention was given to Bucquoy,
Essart, Ablainzeville, and Achiet-le-Grand.

Three groups of artillery were formed—a northern
group, under Lieut.-Col. Southam, a southern group,
under Lieut.-Col. Macdowell, and a wire-cutting
group under Lieut.-Col. Prechtel. The northern and
southern groups were under the orders of the Corps,
and consisted of :

NORTHERN GROUP

3 batteries of 18-pounders (until zero day, then 4
    batteries).
1 battery 4·5 howitzers.
Affiliated at zero to the 169th Brigade.

SOUTHERN GROUP

4 batteries of 18-pounders.
1 battery 4·5 howitzers.
Affiliated at zero to the 168th Brigade.

WIRE-CUTTING GROUP

5 batteries of 18-pounders until zero and then 4
batteries.

1 battery 4·5 howitzers.

Two of the guns of the 4·5 battery will be at the call
of the counter-battery group.

In the preliminary instructions it will be noticed
that a party of officers and men were detailed to act
under the Divisional Gas Officer. Their special duty
was to cover the approach of the infantry by the
discharge of a smoke cloud. It was hoped to
introduce some element of surprise by occasional
discharges of smoke during the preparatory bombardment, and so the Corps ordered that the bombardment should be carried out for a period of five
days, and the attack would take place on the
sixth. These days would be known as U, V, W, X,
Y, and Z days.

"Smoke discharges lasting for a period of ten
minutes will take place on the days and at the hours
mentioned below. They will coincide with the intense
artillery bombardment of the enemy trenches. These
bombardments will commence thirty minutes before
the smoke, and will reach their maximum intensity
during the ten minutes that it is being discharged :

U day, no discharge.
V day, no discharge.
W day from 10.15 a.m. to 10.25 a.m.
X day from 5.45 a.m. to 5.55 a.m.
Y day from 7.15 a.m. to 7.25 a.m.

On Z day the smoke cloud will commence five
minutes before zero. On the 46th and 56th Divisional fronts its duration will be as arranged by

4

divisions. On the 37th Divisional front it will continue for one hour."

U day was the 24th June, but the whole of the great attack was postponed for two days, so that, instead of having five days of the preliminary bombardment, there were seven.

Naturally the Germans did not sit still under this destructive fire, but retaliated on our front line and trench system, and on our rear organisation. The enemy artillery had been active during the month of May, and the division had suffered in casualties to the extent of 402 ; for the month of June casualties leapt up to 801. The end of June was a prolonged crash of guns. Only for one half-hour, from 4 p.m., did the guns cease so that aeroplanes might take photographs of the German lines, and then the sky was speckled with the puffs of smoke from the German anti-aircraft guns.

The guns of the 56th Division fired altogether 115,594 rounds, of which 31,000 were fired on Z day. To this total must be added the work of the Corps heavy artillery. The 6-inch, 9·2-inch, and 15-inch fired on V day 3,200 rounds, on W day 2,200 rounds, on X day 3,100 rounds, and on Y day 5,300 rounds (which was repeated on the two extra days) at the front-line trenches and strong points. 6-inch, 9·2-inch, 4·7-inch, 4·5-inch, and 60-pounder guns also dealt with the villages of Bucquoy, Achiet-le-Grand, Essart, and Ablainzeville, but in nothing like the same proportion of rounds.

The first smoke cloud was discharged on the 26th June, and drew very little hostile machine-gun fire. The enemy lines were reported to be much damaged on that day. On the 27th the smoke discharge was somewhat spoilt by the premature bursting of a smoke shell an hour before the appointed time. This misfortune caused the enemy to put down a barrage on our front-line and communication trenches, which prevented the smoke detachments getting to their appointed positions. When the cloud was eventually discharged there was a large gap in the centre of it, so it must have been obvious to the enemy that it was only a feint.

The continual bombardment became more intense, and the enemy reply more vigorous. On the 28th the enemy wire was reported as satisfactorily cut in front of their first and second lines. Observers also noted that there was considerable movement of troops behind the German lines.

Every night, the moment it was dark, although the artillery still pounded trenches, roads, and tracks, patrols crept forward to ascertain what progress had been made in the battering down of defences. 2/Lieut. P. Henri, of the 3rd London Regt., raided the front line. He found the Germans working feverishly to repair their trench, and succeeded in capturing one prisoner, who proved to be of the Labour Battalion of the 2nd Reserve Guards Division. He reported that the wire in some places still formed a considerable obstacle.

A patrol of the 1st London Regt. reported, on the 29th, that new French wire and some strands of barbed wire had been put up. Up to the last moment the Germans worked at their defences. Great activity was seen on the morning of the 30th.

The artillery grew more furious. A hail from heavy and field-gun batteries descended on trenches

and strong points.   Lieut.-Col. Prechtel's wire-cutting
group pounded away at the wire.   The trench mortar
batteries added their quota, though they were chased
from pillar to post by German retaliation.   And as the
evening shadows fell on the last day, the usual night
firing was taken up by the never-wearying gunners.

.   .   .   .   .

The main object of this attack was to divert
against the VII Corps enemy artillery and infantry,
which might otherwise have been used against the
left flank of the Fourth Army at Serre.   To achieve
this result the two divisions, 46th and 56th, were
given the task of cutting off the Gommecourt salient.

From the 24th to the 30th June the line of the
56th Division was held by the 167th Brigade.   The
other two brigades then practised the assault on a
replica of the German defence system near Halloy.
In the early morning of the 1st July the 168th and
169th Brigades took over the line, and the 167th
withdrew to Hébuterne.

The 5th Cheshire Regt. had a company with each
of the assaulting brigades ; the Royal Engineers sent
a section of the 2/1st London Field Coy. with the
169th Brigade, and a section of the 2/2nd London
Field Coy. with the 168th Brigade.

The London Scottish attacked on the right with
the Kensingtons in support ; then came the Rangers
with the 4th London Regt. in support.   The rôle of
these battalions of the 168th Brigade may be briefly
described as a half-wheel to the right.   They had to
capture the strong point round about Farm and
Farmer trenches, and establish other strong points at
Elbe and Et, south-east of Nameless Farm, and the
junction of Felon and Epte.

On the extreme left of the division was the London
Rifle Brigade, and next to them the Queen Victoria's
Rifles. Again as a rough indication of their task,
they had to make a left wheel and hold the line of
the edge of Gommecourt Park, establishing strong
points. The Queen's Westminster Rifles would then
push straight on, carrying the attack forward, as it
were, between the right and left wheels, and capture
the strong point known as the Quadrilateral.

At 6.25 a.m. every gun opened on the German
lines, and for one hour the enemy was pelted with
shells of all sizes, the maximum speed of fire being
reached at 7.20 and lasting for ten minutes. At this
moment smoke was discharged from the left of our
line near Z hedge, and in five minutes the smoke was
dense along the whole front. Then the assaulting
battalions climbed out of their trenches and advanced
steadily into the heavy fog.

The German front line was reached with little loss—
there was machine-gun fire, but it was apparently
high. Almost immediately, however, the Germans
gave an indication of their counter-measures—they
were reported by the London Scottish to be shelling
their own line. This gallant regiment succeeded in
gaining practically the whole of its objectives, but
they were never very comfortable. Owing to the
smoke the two left companies lost direction, the flank
company being drawn off in the direction of Nameless
Farm, and the inner company failed to recognise its
position and overran its objective. This was in no
way surprising, as it was extremely difficult, owing
to the heavy bombardment, to find, in some places,
any trench at all.

Next to the London Scottish the Rangers met with

strong resistance, and probably strayed a bit to their
left. They were soon in trouble, and two companies
of the 1/4th London Regt. were sent forward to
reinforce them. Together these two units succeeded
in reaching the junction of Epte with Felon and Fell,
but there was a gap between them and the London
Scottish.

On the left of the attack the London Rifle Brigade
had swept up to the edge of Gommecourt Park and
commenced to consolidate their position. The Queen
Victoria's Rifles, on the other hand, were meeting
with fierce resistance, and were short of the Cemetery.
The Queen's Westminster Rifles, advancing in rear,
soon became hopelessly mixed up with the Queen
Victoria's Rifles. Within an hour it became clear
that the infantry were everywhere engaged in hand-
to-hand fighting.

The German counter-attack plans matured about
an hour after the assault was launched. Their barrage on No Man's Land was increased to fearful
intensity, and from Gommecourt Park, which was
apparently packed with men in deep dugouts, came
strong bombing attacks. The London Rifle Brigade
called for reinforcements, but platoons of the reserve
company failed to get through the barrage and
across to the German front line.

The assaulting companies had been provided with
boards bearing the names of the trenches to be
captured, and as they fought their way forward, these
boards were stuck up to mark the advance. At
about 9.30 a.m. the artillery observers, who did most
useful and gallant work during the whole action,
could report that all objectives were gained with the
exception of the Quadrilateral. But the troops in the

German lines were now held there firmly by the
enemy barrage ; they were cut off from all communication by runners, and from all reinforcements. On
the right the Kensingtons had failed in an attempt
to reinforce the London Scottish. Captain Tagart,
of the former regiment, had led his company out, but
was killed, and of the two remaining officers, one was
killed and the other wounded. A confused message
having reached headquarters, a fresh officer was sent
down with orders to rally the men and make another
attempt to cross the inferno of No Man's Land. He
found that there were only twenty men left, and
that to cross with them was impossible.

The Royal Flying Corps contact machine, detailed
to report on the situation, sent constant messages
that the Quadrilateral was empty of troops of either
side. The artillery observers, however, reported
seeing many parties of hostile bombers moving
through the Park, and enemy troops collecting behind
the Cemetery.

It seemed as though all battalions had at one time
gained their objectives except the Queen's Westminster Rifles, but no blame falls on this fine regiment. Lieut.-Col. Shoolbred says in his report,
" As no officer who got as far as this (first line) ever
returned, it is difficult to know in detail what happened." The three captains, Cockerill, Mott, and
Swainson, were killed before reaching the second
German line. Apparently the wire on this section
of the front was not satisfactorily dealt with. The
report says :

" A great deal of the wire was not cut at all, so that
both the Victorias and ourselves had to file in, in

close order, through gaps, and many were hit. . . .
The losses were heavy before reaching the bank at
the Gommecourt–Nameless Farm road. At this point
our three companies and the two Victorias were
joined up and intermixed. . . . Only one runner ever
succeeded in getting through from the assaulting
companies."

There were a few brave young officers of the
Queen's Westminsters left at this point—2/Lieuts.
J. A. Horne, A. G. V. Yates, A. G. Negus, D. F.
Upton, E. H. Bovill. They proceeded to collect their
men and lead them forward, and while doing this
2/Lieuts. Yates and Negus were killed. 2/Lieut.
Upton, having then reorganised a bombing party,
bombed the enemy out of Fellow and reached the
Cemetery. To do this they had to run over the open
and drop into Fellow. Another party tried at the
same time to bomb their way up Etch, but found it
was too strongly held by the enemy. Meanwhile,
2/Lieut. Upton had stuck up his signboard, and more
men doubled up over the open and dropped into
Fellow Trench. 2/Lieut. Horne then mounted a
Lewis gun, under cover of which a platoon of the
Cheshire Regt. and some Royal Engineers blocked
Etch and also Fell (it would seem doubtful, from this
statement, whether Fell was ever held).

Sergt. W. G. Nicholls had kept a party of bombers
together and, led by a young lieutenant of the
Cheshire Regt., whose name unfortunately is not
mentioned [we believe it was 2/Lieut. G. S. Arthur],
this party forced its way from the Cemetery to the
Quadrilateral. The names of some of the men are
given by Col. Shoolbred :

" Cpl. R. T. Townsend, L/Cpl. W. C. Ide, Cpl. Hayward, Rfn. F. H. Stow undoubtedly did reach the Quadrilateral, where strong enemy bombing parties met them, and the Cheshire lieutenant ordered the party to retire, apparently trying to cover their retirement himself, as he was not seen again."

In any case this advance into the Quadrilateral was but a momentary success, and it may be said that the attack never got beyond the German third line. Signals were picked up by the artillery observers calling for bombs. As early as 10 a.m. two parties of London Scottish, each fifty strong, attempted to take bombs across to their comrades. None got to the German first line, and only three ever got back to ours.

About midday the enemy was launching concerted counter-attacks from all directions. He was coming down Epte, Ems, and Etch, he was coming from Gommecourt Park, he was in Fall on the right. More desperate attempts were made to reinforce the hard-pressed troops. Capt. P. A. J. Handyside, of the 2nd London Regt., led his company out to try and reach the left of the line. He was hit, but struggled on. He was hit again and killed as he led a mere half-dozen men into the German first line.

Capt. J. R. Garland, also of the 2nd London Regt., attempted the same feat with his company, and met with a like fate. All the officers of both companies were casualties.

At 2 p.m. the London Scottish still held firm on the right and the London Rifle Brigade on the left—indeed, 2/Lieut. R. E. Petley, with thirty men, hung on to Eck three hours after the rest of his battalion had been ordered to fall back on Ferret, the German first line. But, although the two flanks held, the troops in the centre were gradually forced back until isolated posts were held in the second German line. By 4 p.m. nothing more was held than the German first line.

By 9 p.m. everyone who could get there was back in our own lines.

But we must not leave our account of the fighting with the story of the 46th Division untold. It was not unreasonable for the men of the 56th Division to hope, while they were being hardly pressed, that the 46th Division might suddenly come to their aid. Perhaps luck would favour that division!

The attack from the north was launched between the Gommecourt road and the Little Z. The 137th Brigade, with the 6th South Staffordshire Regt. on the right and the 6th North Staffordshire Regt. on the left, had Gommecourt Wood in front of them. The 139th Brigade, with the 5th Sherwood Foresters on the right and the 7th Sherwood Foresters on the left, carried the attack up to the Little Z.

The account of this action is one long series of disasters. It seems that the South Staffords on the right started by getting bogged in the mud. A new front line had been dug, but they could not occupy it for this reason. They filed out through gaps in their wire, and if any succeeded in reaching the German front line it was for a period of minutes only. The North Staffords fared no better, though a few more men seem to have gained the enemy first line, but were, however, quickly forced out. The utmost confusion reigned in that part of the line, and the attack, from the very start, was futile.

The 5th and 7th Sherwoods got away to time (7.30), but

" there was a little delay in the fourth wave getting
out, owing to the deep mud in the trenches, and still
more delay in the carrying parties moving up (due
to a similar reason), and also on account of the
enemy barrage of artillery, rifle, and machine-gun
fire which became very heavy on our old front line.
. . . Of the 5th Sherwoods the first and second waves
reached the enemy first line fairly easily, but were
scattered by the time this occurred. The third and
fourth waves suffered severely in crossing from
machine-gun fire. The majority of the first and
second waves passed over the first-line trenches, but
there is no evidence to show what happened to them
there, for not a man of the battalions that reached
the German second line has returned. The remaining
waves . . . found that the enemy, who must have
taken refuge in deep dugouts, had now come up and
manned the parapet in parties. The Germans were
noticed to be practically all bombers. . . . The first
three waves of the 7th Sherwoods (the left of the
attack) moved out to time and found the wire well
cut. So far as is known, only a small proportion of
these three waves reached the German second line, and
after a bomb fight on both flanks, the survivors fell
back on the German first line, where they found
other men of the battalion consolidating. After
expending all their bombs in repelling a German
counter-attack, the survivors retired over the
parapet."

One can therefore say that, half an hour after the
attack was launched, the Germans in the Gommecourt
salient had only the 56th Division to deal with. We
know that the Cemetery was seen to be occupied by
our troops about nine o'clock, and it was probably
shortly after this that the party of Queen's Westminster Rifles, led by the gallant lieutenant of the

Cheshires, reached the Quadrilateral. But the Germans were then masters of the situation on the north of the salient and, freed from all anxiety in that quarter, could turn their whole attention to the 56th Division. Up to this time fighting had been hard, but slow progress had been made, and with even moderate success on the part of the 46th Division, depression and bewilderment might have seized the enemy. But he turned with elation to the southern attack, and shortly after 9.30 a.m. small parties of bombers were seen moving through Gommecourt Park to attack the London Rifle Brigade, and strong attacks were launched from the east of Gommecourt village.

For the rest of the day no help came from the 46th Division, though a new attack was ordered, postponed, and postponed again. The plan was to reorganise assaulting waves from the carrying parties, and at 3.30 in the afternoon it seemed probable that an attack would materialise, but it did not. It was perhaps as well, for by that time the 56th Division occupied the German front line only, and that in very weak strength.

As night fell all became quiet. The 167th Brigade relieved the 168th on the right ; the 169th reorganised.

General Hull's conclusions on this action are that

" the primary reason for failing to retain the ground was a shortage of grenades. This shortage was due to :

(a) The enemy's barrage, and in a lesser extent the machine-gun fire from the flanks, which prevented supplies being carried across No Man's Land.

(b) To the breadth of No Man's Land.

(c) Possibly to insufficient means of collecting

grenades and S.A.A. from men who had become casualties, and from German stores.

I understand that our counter-battery groups engaged a very large number of German batteries—the results were not apparent, and I think this was due to the limited number of guns available, and also to the small calibre of the majority employed (60-pounders, 4·7 guns, and 4·5 howitzers). I consider it would be better to employ the heavy (9·2) and medium (6) howitzers, and even the super-heavy.

It was particularly noticeable that, once our attack was launched, the Germans attempted practically no counter-work.

The preliminary bombardment started on the 24th June, and continued for seven days. During this period the enemy seemed to have increased the number of his batteries. . . . The effect of the bombardment on the German trenches was very great . . . on the dugouts the effect was negligible. On the *moral* of the enemy the effect was not so great as one would have hoped. . . .

I am doubtful of the value of these long bombardments, which give the enemy time to recognise the points selected for the attack, and possibly to relieve his troops, and to concentrate guns, and to bring up ammunition.

The intense bombardment prior to the attack lasted sixty-five minutes, considerably longer than any of the previous bombardments. I am in favour of having as many false attacks and lifts of artillery fire as possible, but consider there should be no difference. . . .

The German attitude and *moral* varied considerably—some of the enemy showed fight, but other parties were quite ready to surrender as soon as they came up from their dugouts. But it cannot be said that their *moral* was any more shattered by the bombardment than were their dugouts. Later

in the day German bombers advanced with great
boldness, being assisted by men who advanced over
the open. Our men appear to have had no difficulty
in dealing with enemy bombers at first—it was only
when bombs were scarce that the enemy succeeded
in pushing us back. The counter-attacks on the
right were never made in great strength, but were
prepared by artillery fire which was followed up
closely and boldly by bombers. On the left the
enemy appeared to be in greater strength, and came
out of Gommecourt village and through the Park in
great numbers."

The men of London had done well, although the
salient remained in the hands of the enemy. The
effort of the infantry was valiant, and they were
supported with devotion by the artillery. The
artillery observers took great risks, and the conduct
of one of Lieut.-Col. Prechtel's wire-cutting batteries
is well worthy of note. It established itself practically in our front line, about W48, and fired 1,200
rounds during X, Y, Y1, Y2 days and on Z day
fired a further 1,100 rounds.

The German plan was, as has been shown, to
prevent all reinforcements from crossing No Man's
Land, and to deal with those troops who had lodged
themselves in their trench system by strong and well-
organised bombing attacks.

There is no doubt that the main object of the
attack had been fulfilled. Unpleasant as it may
seem, the rôle of the 56th Division was to induce the
enemy to shoot at them with as many guns as could
be gathered together, and also to prevent him from
moving troops. The prisoners captured were 141
from units of the 52nd Reserve Division, and 37 from

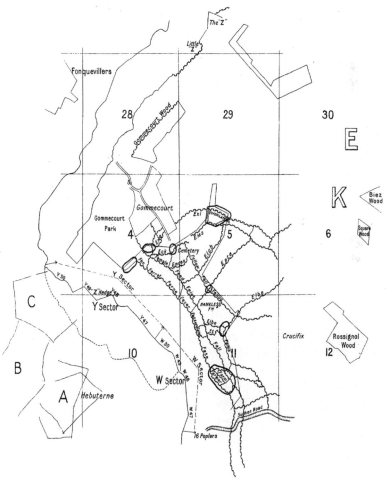

The "Z"

Little Z

Fonquevillers

28   Gommecourt Wood   29   30

E

K   Biez Wood

Gommecourt

Gommecourt Park   Gommecourt   Ex1   White Label

4   Em5   5   Square Wood   6

Cemetery   Eloh

Esh   Ems'n   Eese

Esc   Enm'st   Felix

Felse   Felus   Felen

Y 50   Par Trench   Felix Trench   Elbe

Y Sector   Fence Trench

Y 49 - 'Z' Hedge Y 48   Fence Trench

C   HAMELESS FM   Rossignol Wood

Y Sector   Vote Label   Elbe   Crucifix   12

Y 47   Elbe   Ett

W 30   Felr   Fall

10   W 29 W 28   W Sector   11   Kern Redoubt

B   W Sector   Sunken Road

A   Hebuterne   W 47

16 Poplars

I. THE GOMMECOURT SALIENT.

The dotted line is the old British line.

46)

GOMMECOURT, JULY 1916

the 2nd Guards Reserve Division, so that no movement of troops had occurred on that front, and we know that the number of batteries had been increased. There were many more prisoners than this, but they were caught in their own barrage as they crossed No Man's Land, and large numbers of dead Germans were afterwards found in that much-battered belt.

The main attack of the Fourth Army, launched on the same day, succeeded on the right. North of the Ancre as far as Serre our losses were severe, and the initial gains of the assaulting troops could not be maintained. After five days' fierce fighting, the enemy's first system of defence farther south had been penetrated to a depth of a mile over a front of six miles. But north of the Ancre, after the first day, operations were confined to maintaining a steady pressure on the enemy.

This battle, with the subsidiary attack on the Gommecourt Salient, is known as the battle of Albert 1916.

.   .   .   .   .

The division was not relieved. It had suffered in casualties 182 officers and 4,567 other ranks. The London Scottish had sent 24 officers and 847 other ranks into battle, and 9 officers and 257 other ranks had come out. The Rangers had sent in 23 officers and 780 other ranks—6 officers and 280 other ranks came out. The Queen Victoria's Rifles came out with 22 officers and 160 other ranks; the London Rifle Brigade, 18 officers and 300 other ranks; the Queen's Westminster Rifles, 19 officers and 160 other ranks. The supporting battalions suffered only slightly less.

When the fighting had abated the enemy seems to

have initiated a truce to gather in the wounded. His
own stretcher-bearers came out, on seeing which
ours also went out. This state of affairs lasted for
an hour, when our men were warned to get back to
their lines.

The state of the line was extraordinary. The front
line, over which so much labour had been expended,
had ceased to exist, and could only be held by means
of patrols and a few small posts. Our main line was
now what was known as the R Line, the original line
when the 56th Division arrived in the sector. And
the front held by the division was gradually increased.
From the 3rd July onwards the division took over
the line to the left until on the 8th the 169th Brigade
was north of Fonquevillers with its left opposite
Little Z. Each brigade held its front with two battalions in the line, one in brigade reserve and one
in divisional reserve.

During the night of the 13th the artillery made a
" demonstration " in order to help the Fourth Army,
which was again attacking in the south. On this
night a patrol of the Queen's Westminster Rifles
captured a prisoner who proved to be of the 91st
Regt.—a normal unit.

On the 17th of the month all three brigades
attempted raids, but the enemy were found to be too
alert, and no prisoners were obtained.

The division remained on this front, keeping the
enemy busy, until the 20th August, when it was
relieved by the 17th Division, and marched first to
Doullens, then to Fromer-le-Grand, then to St.
Riquier, where it proceeded to refit and train under
the orders of the X Corps.

CHAPTER II

THE SOMME

THE move to St. Riquier, in the neighbourhood of Abbeville, revealed to some of the officers that their men were not very fit for marching. This knowledge appears to come as a revelation to some people. Those on active service very soon discovered that a long period of trench duty, though it hardened the men to those particular conditions, made them unfit for any strenuous marching. It was probably never understood by people in England. They were, then, weary battalions that arrived at St. Riquier.

When it is said that a battalion or a division was "resting," that word must not be taken in too literal a sense. One might define it with greater truth as being a change of location, sometimes a mere matter of a mile or so, at others perhaps fifty miles. There were, it is true, no trenches to man, no sentry groups by day and night, but there was always work to be done. And the work, very naturally, had always the one end in view—the defeat of the Germans.

The training was almost exclusively of an aggressive nature. Unless there was some special object in view, when trenches would be dug to represent our own and those occupied by the enemy, the optimistic

nature of the Higher Command always leaned to open
warfare training. Companies wandered about, as
they do in England, attacking villages, strong points,
and woods, and indulged in vast schemes of pursuit
after phantom armies called Red or North or South
Armies. But this short period at St. Riquier gave the
56th Division a surprise in the matter of training.

Battalions had been reinforced since the Gommecourt action, and there was some grumbling about
the nature of the reinforcements. Batches of men,
from all sorts of units, were drafted to battalions, and
General Hull made great efforts to get this system
altered. Battalions, however, were of fair strength.

We know that very early in the war the problem
of barbed wire had been exercising the minds of the
Staff in general. Long after the Press campaign for
high explosives, when this form of shell was provided
in large quantities, wire-cutting was still ordered
with quite a high percentage of shrapnel. But whatever you did, however long the time you gave to
cutting the wire, it never disappeared entirely ; vile,
treacherous strands stuck out of the earth like
brambles, stakes remained miraculously upright with
waving lengths of wire to grab you by the sleeve or
the trousers ; and when the cutting was well done,
there had been a mere substitution of obstacles—
the state of the ground, blasted into holes, pits,
mounds, and mud made progress very slow and
difficult.

How was wire to be removed ?

Mr. Winston Churchill let his mind wander round
steam-rollers linked up with chains. Other minds
thought of tractors. At the same time, inventors
were considering the old question of moving forts.

In August 1916 there came from England a weird and fearful-looking machine known as a Tank.

On the 26th August the 7th Middlesex practised an attack in conjunction with five Tanks. One can easily imagine the Middlesex men, and everybody else who had wind of what was afoot, all agog at this new form of field training! What were the criticisms of the London men on this . . . machine?

The Tanks had only been landed in France on the 25th, and it is not surprising that two of them broke down. But the practice was continued on subsequent days until each brigade had acquired experience. Sir Douglas Haig, Marshal Joffre, and H.R.H. the Prince of Wales were interested spectators of these evolutions.

The orders for this exercise were that the Tanks would cross our front line at zero hour, and would be followed by the first infantry wave one minute later. The second wave would start at zero plus three minutes; the third wave at zero plus five minutes; the fourth wave at zero plus six minutes. The infantry were instructed to advance in short rushes up to, but not beyond, the Tanks—unless a Tank broke down, when they were to proceed as if it was not there.

Everyone seems to have been much impressed by the behaviour of the Tanks.

On the 31st August, General Hull received a warning order that his division would move to Corbie and come under the XIV Corps (Cavan). And on the following day the artillery was ordered forward. The 168th and 169th Infantry Brigades left St. Riquier on the 3rd, and the 167th Brigade on the 4th. Events came tumbling over one another.

On the 4th September the leading troops of the division were at the Citadel and Happy Valley, near Carnoy; on the 5th at Maricourt Siding. And on the 6th September the 56th Division was ordered to relieve the 5th Division that night in the front line.

No one will ever be able to describe in adequate fashion the scene behind the Somme battle front. Piccadilly in the height of the season, with its slow-moving and ever-stopping traffic, may give some idea of the state of the roads—only one must substitute army carts, limbers, lorries, for smart limousine cars and buses, one must substitute a loose stone road covered with six inches of mud, and holes three feet deep filled with water, for the smooth wood paving of that thoroughfare. And there were no pavements, no sidewalks. The infantry threaded its way in single file through this mass of dirty carts, and sweating men and horses, and overheated motor-lorries, halting sometimes for hours; or broke away across-country where, although the traffic was not so congested, obstacles such as cavalry lines, transport lines, camps, and, as the forward area was penetrated, lines of heavy guns and howitzers were met with.

The whole country seemed pulsing with life and effort. Here was no labour-saving device of peaceful civilisation, but a continual strain of muscle and sinew. Difficulties were overcome by straining horses, straining men, for where the greatest difficulty existed the engine was of no use. And through the midst of all this, threading its way in long files, passed the 56th Division.

.   .   .   .   .   .

We have said that the results of the first five days of fighting, which started on the 1st July, was an advance of one mile on a front of six miles. This was followed by minor engagements to adjust the line. The two northern Corps of the attacking Army were given to Sir Hubert Gough, with instructions to keep the enemy busy while Sir Henry Rawlinson battered his way through farther south.

On the 14th July the Fourth Army was again launched on a front from Longueval to Bazentin-le-Petit Wood. This battle was continued for several days, and established the Army on a line from Maltz Horn Farm (Montauban), where it joined on to the left of the French, along the eastern edge of Trones Wood to Longueval, then westward past Bazentin-le-Grand to the northern corner of Bazentin-le-Petit (and the wood), and so to the north of Ovillers. Over 2,000 prisoners were taken, which brought the total since the opening of the offensive to more than 10,000, also in this battle we captured 4 heavy guns, 42 field-guns, 30 trench mortars, and 52 machine guns. [Battle of Bazentin Ridge.]

But our line from Pozières to Delville Wood and Longueval, and then south of Maltz Horn Farm, where it was carried still south by the French to the village of Hem, made a most unpleasant salient. The enemy had excellent observation from Guillemont, and could bring a mass of surrounding artillery to bear on a comparatively small area packed with troops, guns, and supplies. To relieve this most uncomfortable position, it was arranged that the right of the British Army should swing forward in conjunction with the French. To do this the French would have to capture the strongly fortified villages of Maurepas, Le Foret, Rancourt, and Frigicourt, while we would have to take all the

country up to Sailly-Saillisel and Morval, which
included the capture of Flers, Gueudecourt, Ginchy,
Guillemont, and Les Bœufs. Before this could be
done, the enemy, on the 18th July, launched a strong
counter-attack on Delville Wood–Longueval–Waterlot
Farm. And this was the prelude to much fierce and
very confusing fighting. [The battle of Delville
Wood commenced on the 15th July and ended
3rd September.]

On the 30th July we attacked Guillemont and
Falfemont Farm in conjunction with our Allies, but
without success ; and on the 7th August our troops
again entered Guillemont and were again driven out.
Guillemont was the important point to be gained,
but it was evident that it could not be won in a small
engagement, and as the only objective, without heavy
loss. So we and the French made a series of attacks,
advancing foot by foot on Maurepas, Falfemont, Guillemont, Leuze Wood, and Ginchy. But no great progress was made. And so the month of August passed.

On the 3rd September a combined French and
British attack was made on a wide front extending
on the left to the Ancre, so that both the Fourth and
Fifth Armies were engaged. The gain in front of
Sir Hubert Gough's Army was small, but the Fourth
Army managed to win the much-disputed Guillemont, and after many assaults Falfemont Farm (which
was only completely captured on the 5th) and the
greater part of Leuze Wood. Ginchy and High Wood
remained in the hands of the Germans, but we had
made a step in the right direction, and had advanced
our right to a depth of one mile on a front of nearly
two miles and captured over a thousand prisoners.
[Battle of Guillemont, 3rd–6th September.]

This was, briefly, the situation when the 56th Division marched forward to take over the line from the 5th Division.

.   .   .   .   .

Brig.-Gen. Loch was ordered to take over a portion of the line, and accordingly the 168th Brigade moved from Maricourt Siding in the direction of Falfemont Farm, and came under the orders of the 5th Division. The local situation was always most difficult to grasp. The Somme field of battle was the most hideous place and absolutely bewildering.   A guide was a treacherous person to trust, or perhaps we should say he was a broken reed to lean on ; for the poor fellow had no treacherous intent in his heart, he was anxious enough, to lead troops in the right direction, but nine times out of ten was completely lost a few minutes after he started.   And there were, perhaps, more mistakes made in attempting to trace the front line in that great battle than in any other.

Guillemont was held by us ; Combles was strongly held by the Germans.   Between these two places was Leuze Wood.   We held, with more or less certainty, the line of the road between Leuze Wood and Guillemont, and we also held the country between Leuze Wood and Falfemont Farm, and had pushed troops into the wood itself ; but the situation in the rest of the square marked 27 was very vague (see map)— the only certain thing was that there were many Germans there.   Except for the wood and the line of the road to Guillemont, the Germans held all of squares 20 and 21.   We had a nasty, elongated triangle pushed into enemy territory, and it had a wobbly right side to it.

The Kensingtons went into the front line not very

far from Falfemont Farm, in the lower left corner of
square 27. The London Scottish were supposed to
be in support to the Royal Irish Rifles, and got into
a two-foot scrape, unworthy of the name of "trench,"
about three-quarters of the way through Leuze Wood.
The Royal Irish Rifles were imagined to be holding
the most southern end of Bouleaux Wood across the
road which separated it from Leuze Wood.

The positions were, of course, taken over at night,
and the next day the French attacked Combles. In
order to help our Allies our guns started a bombardment, but unfortunately most of their shells fell
around Leuze Wood. It was one of the unavoidable
accidents of war. Close shooting has to be done,
and there are many possible causes, from faulty
ammunition to wet ground, for guns shooting short.
It is none the less annoying to the infantry. Capt.
A. H. Macgregor, of "C" Company (London Scottish),
made strong remarks in writing, but failed to stop
the energetic gunners.

The Irish were having a much worse time than the
London Scottish, as they were also being heavily
bombarded by the Germans. So they decided to
evacuate their trench.

All this led to some confusion, and on top of it
the enemy launched a bombing attack, which was
probably in support of their counter-attack on the
French. The London Scottish reserve companies,
which were at Wedge Wood, moved up, and the
battalion prepared to defend Leuze Wood, which they
imagined would shortly be heavily attacked. But
the Irish, although they lost heavily, threw back the
German bombers and were relieved by two companies
of the London Scottish.

By midnight everything was re-established as it had been before, and, while probing about in the dark, the London Scottish gathered in two enemy officers and fourteen other ranks of the 107th Infantry Regt. as prisoners.

The position they were in was on the south of the road, and it was decided to try and dig a trench on the edge of Bouleaux Wood, that is, on the other side of the road. A platoon was sent forward the following morning to undertake this work. It was successfully carried out, and the covering party managed to inflict a good many casualties on the enemy—Sergt. Smith, of " B " Company, shot eight—and three further prisoners were taken.

This experience of the London Scottish will give some idea of the conditions which ruled what was officially known as " holding the line." At any moment a post might be wrested from you and have to be fought for again, and all the time you were described as " established " in Leuze Wood.

On the night of the 7th September the Queen Victoria's Rifles took over this bit of line, and the London Scottish went back to Maltz Horn Farm.

On the night of the 6/7th September, General Hull took over command of the divisional front from the G.O.C. 5th Division. There was a slight readjustment of line the next night, and it was then held by the 169th Brigade on the right and in touch with the 1st French Division, and the 168th Brigade on the left and in touch with the 16th Division on the Combles–Guillemont road.

There was to be a big attack on the 9th, but the position from which the 56th Division had to start was not too satisfactory. A study of the battle of

the Somme will show that at some time or other
every unit lost direction. It was exceedingly difficult
to recognise an objective ; even the heaps of ruins
which marked the sites of villages were frequently
mistaken. It is a rolling, featureless country. But
perhaps the chief cause of loss of direction was the
shape of the jumping-off line. The German defence
was very obstinate and the fighting severe. Troops,
having made an advance, had to hang on anywhere,
facing the enemy where he opposed them most
fiercely. The result was a zigzag line, a crazy front,
where troops frequently faced east and west and
were told to attack north. On an ordinary practice
field-day, a platoon commander can get his men out
of a trench and make them wheel in the desired
direction, but in action attacking troops will always
be drawn towards the nearest firing. Men getting
out of a trench and hearing or seeing an enemy in
front of them will go towards him, no matter how
much orders to the contrary have been dinned into
their heads.

Consider the line of the 56th Division. The left
along the Guillemont–Leuze Wood road was facing
due north ; it then curled round the wood and faced
south-east ; another curl made the extreme right of
the line face north-east. The attack on the 9th was
to be in a north-easterly direction.

To get a better line and form a strong flank facing
Combles, an attempt was made to clear the enemy
from the trenches south-east of Leuze Wood.

The London Rifle Brigade had relieved the Kensingtons on the right of the line, and companies were
somewhat puzzled by their position, which is described
as " most obscure." On the night of the 8th they

made a bombing attack to clear the trenches on the south-east of the wood. At first this met with some success, but in the early morning of the 9th the enemy came at them again in large numbers, and they were driven back to their former position. It was not thought advisable to try to regain the lost ground.

The attack on the 9th September (the battle of Ginchy) was by the whole of the XIV Corps in conjunction with the XV Corps on the left. The XIV Corps held Guillemont; and Delville Wood was held by the XV Corps. The object was to capture Ginchy and bring the line up to point 141·7, and from there down to Leuze Wood. Incidentally it meant clearing the ground to the south-east of the wood, but in following the actions from this date it must be remembered that the Higher Command intended to work round Combles, and so the right of the British Army was always working to form a defensive flank, until the advance reached a point which would enable troops to join hands with the French on the far side of Combles.

The task of the 169th Brigade was the forming of a flank against Combles by capturing the trenches south-east of the wood (the trenches they had failed to take by bombing) and to advance their line a short way through Bouleaux Wood.

The 168th Brigade, who were on the line of the Guillemont–Leuze Wood road, were to pivot on their right (the advance from the northern end of the wood was very slight) and bring their left up to point 141·7. This " right form " was to be done in two stages, the road to Ginchy marking the halfway line.

The artillery were ordered to put up a creeping and stationary barrage. Fifty per cent. of guns were to fire on a known position as a stationary barrage ; the other 50 per cent. were to start just ahead of the infantry and creep forward at the rate of fifty yards a minute, until the stationary barrage was reached, when the latter would be jumped forward to the next stationary barrage line.

It will be gathered from the foregoing account of how the 56th Division took over the line that the conditions under which the infantry waited for the resumption of attack were not dissimilar to those at the end, though not the actual termination, of an engagement—when nobody knows within a few hundred yards where any unit really is. And, indeed, that was always the situation during the battle of the Somme. There was perpetual unrest in the line.

The battle on the 9th has always seemed like a wild rush in fast-fading light. It was to open at 4.45 p.m., but on the left of the Corps it seems to have been delayed. Nowhere was it entirely successful in the assault. The situation remained obscure and fighting continued for several days.

The truth of the whole matter was that the enemy defended Combles with desperation. The right of the 56th Division had as hard a task as was ever set for any troops, and on their left was a German strong point bearing the ominous name of " the Quadrilateral," the strength of which was only learned at bitter cost. We will follow the fortunes of the division from the right of the line.

The 169th Brigade was on the right with the London Rifle Brigade and the Queen Victoria's Rifles attacking. Leuze Wood, as we know, was always a dangerous spot, and the task of the London Rifle Brigade was to capture those trenches on the south-east of the wood and start the building up of the flank facing Combles. But the moment the men left their jumping-off trenches, their attack was met and destroyed by a hail of rifle and machine-gun fire.

On the left of the London Rifle Brigade the Queen Victoria's Rifles, whose objective was the enemy trench on the far side of the Combles road, met with more success and gained a precarious footing in a part of that line. But no troops of the 169th Brigade could be said to be established anywhere on their objective.

Part of the 2nd London Regt. was given to the London Rifle Brigade, and a second attack was launched on the trenches south-east of the wood, almost simultaneously with a counter-attack by the enemy from his Bouleaux Wood defences. The Queen Victoria's Rifles held on to their gains, but the second attack on the trenches south-east of the wood failed. The Queen's Westminster Rifles, who were in reserve, were sent for.

The 168th Brigade, on the left of the division, attacked with the 4th London Regt. on the right and the Rangers on the left. The 4th Londons, pivoting on the north end of Leuze Wood, gained their first objective under close cover of our barrage and with little loss. But the Rangers came under heavy machine-gun fire from their left. It was ascertained from a prisoner, captured later, that a whole battalion of his regiment, the 161st of the 185th Division, was in the centre of the square marked 20.

The left company of the Rangers, with the troops of the 16th Division on their left, met a strong force of the enemy and were driven back to their point of departure. The right company, however, after hard

fighting which lasted until 6 p.m., reached their first
objective, the line of the road from Leuze Wood to
Ginchy.

Meanwhile the 4th London Regt., sticking close to
the artillery barrage, had again advanced at 5.25 p.m.
and gained their final objective. But their losses
were severe. The machine-gun fire was tremendous,
and its effects can be gathered from the fact that a
post, which was left to construct a strong point in
the first objective, was entirely wiped out.

The right company of the Rangers, having gained
their first objective, again advanced, though the
opposition they had met with had caused them to be
late on the barrage. Again the murderous fire was
poured on them from the left, and they swerved so
that they came up on the centre of the 4th London
troops. These two battalions were now on the line
of the trench leading to point 141·7, but exactly how
near that point was only determined later. On the
right they were in touch with the Queen Victoria's
Rifles.

By this time it was quite dark; and the left of
the 56th Division was so much in the air that the
enemy was on all but one side of it. The 16th
Division had fared badly.

The right brigade of the 16th Division had not
been able to advance at all, and were scattered about
in front of Guillemont. The left brigade had secured
a footing in Ginchy, and the 3rd Brigade of the
Guards Division was already on its way to relieve the
whole of the 16th Division. But the situation was
far from good.

The Kensingtons, who were in support to the 168th
Brigade, had moved forward to occupy the departure

trenches, and the commanding officer, seeing something of what had happened, promptly tried to strengthen the flank of the 4th London Regt. and the Rangers. He disposed of his battalion in forward positions with the object of protecting the left flank. The London Scottish were sent for.

Before 11 p.m. the two reserve battalions, the London Scottish and the Queen's Westminster Rifles, had arrived in the vicinity of Leuze Wood. But the situation which faced General Hull at midnight was not a comfortable one. His left was surrounded by Germans, and probably only protected by the night, and his right was uncertain; there had been reports of enemy snipers in Leuze Wood, and the enemy was certainly pressing strongly with his bombers.

Both brigades were ordered to attack again.

Following events from the right of the line, the Queen's Westminsters were ordered to attack and capture the trenches south-east of the wood before dawn. The night was pitch dark, and the Germans were pouring shells into the wood. The exact bearing of the trench and its distance from the wood were unknown to the battalion. It was impossible to arrange an earlier hour than 7 a.m. for the attack.

Patrols were sent out to get in touch with the enemy and reconnoitre the ground, and while the battalion waited casualties mounted up. At last came the dawn, but it brought no light; a thick mist had settled over the country. At 7 a.m. the attack started.

Two companies attacked. The right company went straight ahead, and the left was told to swing to their left and take a trench beyond the sunken road leading to Combles. The barrage was described as ineffective, which was, maybe, due to the fog. At any rate, neither company reached its objective. The enemy was lining his defences in force and poured in a hot fire with rifles and machine guns.

Later in the day a further attack was launched, but met with no success, and the situation during the whole of the morning, complicated by the thick mist, remained extremely uncertain.

On the 168th Brigade front the London Scottish had not waited till dawn for their attack. They formed up in six waves, in trenches dug by the 5th Cheshires on the extreme left of the original line of departure, and were ordered to thrust through, moving due north, and fill the gap between the 4th London Regt. and the troops of the 16th Division in Ginchy. It was hoped that all the enemy troops in square 20 would be cut off.

A quarter of an hour after midnight, in pitch darkness, the battalion started to advance. The first three waves progressed some 600 yards, and then, failing to see any landmarks or recognise where they were, they halted and sent out patrols. The last three waves were nowhere in sight; they had lost direction and joined the 4th London Regt. and Rangers on their right. But while the leading waves waited for their patrols to get in touch with either friend or foe, they were attacked by about a hundred Germans from their rear. The London Scottish whipped round and scattered them at the point of the bayonet. The enemy vanished, but left a considerable number of dead on the ground.

The London Scottish were now completely lost, and so marched south to pick up their position again.

The attempted attack, however, was not repeated,

but two and a half companies were sent to the trench occupied by the 4th London Regt. and the Rangers (Bully), where they attempted, by bombing, to reach point 141·7. Their efforts were not successful.

Meanwhile the situation to the left of the 56th Division was no less obscure. The 3rd Brigade of the Guards Division had been hurried up in the dark to relieve the 16th Division. The guides of the left brigade of the latter division led a relieving battalion into Ginchy, but had only the haziest idea where their own troops were. Part of the 16th Division on the east of the village was not relieved until midday on the 10th. Ginchy was repeatedly attacked by the enemy, and no one knew with any certainty what was happening.

The right brigade of the 16th Division was not relieved for some time. The guides to the relieving battalion lost themselves completely, and a big gap existed between Ginchy and Guillemont. During the 10th this gap was made good, but the whole of that day was occupied by repulsing enemy attacks and trying to establish a definite line.

On the 56th Division front there were repeated bombing attacks by the enemy, and the S.O.S. was sent up several times. We may say that the battalion reports of positions were only relatively accurate, and that nothing was clear to Gen. Hull until the weather improved and air reports could be made.

Relief of the 168th Brigade by the 167th, and of the 169th by a composite brigade of the 5th Division, took place, and it was then ascertained that the London Scottish had, as related above, lost direction in their attack and that no one was near the Ginchy–141·7 road. The enemy still held the Quadrilateral

6

in force, and the most advanced troops of the 56th
Division were some way from it, though they were
strongly established in Bully Trench; and the
enemy were still in square 20. But the 56th and
Guards Divisions were now in touch and a firm line
was held along the Guillemont–Leuze Wood road, and
from the cross-roads to Ginchy, which was also firmly
held.

The Quadrilateral was the danger-point, and it
defied all attempts to take it by bombing, and
successfully withstood the Corps heavy artillery.

. . . . .

Sir Douglas Haig sums up the situation at this
point as follows :

". . . The French had made great progress on our
right, bringing their line forward to Louage Wood
(just south of Combles), Le Foret, Cléry-sur-Somme,
all three inclusive. The weak salient in the Allied
line had therefore disappeared, and we had gained
the front required for further operations.

Still more importance, however, lay in the proof
afforded in the results described of the ability of our
new armies not only to rush the enemy's strong
defences—as had been accomplished on the 1st and
14th July—but also to wear down and break the
power of resistance by a steady relentless pressure,
as had been done during the weeks of this fierce and
protracted struggle. As has already been recounted,
the preparations made for our assault on the 1st July
had been long and elaborate ; but though the enemy
knew that an attack was coming, it would seem that
he considered the troops already on the spot, secure
in their apparent impregnable defences, would suffice
to deal with it. The success of that assault, combined
with the vigour and determination with which our
troops pressed their advantage, and followed by the

successful attack on the night of 14th July, all served to awaken him to a fuller realisation of his danger. The great depth of his system of fortifications, to which reference has been made, gave him time to reorganise his defeated troops, and to hurry up numerous fresh divisions and more guns. Yet in spite of this he was still pushed back, steadily and continuously. Trench after trench, and strong point after strong point, were wrested from him. The great majority of his repeated counter-attacks failed completely, with heavy loss; while the few that achieved temporary success purchased it dearly, and were soon thrown back from the ground they had for the moment regained.

The enemy had, it is true, delayed our advance considerably, but the effort had cost him dear; and the comparative collapse of his resistance during the last days of the struggle justified the belief that in the long-run decisive victory would lie with our troops, who had displayed such fine fighting qualities and such indomitable endurance and resolution.

Practically the whole of the forward crest of the main ridge, on a front of some 9,000 yards from Delville Wood to the road above Mouquet Farm, was now in our hands, and with it the advantage of observation over the slopes beyond. East of Delville Wood, for a further 3,000 yards to Leuze Wood, we were firmly established on the main ridge; while farther east, across the Oombles valley, the French were advancing victoriously on our right. But though the centre of our line was well placed, on our flanks there was still difficult ground to be won.

From Ginchy the crest of the high ground runs northwards for 2,000 yards, and then eastward, in a long spur, for nearly 4,000 yards. Near the eastern extremity of the spur stands the village of Morval, commanding a wide field of view and fire in every direction. At Leuze Wood my right was still 2,000

yards from its objective at this village, and between
lay a broad and deep branch of the main Combles
valley, completely commanded by the Morval spur,
and flanked, not only from its head north-east of
Ginchy, but also from the high ground east of the
Combles valley, which looks directly into it.

Up this high ground beyond the Combles valley
the French were working their way towards the
objective at Sailly-Saillisel, situated due east of
Morval, and standing at the same level. Between
these two villages the ground falls away to the head
of the Combles valley, which runs thence in a south-
westerly direction. In the bottom of this valley lies
the small town of Combles, then well fortified and
strongly held, though dominated by my right at
Leuze Wood, and by the French left on the opposite
heights. It had been agreed by the French and
myself that an assault on Combles would not be
necessary, as the place could be rendered untenable
by pressing forward along the ridges above it on
either side.

The capture of Morval from the south side presented a very difficult problem, while the capture of
Sailly-Saillisel, at that time some 3,000 yards to the
north of the French left, was in some respects even
more difficult. The line of the French advance was
narrowed almost to a defile by the extensive and
strongly fortified wood of St. Pierre Vaast on the one
side, and on the other by the Combles valley, which,
with the branches running out of it and the slopes
on either side, is completely commanded, as has been
pointed out, by the heights bounding the valley on
the east and west. . . .

The general plan of the combined Allied attack
which was opened on the 15th September was to
pivot on the high ground south of the Ancre and
north of the Albert–Bapaume road, while the Fourth
Army devoted its whole effort to the rearmost of the

enemy's original systems of defence between Morval
and Le Sars.

Should our success in this direction warrant it, I
made arrangements to enable me to extend the left
of the attack to embrace the villages of Martin'puich
and Courcelette. As soon as our advance on this
front had reached the Morval line, the time would
have arrived to bring forward my left across the
Thiepval Ridge. Meanwhile our Allies arranged to
continue the line of advance in close co-operation
with me from the Somme to the slopes above Combles ;
but directed their main effort northwards against the
villages of Rancourt and Frigicourt, so as to complete
the isolation of Combles and open the way for their
attack on Sailly-Saillisel."

That much was hoped from the big attack, to take
place on the 15th, there can be no doubt.   Brigades
resting in the rear of the divisional area could see
quantities of cavalry still farther back.   It suggested
big results.

The limits of the Fourth Army attack were Combles
Ravine and Martinpuich, and it was to capture
Morval, Les Bœufs, Gueudecourt, and Flers.   The
Cavalry Corps was to have its head on Carnoy at
10 a.m., and as soon as the four villages had been
captured it would advance and seize the high ground
round Rocquigny, Villers-au-Flos,   Riencourt-les-
Bapaume, and Bapaume.

And it was the first battle in which Tanks were
employed !   [The battle of Flers-Courcelette.]

Even in the midst of the struggle round about the
Quadrilateral a steady bombardment had been going
on, in preparation of a further attack, since the
12th September.   Day firing commenced at 6 a.m.
and went on until 6.30 p.m., when night firing started.

During the night bombardment lethal shells were used.

On Z day the preliminary bombardment was to be the same as on former days, with no increase until zero hour. When the intense fire, or barrage, commenced, there were gaps left in it for the advance of Tanks.

For the XIV Corps there were, taking part in this attack, fifteen Tanks. Nine were allotted to the Guards Division, three to the 6th Division, and three to the 56th Division.

The instructions given to Tanks were that they should start their attack at a time which would enable them to reach the first objective five minutes before the infantry. When they had cleared up the first objective, a proportion of them was to push forward a short way, to prearranged positions, and act as strong points. Departure from this programme to assist any infantry held up by the enemy was left to the discretion of the Tank Commander.

On the second objective Tanks and infantry would advance together and pace was to be regulated to " tank pace," which was given as from 30 to 50 yards a minute. For the third and fourth objectives there would be no creeping barrage, and Tanks would start in time to reach the objectives before the infantry. In all cases their action was to be arranged so as to crush wire and keep down hostile rifle and machine-gun fire.

Signals between Tank and infantry were arranged for by means of coloured flags—a red flag meaning " out of action," and a green flag " am on objective."

The main task of the 56th Division was to clear Bouleaux Wood and form a strong protective flank, covering all the lines of advance from Combles and the valleys running from the north-east of Combles. The 167th Brigade were ordered to advance as far as the bit of Beef Trench running through Bouleaux Wood, and to Middle Copse on the left of the wood ; a flank was also to be formed to the south-east and clear of the wood. The 168th Brigade were to pass through the 167th and carry on the advance by further bounds. The 169th Brigade were to hold the line through Leuze Wood and the left of square 27, and to capture the well-known trench (Loop Trench) to the south-east of the wood which runs into the sunken road to Combles.

One Tank was to advance on the right of Leuze Wood and assist the 169th Brigade to drive the enemy beyond the sunken road ; it would then establish itself in the Orchard as a strong point. This Tank was called the Right Tank.

Two Tanks were to work from the north of Leuze Wood along the left of Bouleaux Wood and assist the 167th and 168th Brigades. These were known as the Centre and Left Tanks, and were eventually to proceed to a railway cutting north-east of Bouleaux Wood, which promised to be a point of some difficulty.

The Right Tank, having seen the 169th Brigade safely in its objectives, was to move along the south-east of Bouleaux Wood and take up a position on the cutting in the top end of square 22.

In the XIV Corps area the Tanks were by no means a success. It is only right to say that this was not the fault of their crews. Every excuse must be allowed, for the Tank was not only a new invention, and, like most new inventions, somewhat clumsy in the first design, but the ground was absolutely vile.

We have not alluded to the weather, which, however, was a most important factor just now. The field of battle was a field of mud; the resting area of the division was a field of mud; the roads and tracks were rivers of mud; anyone can paint a picture of the battle of the Somme provided he can paint miles of mud. And the Army had simply blasted its way forward so that the shell-holes cut one another in the mud.

The scene round Leuze Wood, Guillemont, and Ginchy was a nightmare. There had been little time to devote to the burial of the dead, and corpses lay literally in heaps where the fighting had been severe. One has only to imagine the results of repeated and obstinate attempts to capture a position to realise what it must look like before it is finally taken. An attack is launched and fails. Why does it fail? Perhaps twenty men of a company get back to the trench from which they attacked, and where are the others? On the ground. After five or six attacks, each going out strong and coming back weak, each heralded by a " barrage," what will the place look like?

We may mention here that the stretcher-bearers worked with eight men to each stretcher, and each ambulance required six horses to drag it through the mud.

Just before 1 a.m. one of the Tanks allotted to the 56th Division broke down on its way to the assembly position. This accident left the division with one Tank working on either side of the Bouleaux Wood.

The assault commenced at 6.20 a.m., and was followed by some of the fiercest fighting in the history of the war. On the right of the division the 2nd

London Regt. succeeded, after some hours of gallant
and determined effort, in driving the enemy from
the greater part of Loop Trench, the enemy clinging
to the junction with the sunken road. The Tank,
which was some time before reaching the sunken
road, gave valuable assistance, but was set on fire by
a direct hit from a field gun. The fight then turned
to the sunken road and the trench on the far side of
it ; but the enemy was strong and no less determined
than the men of the 169th Brigade. No further
advance was gained in this direction.

On the left of the division the 167th Brigade
attacked, with the 1st London Regt. in line and the
7th Middlesex in support in Leuze Wood. The 1st
London Regt. captured that portion of Beef Trench
outside Bouleaux Wood and, together with the 7th
Middlesex — who were to advance through them, but
both units became mixed—occupied Middle Copse.

So far as the 56th Division was concerned, the
result of the day's fighting remained with the advance
on the south-east of Leuze Wood as far as the Combles
road, and on the north-west of Bouleaux Wood to
Beef Trench and Middle Copse. The enemy retained
the whole of Bouleaux Wood and the trenches to the
north of the Combles road, and the road itself. But
the action, certainly of the 167th Brigade, was
influenced by the fortunes of the divisions on the left.

The centre of the horseshoe which had been formed
from the east of Ginchy to the cross-roads east of
Guillemont, and then to the north of Leuze Wood
and along Bully Trench, and which was prevented by
the Quadrilateral from being a complete circle, can
scarcely have been an enviable place for the Germans
who were there. As fighters, these Germans deserve

the highest praise. They were of the 21st and 7th
Bavarian Regts., of the 5th Bavarian Division. They
were well wired in, and had in the Quadrilateral deep
dugouts in their front lines and others in the ravine
behind the position. But though we grant them a
perfect position and well-constructed defences, we
must also admit they performed a fine feat of arms.
Those in the Quadrilateral had resisted all efforts of
the 56th and Guards Divisions to bomb them out,
and those in the horseshoe had repulsed the 16th
Division and the 6th Division, which attacked them
on the 13th. They had actually been under severe
artillery fire and subject to repeated assaults since
the 9th September, and on the 15th, in spite of Tanks,
of creeping barrages, and of the heavy artillery, they
remained immovable.

The worst kind of luck had attended the Tanks of
the 6th Division—only one managed to reach the
jumping-off line. This Tank went on with the
infantry for a short way, had all its periscopes shot
away, was pierced by most of the bullets which hit
it (and a perfect stream of fire was directed on it),
and, the driver being badly wounded, it retired through
the ranks of the 6th Division. Had the three Tanks
attacked, something might have been done, anyhow
with the enemy to the south-west of the Quadrilateral; but with only one, the barrage, arranged with
gaps for three, became ineffective, and a concentrated
fire on the one Tank soon put it out of action—it
also drew attention to the infantry attack. Briefly,
the 6th Division failed.

There was still a chance that the Guards would
advance and render the position of the Bavarians
impossible. But this chance was not realised. The

Quadrilateral was a mass of machine guns, and, taking the Guards Division in flank, inflicted fearful casualties. The first objective was taken and held—on the left the second objective was reached—but already the assaulting troops were being shot in the back by the Bavarians, and no further progress was made. Tanks do not seem to have helped in that direction either.

With this state of affairs on the left of the 56th Division, the attacking brigades were not likely to progress very far in the building up of a flank facing Combles. Until the Quadrilateral was taken the 167th Brigade could not possibly move. The 7th Middlesex had lost a lot of men from machine guns firing into their left rear as they advanced behind the assault of the 1st London Regt. And finally their Tank had broken down and was being attacked by the enemy.

By 11 a.m. the two reserve battalions of the 169th Brigade were moved forward to be used as reinforcements before the 168th Brigade was sent into action. Gen. Hull was determined to clear Bouleaux Wood, which had resisted so long. But at 1.30 p.m. the Corps Commander, Lord Cavan, telephoned him that the Guards had not made as much progress as he had thought, and that the operation against Bouleaux Wood would not be practicable. But before this order could reach them the 8th Middlesex made a further attempt to get into the wood and failed. All attention was then centred on the Quadrilateral, which was holding up the advance of no less than three divisions.

The division was ordered to consolidate where it stood, but during the night bombing attacks were carried out by the 169th Brigade on the sunken road and end of Loop Trench, and by the 167th Brigade on the trench in Bouleaux Wood—neither met with success.

On the 16th the 6th Division again attacked the Quadrilateral and failed, but they were now well up to the stronghold. The Guards Division had also crept in from the north.

The 17th September was devoted to preparations for attacking on the 18th. The 169th Brigade made a trench parallel to the sunken road to Combles, and also managed to occupy some 200 yards more frontage along the road. Many dead Germans of the 26th Regiment were found.

The attack on the 18th was in conjunction with the 6th Division. The task of the 56th Division was to capture the trench on the north of the sunken road to Combles, and the south-west face of Bouleaux Wood, to a point beyond Beef Trench, and from there through the wood to Middle Copse, where touch would be obtained with the 6th Division, who were making another effort to clear the Quadrilateral. The attacking brigades of the latter division declined the aid of Tanks on this occasion.

The weather was appalling. The state of the ground was rather worse than what is so frequently called a quagmire—troops could not get along.

The 167th Brigade had lost heavily, and was not in sufficient strength to attack, so the London Scottish were attached to that brigade. But the battalion was unable to reach the assaulting line.

Zero hour was 5.50 a.m., and on the right the 169th Brigade, with the Queen's Westminster Rifles and the London Rifle Brigade attacking, failed to cross the fatal sunken road, which was not surprising,

as the mud by itself was an almost perfect obstacle
from the German point of view. While on the left
the London Scottish failure to reach the assembly
trench caused the attack to be abandoned.

But the 6th Division was successful, and the
Quadrilateral, which gave such strong support to the
enemy troops holding Bouleaux Wood, was captured.
The news was received by everyone with a sigh of
relief.

Of the fighting as a whole on the 15th September
and subsequent days Sir Douglas Haig reported :

"The advance met with immediate success on
almost the whole of the front attacked. At 8.40 a.m.
our Tanks were seen entering Flers, followed by a
large number of troops. Fighting continued in Flers
for some time, but by 10 a.m. our troops had reached
the north of the village, and by midday had occupied
the enemy's trenches for some distance beyond. On
our right our line was advanced to within assaulting
distance of the strong line of defence running before
Morval, Les Bœufs, and Gueudecourt, and on our
left High Wood was at last carried after many hours
of very severe fighting, reflecting great credit on the
attacking battalions. Our success made it possible
to carry out during the afternoon that part of the
plan which provided for the capture of Martinpuich
and Courcelette, and by the end of the day both these
villages were in our hands. On the 18th September
the work of this day was completed by the capture of
the Quadrilateral, an enemy stronghold which had
hitherto blocked our progress towards Morval.

The result of the fighting on the 15th September
and the following days was a gain more considerable
than any which had attended our arms in the course
of a single operation since the commencement of the
offensive. In the course of one day's fighting we had

broken through two of the enemy's main defensive
systems, and had advanced on a front of over six
miles to an average depth of a mile. In the course
of this advance we had taken three villages, each
powerfully organised for prolonged resistance. . . .
The total number of prisoners taken by us in these
operations amounted to over 4,000, including 127
officers."

The 168th Brigade, on the left of the divisional
front, was responsible for holding Middle Copse. On
the two nights of the 19th and 20th September the
London Scottish provided covering parties for the
5th Cheshire Regt., who connected Beef Trench with
Middle Copse, and carried on two lines of trench in a
north-easterly direction as far as the rail or tram
line ; companies of these pioneers also connected the
Copse with the south-east side of the Quadrilateral.
This work resulted in a firm line some 900 yards in
length facing Bouleaux Wood, and gradually working
round Combles.

Prisoners captured by the London Scottish while
covering the digging parties were from the 2nd Battalion, 235th Regiment, Reserve 51st Division.

The right wing of the British Army had not yet
reached the line desired by Sir Douglas Haig. Morval, Les Bœufs, and Gueudecourt were still in the
hands of the enemy, and on the right Combles still
held out at the junction of the Allied Armies. An Allied
attack from the Somme to Martinpuich was arranged
for the 23rd September, but the weather was so bad
that it had to be postponed until the 25th. [The battle
of Morval.]

The 168th Brigade were relieved by the 167th, and
obtained a little rest from the night of the 22nd to

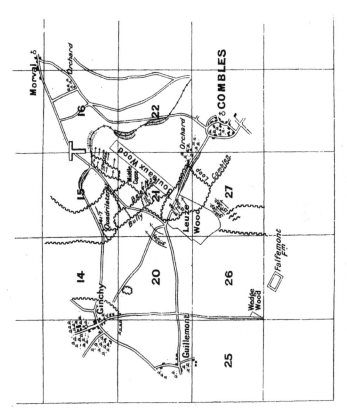

2. GINCHY & MORVAL.

THE BATTLES ON THE 9TH, 15TH, & 25TH, SEPR.

78)

the night of the 24th. The battle front of the division was then the 169th Brigade on the right between Leuze Wood and Combles, the 167th Brigade in Beef and Bully Trenches, and the 168th Brigade in the new trenches ready to attack Bouleaux Wood from the north-west, or rather to envelop it, as the wood was not to be entered.

The main task of the 56th Division was to continue building up the flank, to neutralise the German detachments in Bouleaux Wood, and to get touch with the 5th Division on the left. The actual objectives of the 168th Brigade were some trenches between the north-east of the wood and the tram-line, also the bank and cutting of the tram-line. The 167th Brigade were to help by directing machine-gun and trench-mortar fire on the wood, and the 169th Brigade by firing on the north and north-east exits of Combles.

The whole Corps attacked at 12.35 p.m., and the German resistance crumbled away.

The 4th London Regt. on the right and the London Scottish on the left advanced under " a most efficient enfilade artillery barrage." All objectives were reached. The 4th London Regt. killed a large number of Huns in shell-holes round the north end of the wood, and suffered themselves somewhat from enemy snipers in the southern part of the wood. The London Scottish had some trouble and quite a stiff fight to clear the railway embankment, during which the left company suffered severely. But four machine guns were captured there and eighty prisoners. These two battalions overran their objectives and curled round the end of Bouleaux Wood.

The 5th, 6th, and Guards Divisions on the left

swept through all their objectives—Morval and Les
Bœufs were captured.

For some time the London Scottish were out of
touch with the 5th Division, which had swerved too
far to the right, but the complete success of the operations enabled the 56th Division to improve the position
round Combles. By three o'clock in the afternoon
the 4th London Regt. had two companies in the north
end of Bouleaux Wood, and both the attacking battalions of the 168th Brigade had pushed out patrols
towards Combles. Artillery observation officers reported to Gen. Hull that the enemy could be seen
hurrying, in small parties, from Combles in an easterly
direction.

A steady pressure was kept on the Germans in
Bouleaux Wood. The centre of resistance here was
round the derelict Tank on the left edge of the wood.
The 1st London Regt. was on one side of the Tank
and the enemy on the other. On the right the London
Rifle Brigade and the Queen Victoria's Rifles gave the
enemy no rest in the sunken road and the trench
leading to Combles.

By midnight the 168th Brigade had posts east of
Combles, the 167th Brigade had cleared the lower end
of Bouleaux Wood and got behind the Tank, and
the 169th Brigade had captured all of the sunken
road trench and the Combles trench. And at dawn
an officer's patrol of the 168th Brigade had met a
French patrol on the east of Combles. The London
Rifle Brigade had already entered the town at
3.30 a.m. and secured touch with the French there.

The line desired by Sir Douglas Haig had been
captured and there was a momentary pause. The
line held by the 56th Division at midday on the 26th

was some 1,500 yards to the east of Combles. The 167th Brigade were in the front line and in touch with the 5th Division and the French ; the 168th Brigade were a short distance in rear, round about the railway cuttings ; and the 169th Brigade were half in Combles and half to the west of it. The Germans were some distance away, holding what was known as Mutton Trench in force, and it was arranged that the 168th Brigade should attack with the assistance of five Tanks. But the Tanks failed to put in an appearance, and after waiting twenty-four hours, the Rangers were told that the attack was cancelled.

Meanwhile our Allies on the right had captured Frigicourt and had the hard nut of Sailly-Saillisel to crack. To assist them in securing this very important position, Sir Douglas Haig agreed to hand over the line as far as Morval, so on the 28th the division was relieved and marched for a few days' rest to the neighbourhood of Ville-sur-Ancre and Meaulte.

The battle, however, still raged. Sir Douglas Haig was pushing the enemy hard :

" The success of the Fourth Army had now brought our advance to a stage at which I judged it advisable that Thiepval should be taken, in order to bring our left flank into line and establish it on the main ridge above that village, the possession of which would be of considerable value in future operations.

Accordingly, at 12.25 p.m. on the 26th September, before the enemy had been given time to recover from the blow struck by the Fourth Army, a general attack was launched against Thiepval and the Thiepval Ridge. . . . The attack was a brilliant success. On the right our troops reached the system of enemy trenches which formed their objective without great difficulty. In Thiepval and the strong works to the north of it the enemy's resistance was more desperate. . . . On the left of the attack fierce fighting, in which Tanks again gave valuable assistance to our troops, continued in Thiepval during the day and the following night, but by 8.30 a.m. on the 27th September the whole of the village of Thiepval was in our hands."

The rest for the division, however, was not for very long. Reinforced, though hardly refreshed, the brigades began to move back to the line. On the 29th September the 167th Brigade was in Trones Wood, west of Guillemont, and the 169th in a camp near by. On the last night of September the latter brigade took over the line from the 6th Division, with the right in touch with the French, while the 167th relieved the 2nd Guards Brigade on the left.

The position taken over was outside Les Bœufs, in the trenches called Foggy and Windy. Battalions in line from the right were the Queen's Westminsters, Queen Victoria's, 1st Londons, and the 7th Middlesex. The orders were that they should send out patrols and occupy a line of posts over the crest of the ridge—the 169th Brigade posts A, B, C, D, and the 167th Brigade E, F, G, H, and K.

On October 2nd the 167th Brigade reported having joined up a line of posts, but we cannot make the map-readings given agree with what is known of positions in subsequent events. The country was more than ever devoid of landmarks—it was just a wide expanse of shell-holes in a dark brown, almost black, kind of earth—and no one knew either their own position or those of the enemy within a few hundred yards; and the few hundred yards were a matter of importance. Anyhow, the line was not the line of posts, but probably near the line we have sketched on the left of 34. Touch was obtained with the 20th Division on the left.

Gen. Hull was now instructed that the Fourth Army would renew the attack on the 5th October, and that the XIV Corps would establish itself on a line from which the main Transloy defences could be attacked at a later date. The 56th Division would capture Hazy, Dewdrop, Spectrum, and part of Rainbow, and establish a line along the west crest of the ridge ; the Division would then, as a second phase of the attack, establish a line on the forward slope of the ridge from which Le Transloy could be seen. The General ordered that the 169th Brigade should attack on the right, and the 167th Brigade on the left. [The battle of the Transloy Ridges, 1st–18th October.]

The weather became steadily worse and, though water is supposed to run downhill and the division was on the slope of a hill, the troops might just as well have been in the middle of a pond. No one could move, and the operations were postponed for forty-eight hours.

Assembly trenches were dug ; and patrols reported the enemy some 200 yards on the farther side of the ridge. The objectives for the attack were well beyond the line of posts it had been hoped to occupy with patrols, and thé 2/1st London and 1/1st Edinburgh Field Companies R.E., with two companies of the 5th Cheshire Regt., were given to the two brigades to consolidate what was gained.

The assault took place at 1.45 p.m. on the 7th October, and on the left was fairly successful. The

7th Middlesex, on the extreme left, and the left company of the 1st London Regt. drove the enemy out of the northern half of Spectrum and part of Rainbow, where they joined with the 20th Division. The right company of the 1st Londons, however, was held up by machine-gun fire from Dewdrop and failed to reach that end of Spectrum.

The 168th Brigade fared badly on the right. Three battalions attacked in line—the London Scottish, the 4th London Regt., and the Rangers. Two machine guns were in the front line, for covering fire, and four others west of Les Bœufs, for indirect covering fire ; there were also six Stokes mortars in Burnaby to put a barrage on Dewdrop. In some respects the attack was peculiar. As was so often the case, the direction of the attack was at an angle to our front, and the London Scottish, starting the assault from the right at 1.45 p.m., were followed by the 4th London Regt. at 1.47 and the Rangers at 1.49 p.m. ; this was calculated to bring the three battalions into line by the time Dewdrop and the gun-pits were reached.

The leading company of the Rangers, on the left, was knocked out, before it had gone fifty yards, by machine guns in the northern end of Dewdrop, and the reserve companies of the battalion came under a very heavy barrage and did not succeed in carrying forward the attack. The remnants of this battalion lay out in shell-holes until dusk, when they returned to the original line.

The 4th London Regt., in the centre, met with much the same fate. The left company was annihilated, and the right company, managing to reach a patch of dead ground, lay down unable to move. The rear waves were met with intense artillery fire, but advanced most gallantly to the line of the leading troops. From the dead ground attempts were made to outflank the gun-pits, from which the hostile machine-gun fire was directed, and small parties managed to work well round to the south.

The London Scottish advanced well for about 400 yards, and occupied the south gun-pits and the southern end of Hazy. The enemy at once attempted a counter-attack from the northern end, but this was driven off. But it was found that a wide gap existed between the right of the battalion and the French, who had attacked east instead of north-east, and small parties of the London Scottish were successively pushed out to fill the gap and get touch. At six o'clock they had succeeded in establishing a thin but continuous line in touch with our Allies. But the situation was a very difficult one. The enemy had received reinforcements in Hazy and the north gun-pits—from all appearances fresh troops—and both flanks of the London Scottish were in the air and exposed to the immediate presence of the enemy.

At 8.30 p.m. the German counter-attack developed, and, though heavy casualties were inflicted on the enemy, he succeeded in forcing the London Scottish and the right of the 4th London Regt., which was creeping round the gun-pits, to retire to our original line.

The division, at nightfall, was left with a net gain of part of Spectrum and Rainbow. Gen. Hull then ordered a renewal of the attack on the next day, and sent up the London Rifle Brigade and the Queen Victoria's Rifles to the 168th Brigade, and the Queen's Westminster Rifles to the 167th Brigade.

The assault took place at 3.30 p.m. on the 8th

October, and almost at once Brig.-Gen. Freeth
reported that the barrage was very feeble.

On the 168th Brigade front the attack was arranged
this time so that it started simultaneously all along
the line. The London Rifle Brigade on the right
advanced steadily for about 500 yards, and again
gained a foothold in Hazy. But the experience of
the previous day was repeated. The northern gun-
pits, with their garrison of machine-gunners, was held
by the enemy, who poured a devastating fire into the
left flank of the four advancing waves, and on this
occasion there was fire from the right flank as well ;
the attack was in the main held up about fifty yards
from Hazy, where a shell-hole line was established.
The reserve company was sent forward to fill the
gap which existed, as on the first attack, between us
and the French.

The Queen Victoria's Rifles and the 3rd London
Regt., on the 167th Brigade front, failed to make any
appreciable advance. Both Dewdrop and the south
of Spectrum resting on the sunken road were strongly
garrisoned, and the machine-gun fire was withering.
At 10.30 p.m. all troops were withdrawn to the
original line.

The position on the morning of the 9th was that
we held Spectrum to the bend in the trench just
south of the sunken road, and had a strong party of
the Queen's Westminsters in the sunken road. On the
remainder of the front there had been no advance.

On these two days 84 prisoners of the 31st and
84th Reserve Infantry Regts., 18th Division, and
two machine guns were captured. The great difficulty experienced was to know where troops were
situated. The weather was bad, and the effort of

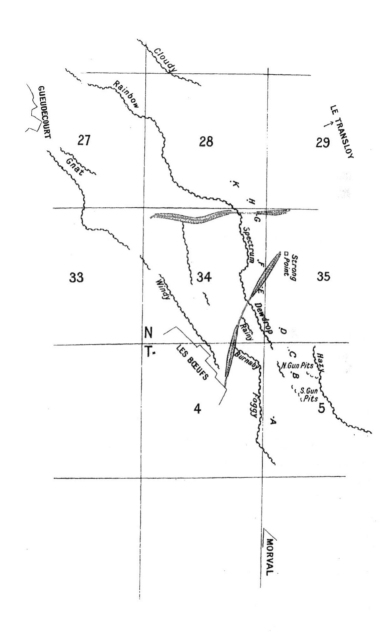

3. THE TRANSLOY RIDGE.

attacking was in itself a gigantic one, but that effort
had been made, and seemed to hang on the brink of
success, and if the artillery could have helped a little
more would have been entirely satisfactory. The
artillery, however, were greatly handicapped. Maps
could not tell them where the new enemy trenches
were, and aeroplanes were unable to take photographs. As to being helped by roads, though these
were clearly marked on the map, they had been
almost completely blown away by shell fire on the
ground and were by no means easy to distinguish.
It was a vile country.

The latter days of the Somme battle were even
worse for the R.A.M.C. Wounded men had to be
carried to Ginchy and frequently from there to Montauban. The medical branch of the division never
experienced a harder time than that on the Somme.

On the night of the 9th October the 56th Division
was relieved by the 4th Division. The battles of
the Somme were practically over. Sir Douglas Haig
wanted to push on in the direction of Le Transloy :

" On our eastern flank . . . it was important to
gain ground. Here the enemy still possessed a strong
system of trenches covering the villages of Transloy
and Beaulencourt and the town of Bapaume ; but
although he was digging with feverish haste, he had
not been able to create any very formidable defences
behind this line. In this direction, in fact, we had
at last reached a stage at which a successful attack
might reasonably be expected to yield much greater
results than anything we had yet attained. The
resistance of the troops opposed to us had seriously
weakened in the course of our recent operations, and
there was no reason to suppose that the effort required
would not be within our powers.

This last completed system of defence, before Le Transloy, was flanked to the south by the enemy's position at Sailly-Saillisel and screened to the west by the spur lying between Le Transloy and Les Bœufs. A necessary preliminary, therefore, to an assault upon it was to secure the spur and the Sailly-Saillisel heights. Possession of the high ground at this latter village would at once give us far better command over the ground to the north and the north-west, secure the flank of our operations towards Transloy, and deprive the enemy of observation over the Allied communications in the Combles valley. In view of the enemy's efforts to construct new systems of defence behind the Le Transloy line, it was desirable to lose no time in dealing with the situation.

Unfortunately, at this juncture very unfavourable weather set in, and continued with scarcely a break during the remainder of October and the early part of November. Poor visibility seriously interfered with the work of our artillery, and constant rain turned the mass of hastily-dug trenches for which we were fighting into channels of deep mud. The country roads, broken by countless shell craters, that cross the deep stretch of ground we had lately won, rapidly became almost impassable, making the supply of food, stores, and ammunition a serious problem. These conditions multiplied the difficulties of attack to such an extent that it was found impossible to exploit the situation with the rapidity necessary to enable us to reap the full benefits of the advantages we had gained."

Two attacks were, indeed, made to assist the French in their operations against the important village of Sailly-Saillisel, which fell to them on the 18th of the month, but by that time the weather had become so bad, and the delay had been so long, that the decisive moment had passed. [The short

and successful battle of the Ancre was fought on the
13–18th November, bringing the total number of
1916 Somme battles up to twelve.]

.   .   .   .   .

Lieut.-Col. A. D. Bayliffe, who commanded the
168th Brigade through this great battle, wrote at the
time an interesting paper which he heads : " Lessons
to be deducted from the Operations on the Somme."
Written with the incidents and conditions fresh on
his mind, and for future guidance, it is not a criticism
of the actions fought, but from his recommendations
we may gather something of the difficulties which
had to be faced and overcome.   We give only some
striking extracts :

" The results of the operations carried out by this
brigade bear out more than ever the necessity for an
assault being made direct at the objective. Failures,
or partial failures, are attributable to present-day
troops being asked to perform a complicated
manœuvre such as a wheel or change of direction
during an assault.

The objectives allotted should be as far as possible
definite, and should be chosen on the ground so that
well-defined landmarks may be included. With the
heavy casualties which occur among the officers, and
considering the partially-trained state of N.C.O.s
and men, it is seldom any use leaving the site of the
objective to the judgment of the assaulting troops.

In order to comply with this suggestion, it is essential
that a proper scheme of assembly trenches should be
thought out, and proper time given for their construction even in the rapid advances which have
been taking place.

In this connection it should be remembered that
troops engaged in holding the line cannot be expected

to do much digging work. Also that, without further training, reinforcement officers are incapable of finding their way over unknown ground, even with good maps, and that they cannot tape out trenches and extend working parties. It is therefore necessary to use pioneers very largely for the digging of assembly trenches if this essential work is to be well done.

Attacks delivered on too broad a front with too little weight fail even against what appears to be inferior hostile defences. The reason is that assaulting troops edge away from the source of hostile fire, and when the lines of men are too thin, they move forward through the gaps in the hostile defences without dealing with them.

It appears that assaults, to be successful, should never be delivered with less than four waves even against near objectives. One hostile machine gun may completely break up the first wave or two; if there are two or more waves in rear they may successfully carry on the assault.

It is desirable to have Battalion Headquarters as far forward as possible, right up in the front assembly trenches if possible, before an attack. But it is no good placing them there unless there is some suitable shelter (however small), and unless time is available to lay communication lines forward. Brigade Headquarters should also be right forward, provided there is some accommodation. This facilitates personal reconnaissance and liaison.

If the efficiency of a brigade is to be maintained as a fighting unit through a period of several weeks of active operations, a far larger proportion of officers and men should be left back than is customary. The average reinforcement officer is quite useless when his first appearance on service is in the middle of a modern battle. I would suggest that a battalion should go into action with from 12 to 16 officers only, and that 4 to 8 more should be kept about the line of Brigad

Headquarters, and the remainder to be at the transport lines. N.C.O.s should be dealt with in the same proportion.

It is well borne out through these operations that, if the artillery barrage is good and the infantry advance close to it, they will probably reach their objective without heavy loss. Usually the standing barrage was put up behind the objective, and it is thought that the standing barrage should be on the objective until the creeping barrage coincides with it and then both move together to their next standing line.

On one occasion (7th October) the three battalions of infantry on this brigade front had to advance at different times; the consequence was that the last to move had to face a very heavy barrage in addition to machine-gun fire. It is thought that the infantry should always move at zero, even if they are not in line with each other, and that the barrage line should be made to conform with the line of the assaulting infantry.

As usual there was a complete lack of touch throughout the operations with the heavy artillery. It is thought that the artillery group system should be extended so as to include some heavy artillery.

It is suggested that a large supply of signboards, painted white or luminous, should be prepared for active operations, and also a supply of trench bridges . . . reliefs were often much complicated and delayed by the lack of good tracks.

The value of the Stokes mortars in the more open fighting we have been having is very doubtful. The results achieved have never been commensurate with the great labour involved in getting the guns and ammunition forward. The trench mortar, from an administrative point of view, is more trouble than any other unit when frequent moves and reliefs occur, as it is not self-contained, and much work and trouble is involved at very busy moments in devising how its stores are to be moved.

The Tanks allotted to co-operate with this brigade were not found to be of any use at all. It is thought that Tanks require select crews of great determination, and officers in charge who have more experience and knowledge of the methods of infantry and artillery in war. If the speed of the Tanks could be increased, it would add very greatly to their value."

The difficulties indicated in this paper were those which faced the actual fighting men. We have already mentioned the zigzag line, and the reader will readily appreciate how the attempt to form a front, moving in a given direction after the men had left the trenches, frequently led to confusion and loss of direction. Col. Bayliffe's statement that men will edge away from the source of fire does not necessarily contravert our assertion that they are drawn towards the sound of fire, which must be read in conjunction with the admitted uncertainty of the exact position of an objective. During an attack no officer or N.C.O. can control more than half a dozen men, and the more usual number is two. On this basis the proportion of officers and N.C.O.s is totally inadequate, and it follows that success depends largely on the men themselves. The assaulting troops will fall naturally under two heads : leaders and followers. The leaders are the men of greater initiative, and in moments of uncertainty, when doubt of their direction seizes them, when no trench is visible, they turn towards the sound of the enemy—the place where the firing comes from. It is one of the factors to be dealt with in keeping direction. A line which has become thin through casualties will, no doubt, swerve from a strongly-held post.

And what a lot is covered by the paragraph on

digging ! The physical effort required to go through a battle like the Somme was colossal. Relief meant only relief from the actual front line, not relief from open trenches, from wet, from mud, from cold, or even from severe casualties ; it was merely a case of moving a short way back to other trenches. After days of this sort of life an assault was a most exhausting experience and, if successful, was not finished with the written message, "We are on our objective." Exhausted men were called upon to dig new trenches at once, under fierce fire, and the trenches dug, they waited for the counter-attack which, on the Somme, inevitably followed. Perhaps the counter-attack succeeded and the men were driven back to their original line—and still there was no rest.

Imagine the condition of mind of the surviving officers and men of a company when they were reinforced by troops straight from home, with no experience of modern or indeed any other form of fighting. The reinforcements came almost as an added anxiety to the old men. And how could the new arrivals be expected to appreciate the advantage of following close on our own barrage, in itself a doubt-provoking thing ? There was nothing easy for the regimental officer or for his men ; they fought the enemy, the earth, and the sky.

We give the gallant colonel's remarks on Tanks as an interesting light on the early proceedings of the new engines of war. We are well aware that they will provoke a smile from some readers, but they are none the less justifiable. Tanks accomplished very little on this part of the battle front. To the infantry they seemed only to attract the attention of the enemy with the appalling noise they made and the very definite target they afforded, and then they broke down ! Col. Bayliffe's opinion, which does not absolutely condemn the use of Tanks, was shared by two Brigadier-Generals of the 16th Division, and most of the infantry in less exalted positions. That they afterwards accomplished the object of their inventors is beside the point.

Heaven forbid that we should appear to offer excuses for the 56th Division—none are needed. But we find it impossible to give a true picture of the conditions under which men fought, and by placing a few of the difficulties before the reader, hope to enable him to appreciate the truly great fighting qualities of these London men. Success conjures up to the mind a picture of swift movement, and such successes were gained during the war—but not on the Somme. The enemy was strong and determined, and fought to the last. Gen. Falkenhayn, who was the instigator of the Verdun offensive, seems to rather pooh-pooh the battle of the Somme, and give the impression that it had little effect on the Central Powers ; but as he was dismissed at the end of August, one might deduce that other people did not share his views. Hindenburg and Ludendorff, on the other hand, wag their heads gravely over the whole business. The Germans were being badly battered, and were fighting most desperately to arrest disaster. And so, in recording the exploits of the 56th Division, we have to repeat somewhat monotonously the account of attacks being continually delivered on the same trench or point.

The trouble in a battle of this sort is to reconcile the two points of view : that of the Higher Command and that of the infantry. For the infantry there was no break in the fighting—if they did not assault "over the top," they were bombing the enemy out of a trench or being bombed out themselves. And it is not too easy to decide what particular trenches were held at any one moment. The position in Loop Trench, for instance, was continually changing. Combles Trench, the sunken road, and the southern end of Bouleaux Wood were points of continual struggle. The enemy exerted his full pressure on the 56th Division. But for the Higher Command this month of fighting divides itself into five attacks !

The plan on this part of the front was to surround Combles by joining the French on the far side. The junction of two armies of different nationalities might always be considered a point of weakness, and the movement itself was one of which the enemy could take advantage. Lord Cavan explains the position very clearly with a small rough sketch :

" The plan to take Combles was like this :

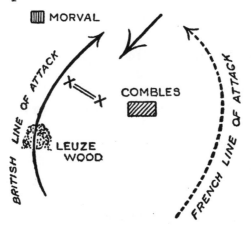

Therefore during the advance the protection of my flank from a possible counter-stroke down the

arrow was most important. This protection from
Leuze Wood to Morval was splendidly and gloriously
afforded. Further, in the actual attack on Morval
and Les Bœufs this protecting flank had to be advanced
to keep pace with the attack. The key of this was
the capture of a trench about X–X. This was captured and held, and the complete success of the battle
was assured. I had every confidence in Hull and his
men, tired though they were, and this confidence was
more than justified."

This grim, determined, and desperate struggle reveals
qualities in the London troops which, though they
existed, would not in a more spectacular success have
been so clearly demonstrated. It requires good men
to attack again and again until their object is gained,
and when these attacks are launched against such
splendidly trained soldiers as the Germans, one can
only marvel that the thing was ever done, and applaud
the steadfast courage, the endurance of body and spirit,
which enabled the men to do it.

True, the battles of the Somme ended with both
sides being stuck in the mud—an inglorious ending to
so much heroism—and the final, and perhaps fatal,
stroke was snatched from our grasp by the weather ;
but those who came through the battle may now
consider dispassionately what it was they had accomplished.

The Central Powers (we must always remember that
we fought more than the strength of Germany) had
decided, as we know, to bleed France white on the
field of Verdun. They were also pressing Italy hard
and had gained important successes. The Entente
Powers replied first with Brussiloff's attack, and
secondly with the Franco-British offensive on the

Somme. Falkenhayn declares that the most dangerous
moment of the Russian offensive had been passed
before the first shot of the battle of the Somme had
been fired. He also maintains that the Austrian loss
of the right bank of the Isonzo had no connection
with the Somme ; that the Germans would not in
any case have sent troops to help their ally in Italy.
As for Verdun, he deals with it in a somewhat unsatisfactory paragraph :

" The only tangible gain, then, of this battle to the
enemy remains in its effect on the situation on the
Western Front. As a matter of course, an expenditure of strength such as the enemy favoured de-
manded the use of corresponding forces for the
defence. The operations in the Meuse area were not
yet, however, immediately affected. On the 11th July
we were still able, by a strong thrust, to advance our
line on the east bank. . . . After this it was the tension
of the whole situation, and especially the necessity
to husband our *matériel* and ammunition, which
necessitated the abandonment of any big German
offensive operations on the Meuse. The headquarters
of the Crown Prince's Army Group were instructed
to carry on the offensive calmly and according to
plan, so as to give the enemy no good reason for
concluding that he could hope for its cessation.
This, too, was quite successful, for the French were
unable to bring up reinforcements from the Meuse
to the Somme front until September, when, following
on the change of Chief of the General Staff, the
' Verdun-offensive ' had been completely abandoned."

The last sentence is, of course, the bitter pill for
Falkenhayn. It is perhaps only natural that he
would seek to justify his policy, and persist that he
was right and would have succeeded had he been left

8

alone. Hindenburg's memoirs give one a somewhat
different impression :

" Very soon after I took over my new post I found
myself compelled by the general situation to ask His
Majesty the Emperor to order the offensive at Verdun
to be broken off. The battles there exhausted our
forces like an open wound. Moreover, it was obvious
in any case that the enterprise had become hopeless,
and that for us to persevere with it would cost us
greater losses than those we were able to inflict on
the enemy. The battlefield was a regular hell, and
was regarded as such by the troops."

And of the Somme he says :

" The extent of the demands which were being made
on the army in the West was brought before my eyes
quite vividly for the first time during this visit to
France. I will not hesitate to admit that it was only
now that I fully realised all that the Western Armies
had done hitherto. . . . I could now understand how
everyone, officers and men alike, longed to get away
from such an atmosphere. . . . Many of our best and
finest fighting men had to pour out their heart's
blood in destroyed trenches. . . .
   It was only when the arrival of the wet season
began to make the ground impossible that things
became quieter in the battle area of the Somme.
The million of shell-holes filled with water became
mere cemeteries. . . . Over everyone hovered the
fearful spectre of this battlefield, which for desolation
and horror seemed to be even worse than that of
Verdun."

General Ludendorff carries the impression still
further [1] :

----

[1] *My War Memories*, 1914-1918, Ludendorff.

" On the Somme the enemy's powerful artillery,
assisted by excellent aeroplane observation and fed
with enormous supplies of ammunition, had kept down
our fire and destroyed our artillery. The defence of
our infantry had become so flabby that the massed
attacks of the enemy always succeeded. Not only
did our *moral* suffer, but in addition to fearful
wastage in killed and wounded, we lost a large number
of prisoners and much material. . . .

The 25th saw the beginning of the heaviest of the
many heavy engagements that made up the battle of
the Somme. Great were our losses. The enemy took
Rancourt, Morval, Gueudecourt, and the hotly-
contested Combles. On the 26th the Thiepval
salient fell. . . .

The fighting had made the most extraordinary
demands both on commanders and troops. . . .
Divisions and other formations had to be thrown in
on the Somme front in quicker succession, and had
to stay in the line longer. The time for recuperation
and training on quiet sectors became shorter and
shorter. The troops were getting exhausted. Everything was cut as fine as possible. The strain on our
nerves in Pless was terrible. . . ."

We may conclude, then, that the Somme, as the
chief counter-stroke of the Entente Powers, defeated
the Central Powers; France was not bled white; and
although the Russians were driven back, and
Roumania, who had entered the war, was speedily
defeated by the Central Powers, Italy was relieved
and delivered a successful counter-attack on the
Austrians. The situation, as a result of the Somme,
although the individual British soldier may not have
thought it vastly improved, was more than ever
serious for the Central Powers, and one could not at
that stage hope for more.

The total number of prisoners taken by the British Armies on the Somme, from 1st July to 18th November, was over 38,000. Also 29 heavy guns, 96 field guns, 136 trench mortars, and 514 machine guns.

CHAPTER III

ONE might well imagine that the 56th Division was entitled to a rest, but the days when armies retired into winter-quarters had passed—unless a "quiet" bit of the line may be so called. There was a rest for a few days in the neighbourhood of Belloy-sur-Somme, north-west of Amiens. Battalions moved there, after a night at Bernafay Wood, Mansell Camp, or the Citadel, by bus, and all moves were complete by the 12th October. Then they rested and cleaned up.

There was a slight rearrangement on the 20th, which brought Divisional Headquarters to Hallen-court, and some of the units into other villages, but the division was once more on the move almost immediately, and on the 24th October was behind the 61st Division in the country round Lestrem. Three days later brigades commenced the relief of the 61st Division in the Richbourg l'Avoué–Laventie line.

This bit of country was exceedingly flat, and in normal times was drained by innumerable ditches. It was one of those bits of country where trenches are an impossibility—soil and water seem to be combined in equal proportions. Naturally war conditions did not improve the draining, and at times large tracts of the country were flooded. Our defences were breastworks, and the system of holding the line was by a combination of posts. There were certain advantages about this line, matters of space and of easy approach, but they were only apparent when the weather was fine ; when it was cold and wet, shelter was very difficult to find.

At first all three brigades were in line, but on the 27th November the 5th Division was put in on the right and the front was shortened, so that two brigades held the line and one was in reserve.

The whole of the division, however, did not arrive in this sector at once. The artillery had been left on the Somme battlefield covering the left of the French. Of this time Brig.-Gen. Elkington writes :

" During the whole of the month of October the heavy and incessant rain had made the going so bad that it was almost impossible to get vehicles up to the positions. Improvised ammunition carriers were made out of the baskets from the ammunition wagons, and for the last part of the operations all ammunition, rations, and water went up on pack animals. It was most difficult to get material for dugouts up to the guns, and in consequence officers and men suffered a great deal of discomfort. The horses also suffered very much from the constant hard, heavy work. The 56th Divisional Artillery were relieved on the 31st October by the 8th Divisional Artillery. Owing to the heavy going, the withdrawal of the guns was a difficult job, and one section of A/280, which got stuck in deep mud, took two days to get out. The 56th Divisional Artillery marched from the Somme on the 1st November, badly in need of a rest and refit in the way of clothes, etc., and on the 5th we arrived on the Neuville–St. Vaast front, and went into the line, covering the 3rd Canadian Division facing the Vimy Ridge, on the 6th. The headquarters of the artillery was established at Aubigny, where the headquarters of the Canadian Division, under Major-Gen. Lipsett, were.

From the 7th November to the 1st December we remained covering the Canadian Division. The sector was a very quiet one, but the batteries were very extended, and it was a matter of very long walks going round them, as cars were not allowed forward. We were very well done by the Canadians, and the men were able to get reclothed, and the horses managed to pick up in the good stabling. . . . On the 1st December the 56th Divisional Artillery was relieved by the Canadian R.F.A., and we marched to the Neuve Chapelle area to cover our own division."

Meanwhile the 56th Division was covered by the 6th Divisional Artillery.

Reinforcements for the shattered battalions were prompt, and all monthly strength returns show a good average of a thousand men for battalions. Horses remained steadily about 5,100, although the number fell during the battle of the Somme. In actual numbers the division was of average strength, but the quality had suffered. We find, for instance, a record that a draft of over a thousand men arrived about this period, and that they had not been instructed in musketry! With all the will in the world such men were not of very great use. Provision was made, however, for their instruction.

Almost at once the reputation of this Neuve Chapelle front began to change. It had been considered a quiet bit of line with nothing much happening beyond mining and counter-mining. On the 28th October the enemy opened a trench-mortar bombardment which Australian miners declared to have been the heaviest they had experienced during their stay in that line. The system of holding the line by means of posts, too, gave many opportunities for patrol work, as it was a system adopted by both sides. The advantage of position, as was so often the case, was with the Germans, who were on the Aubers Ridge, with better observation and drier ground.

The month of November was a quiet month, cold and wet. No Man's Land was flooded and patrols found it very difficult to move about, as they could not avoid splashing and consequent betrayal of their presence.

On the 30th November the enemy raided the 7th Middlesex, who occupied as part of their line a mine-crater. Major Emery was on the spot, and with two men drove them off. They failed to secure identification. The next day, however, we secured identification in the shape of a Lieut. Steinhardt, 19th Bavarian Regt., who was in charge of a patrol which was dispersed by one of our Lewis-gun teams—an experience which the lieutenant found so bewildering that he lost his way and entered our lines, under the impression that they were his own.

Two lance-corporals, Millar and Wodley, of the 2nd London Regt., also secured identification by chasing a German patrol of five men, of whom they killed one and the remaining four put up their hands. These men were of the 7th Bavarian Regt., 5th Bavarian Division, III Bavarian Corps.

The policy of the XI Corps (Gen. Haking) was to annoy the enemy on all occasions and keep him always uneasy. The month of December was therefore devoted to most active patrolling, and the enemy lines were entered again and again only to be found empty. There is only one record of finding the line occupied, when the Queen Victoria's Rifles captured two prisoners. The reason, of course, was the state of the ground, and it affords an interesting sidelight on the endurance shown by the men of the 56th Division, as the trenches, or rather defences, they occupied were similar to those of the Hun.

The operations of the winter are, in fact, only of interest as showing the endurance, the determination, and the spirit of the 56th Division. There was nothing in the nature of an attack or even a raid of any magnitude—it was a matter of small parties of men resisting the fearful conditions of climate, and penetrating with the greatest boldness into the enemy lines.

Having ascertained that the enemy was not occupying his line, but merely patrolling it, a more aggressive attitude was adopted from the 1st January, 1917. On the first day of the year snipers, from the battalions in line, established themselves in the German front line and remained there all day. They had a few opportunities which they did not miss.

The operations until the 14th January were carried out by battalions of the 167th Brigade; those between the 14th and 29th by the 169th Brigade. Briefly they may be summarised.

On the night of the 3rd/4th January 100 men of a new draft were taken across No Man's Land, in parties of six, to " visit " the enemy trenches; this was no easy matter on account of the state of the ground. On the same night two officers of the 3rd London Regt. penetrated almost to the enemy support lines, when they were held up by deep water.

On the night 9/10th January four posts were

established in the enemy front line, and on the next night two more.

On the 14th a post known as Hampstead Heath was violently attacked by the enemy in very superior numbers. This post was held by the 7th Middlesex, and the men were so cold they could scarcely move ; the Queen's Westminster Rifles were actually half-way across No Man's Land on the way to relieve them when the attack occurred. This relief was apparently driven back by trench-mortar barrage and machine-gun fire. The 7th Middlesex men put up a fight, but their Lewis gun was jammed and useless, and they were forced out of the post. One man was found to be missing. The record of this regiment is particularly fine, and they felt very acutely the taking of this prisoner by the enemy. The 7th Middlesex is one of the two Imperial Service Battalions of the Territorial Force which existed at the outbreak of war. It was the first battalion to leave the country and was sent to hold Gibraltar. In March 1915 it arrived in France and was attached to the 8th Division at La Gorgue—in this same area. From the taking over of the line immediately after the battle of Neuve Chapelle it went through many engagements before joining the 56th Division, and up to this time, in spite of all the attacks on the Somme, it had only lost six men as prisoners. Its casualties in France, to date, were : 28 officers and 338 other ranks killed, 35 officers and 763 other ranks wounded.

On the morning of the 15th January another post called Bertha was attacked under cover of a dense fog, and after four men out of eleven had been killed, the post (of the 1st London Regt.) was driven out—but two were taken prisoners. Almost immediately, however, a patrol of the same regiment, composed of four men, left our front line and reoccupied the post, and by noon our troops had restored the position. The enemy made another attack, but were driven off. This post evidently caused the Germans great annoyance, as they attacked it on the night of the 16/17th January and were again driven off.

From the 17th to the 20th the posts were bombarded by artillery and trench mortars, and on the 21st, under cover of an intense bombardment, the enemy succeeded in occupying Bertha Post. A counter-attack was at once organised, but it failed, owing to two machine guns which the enemy had brought up with them. In the early morning our patrols discovered the enemy leaving it, and it was again occupied.

During the night 22nd/23rd January the enemy made an organised attempt to recapture all the posts. After repeated attacks the garrison of Bertha Post was once more forced to retire, and again reoccupied the spot in the early morning.

The enemy shelled the posts all day on the 23rd and 24th, on the latter with a large percentage of lachrymatory shells, which shelling was followed by four separate attacks. After hand-to-hand and bombing fights they were driven off.

On the evening of the 27th the enemy concentrated his artillery fire on Irma Post, which until then had only received general attention from him, and succeeded in driving the garrison out. We then drove the enemy out by artillery fire, and the post was reoccupied by us.

On the 28th the Army Commander, Gen. Horne, directed that all the posts should be vacated.

One cannot consider these incidents only as small bickerings. The artillery fire which the men had to face was remarkably accurate and very fierce, and there was also the weather. At first No Man's Land was a swamp, or a lake, and then a cold snap set in, which was paralysing to all who had to live in the open. The men had no cover either from shell fire or the weather—the " posts " were only a matter of shell-holes on our side of the German breastworks, and improved with the help of a shovel and a pick. In face of these hardships the courage and determination of the troops of the 56th Division never faltered, although at one time Capt. Newnham felt impelled to write that, "although wiring has been much strengthened, actual consolidation is impossible owing to the frozen ground. The garrison feel they are occupying shell traps. Battalions are on the defensive and not offensive, and the *moral* of the men is suffering. At the same time our existing defences are falling into disrepair." In spite of this dictum the men succeeded, after it was written, in driving off four severe attacks, but it gives an indication of the desperate conditions under which the 56th Division carried out an aggressive policy.

All this work drew from the Corps Commander a personal letter to Gen. Hull :

" I should be glad if you would convey, to the troops of the division under your command, my appreciation of the operations they have carried out so successfully during the last month in establishing posts in the German front line, and holding them in spite of heavy bombardments and hostile infantry attacks.

The effects of the operations are much greater than the troops that took part in them are probably aware of. They have shown the enemy the offensive and enterprising spirit displayed by our troops, and have encouraged other British formations to adopt similar tactics which will have a far-reaching effect.

Brig.-Gens. Loch and Freeth, who conducted the operations at different periods when you were acting in command of the Corps, deserve credit for the determined manner in which they continued the pressure against the enemy in spite of serious opposition. The various counter-attacks by our troops, immediately delivered without waiting for any further orders and simply adhering to the plan laid down by you, show a fine military spirit on the part of officers and men of the battalions engaged.

I was particularly pleased with the action of the scouts of the 1st London Regt. who went across No Man's Land in daylight on the 14th January, and with the prompt action of " B " Company, Queen Victoria's Rifles, under Capt. Brand, on the night of January 22nd/23rd, when the posts were attacked. Also with "A" and "B" Companies of the London Rifle Brigade, under Lieut. Prior and 2/Lieut. Rose, who held Enfield and Barnet Posts in the enemy lines on the night of January 24/25th, when their posts were shelled with lachrymatory shells and our men had to wear respirators. These posts were then heavily attacked, and the supporting platoons quickly traversed No Man's Land before the hostile barrage was put down. I am also glad that the artillery support on all occasions throughout these operations has been prompt and effective.

R. HAKING, Lieutenant-General,
Commanding XI Corps.
3rd February, 1917."

The division then settled down to more ordinary trench routine ; but the active season was approaching.

.   .   .   .   .

Although the first day of the new year seems to mark a definite break in time, no such break was obvious to the British troops in France and Belgium. Sir Douglas Haig was determined to seize every favourable opportunity to push the advantage that had been won at the battle of the Somme. Between the Ancre and the Scarpe valleys the enemy was in a very pronounced salient. A series of operations were undertaken against the flank of this salient, commencing in November 1916. It was, however, necessary to wait on the weather, and although some valuable positions were captured, real advance was not made until January, when actions were won and ground gained at Beaumont Hamel, Grandcourt, Miraumont, Serre, Gommecourt, and Irles. These successes opened the way for a big operation against the Le Transloy–Loupart line. The enemy then made his celebrated retreat to the Hindenburg Line. This line branched off from the original German defences near Arras, ran south-east for twelve miles to Quéant, and then west of Cambrai towards St. Quentin.

The opening of the new year is a most interesting study. The Germans were beginning to feel the lack of men. Their retreat was decided upon for the purpose of shortening their line and avoiding a battle. They knew it would require months of preparation before an army could advance to the attack across the wide area which they had systematically laid waste. Here at least they reckoned on a breathing space. And in Germany itself the Hindenburg programme for production was coming into operation— everywhere they were carefully going over their resources and reorganising.

England reached, in 1917, the height of her fighting

power as regards the number of divisions, and this was known to the enemy. So he waited with some anxiety for developments on the Western Front.

The Germans had started their unrestricted submarine compaign, from which they hoped to gain much benefit, but, on the other hand, they were nervous of Russia—and Russia complicated the situation.

Ludendorff writes :

" How often had I not hoped for a revolution in Russia in order that our military burden might be alleviated ! But my desire had been merely a castle in the air. Now it had come true and as a surprise. It felt as though a weight had been removed from my chest."

The revolution in Russia took place in March, and so, right at the beginning of what promised to be an ominous year for the Germans, they were able, by a stroke of fortune, to save ammunition in the East, and to transfer fresh divisions from the East to the West, and let their worn-out divisions deal with the Russians.

The Entente Powers, however, had no reason to feel more than disappointment, as they dealt the Central Powers a blow by the capture of Baghdad ; and although they had no immediate support from America, that country declared war on Germany as a result of the submarine policy adopted.

The 56th Division opened the new year in very fair strength, as the following return will show :

	Officers.	Other Ranks.
Divisional Headquarters	22	103
167th Brigade Headquarters	2	3
1st London Regt.	34	1,028
3rd London Regt.	32	1,066
8th Middlesex Regt.	22	1,051

	Officers.	Other Ranks.
167th Machine Gun Coy.	11	171
168th Brigade Headquarters	7	25
4th London Regt.	40	1,003
12th London Regt.	47	1,073
13th London Regt.	38	1,043
14th London Regt.	37	963
168th Machine Gun Coy.	11	165
169th Brigade Headquarters	8	26
2nd London Regt.	41	1,012
5th London Regt.	35	1,052
9th London Regt.	34	1,030
16th London Regt.	39	975
169th Machine Gun Coy.	11	182
5th Cheshire Regt.	38	890
193rd Machine Gun Coy.	10	174
56th Divisional Artillery Headquarters . .	4	19
280th Brigade R.F.A.	29	756
281st Brigade R.F.A.	26	748
282nd Brigade R.F.A.	28	705
D.A.C.	24	806
56th Divisional R.E. Headquarters . .	2	10
416th Edinburgh Field Coy.	10	210
512th London Field Coy.	10	212
513th London Field Coy.	10	218
Divisional Signals	6	212
Divisional Train	18	388
Medical Units	26	573
Mobile Veterinary	1	23

But soon after New Year's Day the artillery was reorganised. The 56th Divisional Artillery became two brigades (280th and 281st), each of three (six-gun) 18-pounder batteries, and one (six-gun) howitzer battery. For this purpose A/282 Howitzer Battery was split up, one section going to D/280 and one to D/281. The 282nd Brigade, under the new organisation, became an Army Field Artillery Brigade, and to bring it up to strength it absorbed "B" Battery, 126th Brigade, and one section of "D" Battery, 126th Brigade. This battery and section came from the 37th Division.

In the big operations which were soon to take place, Gen. Hull had Lieut.-Col. Packenham to help him as G.S.O.1.

．　　．　　．　　．　　．

Although we say the division went back to ordinary trench warfare after January, it must not be thought that the policy of aggression had been abandoned. The enemy lines were constantly visited and found on most occasions to be empty. But the 13th London Regt., the Kensingtons, secured five prisoners of the 13th Bavarian Regt., and killed about forty on one occasion ; and the London Rifle Brigade obtained identification and killed three in a subsequent raid. The enemy also made one attempt, and entered our line between two posts, but the posts attacked him vigorously and drove him out, after killing three of the party, who proved to be of the 13th Bavarian Regt.

On the 6th March the line was handed over to the 49th Division, and the 56th Division left the First Army and was transferred to the VII Corps (Snow), Third Army. Brigades marched back to the Flers area, Divisional Headquarters being at Le Cauroy, and battalions scattered about the country between Frevent and St. Pol, in the villages of Beauvois, Hernicourt, Croisette, Pronay, Siracourt, Blangermont, Blangerol, Guinecourt, Héricourt, Framecourt, Petit Houvin, Nuncy, Haute Côte, Sibiville, Séricourt, Honval, etc.

9

CHAPTER IV

THE BATTLES OF ARRAS, 1917

THE Germans had commenced their retreat, and we know that the British Higher Command had planned large movements. On the 14th March the 169th Brigade took over the front line between Achicourt and Agny, to the south of Arras, with the 30th Division on the right and the 14th Division on the left. Two days after a number of fires were seen in the enemy lines to the south. The Hun was moving, but patrols found him very alert on their immediate front.

Brig.-Gen. Coke, 169th Brigade, went round his line on the 15th March, and the diary notes that " trenches in a shocking condition, full of mud and dirt " ! It was a normal condition for trenches, and one might well be excused for wondering if the Italians or the forces in Salonica fared any better in this respect. Did they find mud on the top of a real mountain ? Maybe their position was always in the valley, in the centre of a stream !

As usual, patrols were out on the night of the 17th (the patrolling of the 56th Division is worthy of great praise) and noticed nothing in particular. But some scouts of the 2nd London Regt., lying close to the enemy wire as dawn was breaking on the 18th, came to the conclusion that the enemy line was not normal.

They investigated and found it empty. This was promptly reported to the company commander, who sent out strong fighting patrols and occupied the front line.

Officers in the line acted with the greatest promptitude. Brigades on either side were quick to follow the example of the 2nd London Regt., and all Headquarters were buzzing with excitement, although the situation, in view of what was happening farther south, was not unexpected.

By midday the 2nd London Regt. had occupied Beaurains. The whole Corps was ordered to advance; the German second line was occupied, and on the left the 14th Division were in the third line. The Corps order for the advance, however, was cautious. It pointed out the probability of the enemy withdrawing to a main line of defence, Telegraph Hill, and the east half of Neuville Vitasse. The 169th Brigade were to keep touch with the enemy, but Brig.-Gen. Coke must avoid becoming involved in a serious engagement at present.

By the early morning of the 19th March patrols had established the fact that the enemy were indeed holding Neuville Vitasse, and on the left he was found at Tilloy, the Harp, Telegraph Hill, and Nice Trench. Troops remained in front of Neuville Vitasse and constructed advance trenches.

We have pointed out the salient, between the Ancre and the Scarpe, which was the result of the battles of the Somme; and we have mentioned the actions that had been fought on the right of this salient in preparation to a bigger operation. It was the intention of Sir Douglas Haig to attack the salient from both sides—the Fifth Army in the south operating on the Ancre Front, and the Third Army about Arras. The plan included the pinching off of the whole area, and on the north of the Scarpe the capture of the Vimy Ridge. This latter operation was the task of the First Army.

So far as the Fifth Army was concerned, the German retreat had avoided a battle, but on the Third Army front their retirement must be limited, as the enemy had no intention of giving up the Vimy Ridge on our First Army front. Indeed, there was no retirement on the left of the VII Corps, just south of Arras, which was the flank of the Hindenburg Line.

But adjustments and new orders were necessary to meet the situation. It was most desirable to attract as many enemy troops to our front before the French offensive was launched in the south, and so the Fifth Army was ordered to follow the enemy closely to the Hindenburg Line, where it would exert the greatest pressure, and the Third and First Armies would, with slight modifications of detail, carry out the original attack as planned on their front.

The VII Corps was the most affected. The objectives of the Third Army had been Mercatel, Hill 90, the German third-line system from Feuchy Chapel, and the high ground about Monchy. The effect of the enemy withdrawals on the VII Corps front was

" to change our task from an attack in a south-easterly direction from prepared positions, to an attack in an easterly and north-easterly direction from improvised positions. But the objects of the attack remain the same ; that is, to break through the enemy's defensive line on the right of the Third Army front, to overrun all his defences as far as the Green Line (the far side of the Cojeul River), and to clear and hold the southern side of the gap which the VI Corps, advancing simultaneously with us, will have made."

The VII Corps front was held by the 21st, 30th, 56th, and 14th Divisions in line, with the 50th in reserve. On the right the 21st Division had a very small rôle allotted to it. The first attack was to be delivered by the 56th and 14th Divisions with the VI Corps on their left (no German retreat had taken place here), and gradually the 30th and then the 21st Divisions would take part in the advance.

The first phase of the planned attack gave to the 56th Division the task of capturing Neuville Vitasse (the 30th would conform on the right, but even so would not approach the enemy main line), and to the 14th Division the piercing of the extreme left of the Hindenburg Line and part of the Harp ; the 3rd Division, VI Corps, on the left would capture Tilloy.

The second phase placed the right of the 30th Division on the south of the Cojeul River and in possession of St. Martin-sur-Cojeul, and the left through the Hindenburg (Cojeul Switch) Line, while the 56th and 14th would be in front of Wancourt.

The 56th and 14th Divisions were not to go beyond Nepal Trench, as the 30th Division, pushing up from the south-west, would cross their front and, passing entirely to the south bank of the Cojeul, would join hands with the troops of the VI Corps east of Guemappe. The 21st Division would contribute to the flank thus formed with its right standing fast on Croisilles.

After this Green Line, as it was called, there was the usual hopeful reference to a distant objective, Cambrai, and some talk of cavalry, no doubt a necessary provision, but one which, nevertheless, was greeted with hilarity. One thing, however, seems very certain : the German retreat caused very little inconvenience to the Third Army, and none at all to the First.

Preparations for the attack on the Third Army front were carried on swiftly. The enemy made no further move, but to the south, where he had many miles to go before reaching the Hindenburg Line, he was still being closely pursued by the Fifth Army. By the 2nd April the general line was Sélency, Jeancourt, Epéhy, Royaulcourt, Doignies, Mercatel, Beaurains. Between Sélency and Doignies the enemy still held positions in advance of the Hindenburg Line, and minor engagements were continually taking place on this section of the front.

On the night of the 1st April the 167th and 168th Brigades relieved the 169th Brigade in the front line. The bombardment of the enemy positions commenced on the 4th, and was carried on for five days. Meanwhile troops could study the country they were to attack.

While the 169th Brigade had been in the line, training had been carried on extensively by the other two brigades. Some of the instructions and arrangements are worthy of note. For the men, open fighting was the main practice. Regimental officers were told that

" it must be realised that the maintenance of forward movement depends on the determination and power of direction of sections, platoons, companies, and battalions. The habit of digging a trench and getting into it, or of waiting for scientifically-arranged artillery barrages before advancing, must be discarded.

A slow advance will give time for the German reinforcements to arrive—the greater the rapidity of an
advance the more is resistance likely to lessen. A
few sticky company commanders may not only delay
the whole operation but, by giving the enemy time to
reinforce, will also cause unnecessary casualties."

We quote this for comparison with other instructions given at a later date. There is nothing new in
it, and nothing to criticise in it, but man is a lover
of precedent, and trench warfare, and failure to get
through to open fighting, was the precedent established for him.

Very interesting instructions were issued on the
subject of signals between infantry and artillery.
One of the most curious facts of the war was the
general lack of communication between attacking
infantry and artillery. True, the infantryman in the
front line is not always in the best position to direct
artillery fire, but, on the other hand, he is frequently
the only man who knows anything at all. We learned,
to our cost, the excellence of the German control of
artillery fire, and though our artillery observation
officers performed the most gallant feats, our method
never seemed as good as that of the enemy. The
instructions issued were in imitation of the German
method. Coloured lights were to be fired from any
sort of pistol. Green lights were to mean "open
fire," and white lights "increase the range." These
were the only signals to be employed, either by the
Forward Observation Officer or by the infantry.
The plan does not appear to have answered very well.

There were also definite instructions as to the
strength of battalions and the number of officers,

non-commissioned officers, and men to be left out of
the fight.   We must deal with that in another place,
merely noting here that platoons were now made up
of one rifle section, one Lewis-gun section, one
bombing section, and one rifle grenade section, and
that a Divisional Depot Battalion was formed at
Bouquemaison, where all details left out of the
battle were sent.   The Depot Battalion ensured a
number of trained reinforcements being available.

We have left the 167th and 168th Brigades looking
at Neuville Vitasse.   The way to that heap of ruins
seemed clear, with the exception of a strong point,
Neuville Mill, situated on the right and in a position
to enfilade the attacking troops.   On the 7th the
1st London Regt. attempted to capture the place,
but found it well defended with machine guns, and
failed.   It was decided to deal with it by means of
Tanks.

The attack launched by the Third and First Armies
on the morning of the 9th April was on a front of
fifteen miles, from Croisilles to the northern foot of
the Vimy Ridge.   It included between four and five
miles of the Hindenburg Line.

The 56th Division attacked with the 167th Brigade
on the right, having the 3rd London Regt. and 8th
Middlesex Regt. in line, with the 1st London Regt.
in support and the 7th Middlesex in reserve ; the
168th Brigade was on the left, with the 13th and 12th
London Regts. in line, the 14th in support, and the
4th in reserve.   The Edinburgh Field Coy. R.E.
(less two sections) were with the right brigade, and
the 513th Field Coy. R.E. (less two sections),
one company of the 5th Cheshires, and two sections
of the 193rd Divisional M.G. Coy. with the left

brigade. As the whole success of the operation
depended on the 14th Division, the left brigade had
to be prepared to make a defensive flank—hence the
machine guns and pioneers.

The method of attack was what was sometimes
called leap-frog. The two battalions in line on each
brigade front were to capture Pine Lane and Neuville
Vitasse, and then the supporting battalion would
" go through " them and capture the second defence,
which was the Hindenburg, or Cojeul Switch. In the
case of the 167th Brigade, the reserve battalion, the
7th Middlesex, were to carry on the game of leap-frog
and capture Nepal Trench.

The weather up to this point had been fine, but on
the morning of the 9th dark clouds rolled up, bringing
heavy showers. The attack was started by the Corps
on the left. The 56th Division moved to the assault
at 7.45 a.m.

The first phase of the attack was the capture of
Neuville Vitasse. The 3rd London Regt., on the
right, progressed well—two Tanks worked on this
battalion front and dealt with the strong point,
Neuville Mill—and at 10 a.m. had reached their first
objective—that is to say, they were in a position short
of the Hindenburg Line. The 8th Middlesex Regt.
were delayed at first by uncut wire, but soon entered
the ruined village. Just before reaching the site of
the church they found themselves confronted by a
" pocket " of determined Germans with several
machine guns. Working round the flanks of this
" pocket," bombers and riflemen succeeded in
enveloping the enemy, so that just before eleven
o'clock sixty-eight survivors surrendered with four
machine guns. The battalion then cleared the rest

of Neuville Vitasse and were in touch with the 3rd
London Regt.

The Kensingtons swept through the enemy front
line with little opposition, and soon reached Moss
Trench. Their reserve company, seeing that all was
well, moved south into the village and rendered some
assistance to the 8th Middlesex.

On the extreme left of the divisional line the 12th
London Regt., after going through the first line, met
some uncut wire which delayed them, but soon after
ten o'clock they were in touch with the Kensingtons
in Moss Trench, although their left was thrown back
owing to the right of the 14th Division being held up
by uncut wire.

Of the two Tanks on the 168th Brigade front,
which were supposed to work round the north of the
village, only one ever started, and very soon that one
was on fire.

Meanwhile the artillery, the 281st, 293rd, and " C "
Battery of the 232nd Brigades, had moved across the
old German line and taken positions, about a thousand
yards west of Neuville Vitasse, by ten o'clock. (It
will be noticed that the artillery was " grouped "
again.)

Everything was therefore ready for the assault on
the northern extremity of the Hindenburg Line, and
an advance to Nepal Trench. This, as we have said,
was to be done by the 14th and 1st London Regts.,
who were the supporting battalions to each brigade.

The general plan at this point was that the 14th
and 56th Divisions should attack simultaneously,
and the 30th Division, on the right, was to follow in
echelon. Not until the 7th Middlesex Regt.—which
was in reserve to the 167th Brigade, and was detailed

to attack and capture Nepal Trench after the Hindenburg Line had been made secure—had passed Neuville Vitasse was the 30th Division to move. As the fighting on this right flank of the 56th Division was the most severe, we will deal first with the left flank.

The attack started at 12.10 p.m., and the London Scottish, passing through the Kensingtons and 12th London Regt., were soon engaged in some lively fighting which lasted about two hours. They killed a number of the enemy, captured 100 of them and one machine gun, and overran the mass of trenches by 1,000 yards. On their left they were in touch with the 14th Division, but their right was in the air. As the 167th Brigade had not progressed so well, the London Scottish position was not too good.

On the right of the 56th Division the situation was obscure. The 30th Division—timed to advance after the 167th Brigade—had failed, and this failure enabled the enemy in Egg and the adjacent trenches to give their undivided attention to the flank of the 56th Division. The attack was held up.

Gen. Hull had foreseen strong opposition in this direction, and had given Brig.-Gen. Freeth the 4th London Regt., the reserve battalion of the 168th Brigade, and the Queen Victoria's Rifles from the 169th Brigade. So when it was seen that the 1st London Regt. had failed to make progress, the 7th Middlesex and 4th London Regts. were launched. Some progress was made, but casualties were heavy, and the position remained uncertain and enveloped in a fog of rumour.

In order to give more stability to the line, Brig.-Gen. Loch, 168th Brigade, ordered the Kensingtons forward into that part of the Hindenburg Line which the London Scottish had captured, and the latter battalion to withdraw from their forward position and reorganise.

The situation at 6 p.m. is shown (*A*) on map.

But the 14th Division, on the left, ordered an assault of the Wancourt Line at 6.45 p.m., which attack, owing no doubt to the situation on the 56th and 30th Divisional fronts, failed.

Soon after ten o'clock that night (9th April) the Corps ordered the assault of the Wancourt Line to take place at eight the following morning, but Gen. Hull pointed out that fighting was still going on, that the situation would not be clear until daylight, and that his division would not be able to attack at that hour. The order was, therefore, amended so that the attack should take place when the situation on the 56th and 14th Divisional fronts was clear.

In the darkness of the night the 167th Brigade troops bombed the Germans out of all of the Hindenburg Line on their front, but they were still giving much trouble from the 30th Division area. The London Scottish were now able to advance again on the left and get in touch with the 14th Division about 15.

The position did not seem too favourable unless something was done on the right, but at 10.45 a.m. the Corps issued a more ambitious order : that the attack was to be carried on to the east of Guemappe.

At midday the attack was launched, but now the whole direction was altered. The left of the line, advancing on Wancourt, was held up, and the right, in order to get elbow room, was forced to clear the Hindenburg Line on the 30th Division front. In this maze of trenches the 167th Brigade made steady progress towards the junction of the Hindenburg and

Wancourt Lines. This was good work, and the Corps ordered the occupation of Hill 90, on the far side of the Wancourt Line. Gen. Hull, however, informed the Corps that it could not be done that night.

On the left the position was as uncertain as it had been the previous day on the right. The 14th Division claimed to be in the Wancourt Line, and eventually it was found that they had swerved to their left and created a large gap between their right and the left of the London Scottish, who were lying out in the open.

So the situation (B) remained through the night. The next day, the 11th, nothing was done on the left of the line, but the 167th Brigade carried on their good work and the Queen Victoria's Rifles cleared the Hindenburg Line as far as the Cojeul River, and a long length of Nepal Trench, which was part of the Wancourt Line. The difficulty of the 30th Division was apparently uncut wire. They seemed to be stuck facing the Hindenburg Line, while the Queen Victoria's Rifles cleared it. A Corps telegram to this division reads :

" Not satisfied that the infantry are receiving sufficient support from the artillery. The situation demands that as many batteries as possible be pushed forward so that enemy machine guns be dealt with at decisive range."

The 167th were relieved by the 169th Brigade late in the afternoon, after three days of very severe and successful fighting.

The 169th Brigade were ordered to consolidate Hill 90 and to push patrols into Heninel, and later,

when the 30th Division had occupied the Hindenburg
Line, to cross the River Cojeul and make good the
high ground to the south.

The attack ordered started at 5.15 a.m. on the 12th,
and after stiff bombing fights, the 2nd and 5th London
Regts., working to the north and south of Hill 90,
joined hands on the other side of it. It was found
necessary, during this operation, to have a password,
so that converging parties should not bomb each other.
To the great amusement of the men the words " Rum
jar " were chosen. The Germans, being bombed from
both sides, must have thought it an odd slogan. The
enemy were then seen withdrawing from Heninel,
and the leading company of the 2nd London Regt. immediately advanced and occupied the village. The
30th Division then crossed to the south of the Cojeul
River, and made progress along the Hindenburg Line.
Meanwhile the 2nd London Regt. had pushed
forward patrols and occupied the high ground to
the east of Heninel, where they got in touch with
the 30th Division.

The occupation of Hill 90, which had been made
possible by the 167th Brigade and the Queen Victoria's
Rifles (attached), also caused the enemy to vacate
the village of Wancourt, which was entered by patrols
of the London Rifle Brigade about eleven o'clock.
The 14th Division moved two battalions, one on either
side of the village, with a view to continuing the
advance to the high ground east of the Cojeul River,
and at 1 p.m. the Corps ordered the advance to be
continued to the Sensée River ; but these orders were
modified and the 56th Division was told to consolidate
(C) and prepare for an advance on the 13th.

On the 13th April nothing much was done. The

56th Division held the ridge from 35 to Wancourt Tower; on the right the 33rd Division, which had relieved the 30th, failed to advance; on the left the 50th Division, which had relieved the 14th on the preceding night, also failed to advance, having been held up by machine-gun fire from Guemappe. But the Corps ordered a general advance on the next day, the objective being the line of the Sensée River.

During the night the enemy blew up Wancourt Tower, which seemed to suggest that he was contemplating retirement. At 5.30 a.m. our attack was launched, but almost at once the 169th Brigade reported that the Queen's Westminster Rifles had gone forward with no one on their left. About five hundred yards in front of them were some practice trenches which the enemy had used for bombing. Capt. Newnham writes of the attack dissolving about the line of these trenches. Apparently Guemappe had not been taken on the left, and a perfect hail of machine-gun fire enfiladed the advancing troops from this village. The Queen Victoria's Rifles, who attacked on the right, met with no better fate, the leading waves being wiped out. From the diary of 169th Brigade we learn that

" the 151st Brigade attack on our left never developed, leaving our flank exposed. Enemy met with in considerable strength; they had just brought up fresh troops, and the allotment of machine guns, according to prisoners, was two per battalion. The 151st Brigade attack was ordered with their left flank on Wancourt Tower, which was our left and the dividing-line between brigades. Great confusion consequently on our left front, where two battalions of Durhams were mixed up with the Queen's Westminster Rifles, and the London Rifle Brigade, moving up in support, added to the congestion. Casualties were heavy— Queen's Westminster Rifles, 12 officers, 300 other ranks ; Queen Victoria's Rifles, 15 officers and 400 other ranks."

The attack had not, however, dissolved at all points, as a thin line of troops undoubtedly advanced a thousand yards, and more, beyond the practice trenches. But these gallant fellows soon found themselves in a very lonely position, and as the 30th and 50th Divisions failed to make any ground at all, they had Germans practically on all sides of them. They remained for some time and eventually withdrew.

The next two days, the 15th and 16th, were occupied in consolidating the ground gained. The division had alarms of counter-attack, but nothing developed on their front. On the left, however, the enemy attacked and recaptured Wancourt Tower from the 50th Division. This point was not retaken by us until the next day, but the 56th Division were not concerned. Further advance was postponed until the 22nd April, and on the 18th the 30th Division took over the line from the 56th Division.

This was the opening battle of the Arras series, and is known as the First Battle of the Scarpe, 1917, and is linked up with the Battle of Vimy Ridge. The student would do well to consider the two battles as one. The capture of Vimy Ridge by the Canadians, and of Monchy by troops of the Third Army, gave us positions of great importance and improved the situation round Arras. The feeling of the 56th Division was that it had been a great fight, and that they had proved themselves undoubtedly better men than the Germans. The capture of

Neuville Vitasse and subsequent rolling up of the Hindenburg Line to the south of Heninel was a feat of which they felt proud. And they had killed a lot of the enemy at close quarters. It is an interesting battle, as it undoubtedly inflicted a terrifying defeat on the enemy. Ludendorff says of it [1]:

" The 10th April and the following days were critical. The consequences of a break through, of 12 to 15 kilometres wide and 6 or more kilometres deep, are not easy to meet. In view of the heavy losses in men, guns, and ammunition resulting from such a break through, colossal efforts are needed to make good the damage. . . . A day like 9th April threw all calculations to the winds. Many days had to pass before a line could really be formed and consolidated. The end of the crisis, even if troops were available, depended very largely, as it generally does in such cases, on whether the enemy, after his first victory, would attack again, and by further success aggravate the difficulty of forming a new line. Our position having been weakened, such victories were to be won only too easily. . . ."

Hindenburg also confesses to very anxious moments, and suggests that " the English did not seem to have known how to exploit the success they had gained to the full."

In his dispatch on this battle Sir Douglas Haig said that :

"With the forces at my disposal, even combined with what the French proposed to undertake in co-operation, I did not consider that any great strategical

[1] *My War Memories*, 1914-1918.

10

results were likely to be gained by following up a success on the front about Arras, and to the south of it, beyond the capture of the objectives aimed at. . . . It was therefore my intention to transfer my main offensive to another part of the front after these objectives had been secured.

The front selected for these operations was in Flanders. They were to be commenced as soon as possible after the Arras offensive, and continued throughout the summer, so far as the forces at my disposal would permit."

It must be remembered that the plans for the year were drawn up in consultation with our Allies, and the battles of Arras must be taken as a part only of those plans. The First and Third Armies secured positions which Sir Douglas Haig intended that they should secure ; they inflicted great loss on the enemy, more than 13,000 prisoners and over 200 guns ; they drew German reserves until at the end of the operations there were twice as many enemy troops on that front as at the beginning, which materially helped our Allies, who were on the point of launching a big offensive on the Aisne and in Champagne. On the whole, these battles fulfilled their object and may be viewed with satisfaction.

On the 16th April the French attacked the Chemin-des-Dames, north-west of Rheims, and in the Champagne, south of Rheims. They met with very heavy losses and most obstinate resistance. These were the much-discussed operations under Gen. Nivelle, and, in order to assist, Sir Douglas Haig agreed to continue the operations round Arras longer than was his first intention. Plans, which had been made for a rearrangement of artillery and troops for the operations at Ypres, were cancelled, and orders were issued for a continuance, with shallow objectives, of the fighting at Arras.

The First Battle of the Scarpe and the Battle of Vimy Ridge were, therefore, the original scheme, and the subsequent battles should be considered with this fact in mind. They were: the Second Battle of the Scarpe, 1917, 23rd–24th April; the Battle of Arleux, 28th–29th April; the Third Battle of the Scarpe, 1917, 3rd–4th May. The Battle of Bullecourt, 3rd–17th May, and a number of actions must also be included in the subsequent Arras offensive.

A few days' rest was granted to the 56th Division. The 167th Brigade was round Pommier, the 168th round Couin, the 169th round Souastre. Divisional Headquarters were first at Couin and then at Hauteville. On the 25th Gen. Hull was ordered to hold himself in readiness to move into either the VI or the VII Corps, and the next day was definitely ordered into the VI Corps. On the 27th the 167th Brigade relieved the 15th Division in the front line, and Divisional Headquarters opened in Rue de la Paix, Arras.

.   .   .   .   .

From the Harp, which it will be remembered was the original line, to east of Monchy there runs a ridge of an average height of 100 metres; at Monchy itself it rises above 110 metres. This ridge shoots out a number of spurs towards the Cojeul River to the south. The position taken over by the 167th Brigade was from a small copse south-east of Monchy to the Arras–Cambrai road, about 500 yards from the Cojeul, and on the reverse slope of one of these spurs.

Observation for them was bad, and the enemy trenches were well sited and frequently over the crest of the hill.

On the 29th the 169th Brigade took over the right of the line from the 167th. The front line was then held by the London Rifle Brigade, the 2nd London Regt., the 1st London Regt., and the 7th Middlesex Regiment. The Queen Victoria's Rifles were in support of the Queen's Westminster Rifles in reserve to the right brigade, and the 3rd London Regt. in support and the 8th Middlesex Regt. in reserve to the left brigade.

With a view to the important operations which the French were to carry out on the 5th May, it was decided to attack on an extended front at Arras on the 3rd. While the Third and First Armies attacked from Fontaine-les-Croisilles to Fresnoy, the Fifth Army launched an attack on the Hindenburg Line about Bullecourt. This gave a total front of over sixteen miles. [The Third Battle of the Scarpe, 1917.]

Zero hour was 3.45 a.m., and in the darkness, illumined by wavering star-shells fired by a startled enemy, and with the crashing of the barrage, the men of the 56th Division advanced from their assembly trenches. As soon as the first waves topped the crest, they were met with a withering machine-gun and rifle fire. The ground was confusing and the darkness intense—officers, as was so often the case in night attacks, found it impossible to direct their men. Exactly what happened will never be known in detail. No reports came in for a considerable time.

With daylight the artillery observation officers began to communicate with headquarters. Our men,

they said, had advanced 1,000 yards on the right,
and were digging in near a factory (Rohart) on the
bank of the Cojeul, and the 14th Division on their
right seemed to have reached its objectives. About
300 yards over the crest of the spur was a trench
known as Tool, and this seemed to be occupied by
the enemy.

Soon after this the 169th Brigade reported that the
London Rifle Brigade were holding a pit near the
factory and a trench about the same place ; the 2nd
London Regt. had a footing in Tool Trench. The
latter position is doubtful, but the 2nd Londons were
well forward.

Cavalry Farm, near and to the right of the original
line, was still held by the enemy, and about 10 o'clock
the Queen Victoria's Rifles, after a short bombardment by the Stokes mortars, rushed and secured the
farm. They found a number of dugouts, which they
bombed, and secured 22 prisoners. The farm was
connected with Tool Trench, and they proceeded to
bomb their way up it. It would appear, therefore,
that the 2nd London Regt. held a small section of
this trench farther to the north, if any at all.

We must now follow the 167th Brigade on the
left. The two attacking battalions had been met
with even worse machine-gun fire than the 169th
Brigade. There was no news of them for a long
time. It is clear that neither the 1st London Regt.
nor the 7th Middlesex ever held any of Tool Trench,
but a few gallant parties did undoubtedly overrun
Tool, and, crossing a sunken road known as Stirrup
Lane, reached Lanyard Trench, quite a short distance
from the men of the London Rifle Brigade, who had
lodged themselves in the pit near Rohart Factory.

They were, however, not in sufficient numbers to join hands with the London Rifle Brigade, or some small groups of the 2nd London, who were also in advanced shell-holes, and about 8 o'clock in the evening were forced to surrender. (A small party was seen marching east without arms.) The remaining 1st London and 7th Middlesex men lay out in shell-holes in front of Tool Trench.

Soon after the Queen Victoria's Rifles had captured Cavalry Farm and started to bomb up Tool Trench, with the forward artillery and trench mortars helping them, the 3rd Division on the left of the 56th declared that their men were in the northern end of Tool. They asked that the artillery should be lifted off the trench, as they were going to bomb down towards the Queen Victoria's Rifles. But it appears that they were very soon driven out, as by 3 p.m. the 3rd Division were definitely reported to be in touch with the 7th Middlesex in the original line.

Meanwhile the 14th Division, on the right, which had made good progress at the start, had been violently counter-attacked, and at 11.50 a.m. reported that they had been driven back to their original line.

Brig.-Gen. Coke, of the 169th Brigade, now found his men in a queer position. The troops on either flank of his brigade were back in the line they had started from ; he ascertained that none of his brigade were north of the Arras–Cambrai road, and so he held a long tongue in the valley of the Cojeul open to attack from the high ground on either side of it.

Much movement by the enemy was observed during the afternoon ; reinforcements were assembling in Tool and the sunken road behind it. About 10 o'clock

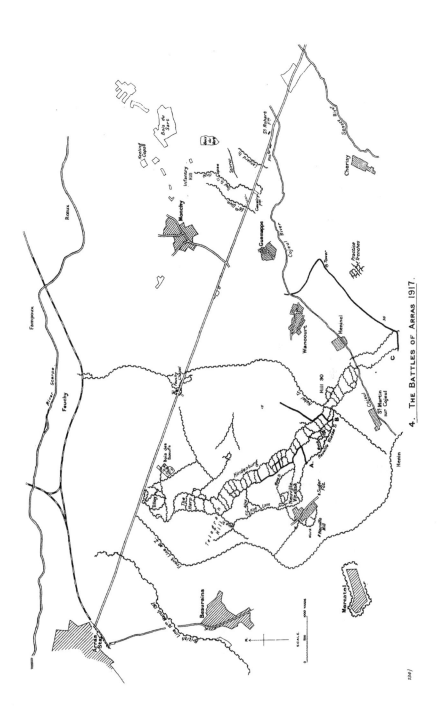

4. THE BATTLES OF ARRAS 1917.

in the evening the Germans started a fierce bombardment of the tongue of land held by the London Rifle Brigades and 2nd London Regts., and, after an hour of ceaseless fire, counter-attacked and drove the troops back to their original lines.

Gen. Hull then ordered them to hold their original line and reorganise, but before the orders could reach them these two fine battalions had attacked again and reoccupied all the positions they had gained in the morning with the exception of Cavalry Farm. But they were in a bad situation. With the enemy holding the Cambrai road in force, the only communication with the advanced troops was down the bottom of the valley, a place of much water and mud. Brig.-Gen. Coke therefore withdrew his men just before sunrise. They brought with them, however, a German officer and 15 men who had surrendered in the neighbourhood of Cavalry Farm.

It had been a day of very hard fighting, and the gain on the whole of the sixteen miles of front attacked was Fresnoy, which had been taken by the Canadians, and a portion of the Hindenburg Line, east of Bullecourt, captured by the Australians. The enemy had been terribly frightened by the successful start of the battles of Arras. Hindenburg and Ludendorff were putting into effect their new system of holding the front in depth, but thin in the forward zones, with many machine guns, and strong supports for immediate counter-attack. It seemed as though their system had broken down at the first test, and, as the Russians were no longer a menace to them, they poured reinforcements across Germany. But, as we know, this continuation of the offensive was with the object of helping our Allies by holding troops and guns which might otherwise have been used against them.

The 167th and 169th Brigades held the line for one day more, and were relieved by the 168th on the 5th May. The latter brigade also took over a stretch of extra line to the north.

The enemy was exceedingly quiet and our patrols very active. If any indication is wanted of the high *moral* of the 56th Division, it can be found in this patrol work. After an action of this kind, when the two brigades lost just on a thousand men, really audacious reconnoitring deserves the highest praise. Again and again attempts were made by patrols to enter Tool Trench, only to find the enemy alert. Cavalry Farm, on the right, and the copse, on the left, were both entered and found unoccupied ; but the exact position of the enemy in Tool Trench was ascertained.

Meanwhile the heavy artillery kept up a steady fire on Tool Trench, causing large numbers of Germans to run over the open and seek safer ground. And troops worked hard on our trenches, which were greatly improved.

At 8.30 p.m. on the 11th May the 4th London Regt. on the right and the London Scottish on the left attacked Cavalry Farm and the trench on the far side of it, and Tool Trench.

A practice barrage on the previous day had drawn heavy fire in a few minutes, and it had been decided not to have a barrage, but to keep the heavy artillery firing steadily to the last minute. The enemy, who held the line in full strength, were taken by surprise. Only Cavalry Farm was visible from our line, and the 4th London Regt. swept into this place with no difficulty. But the right of the enemy line was able to put up a fight, and the left company of the London Scottish suffered somewhat severely. Except for this one point, the trench was vacated by its garrison in a wild scramble. They could not, however, escape the Lewis gunners and brigade machine-gunners, who did some good execution. Quite a lot of the enemy were killed in the trench and a round dozen taken prisoner—they were of the 128th Infantry Regt. and the 5th Grenadier Regt. Eight machine guns were also found.

Tool Trench was only a part of the enemy line which ran up the hill on the east of Monchy. To the south of the copse it was Tool and to the north it was Hook. The very northern end of Tool and all of Hook remained in the hands of the enemy. A block was made by filling in about forty yards of the trench and the new line was consolidated.

The new line had been much damaged by our fire, but it was soon reconstructed, and two communication trenches were dug to the old line. Meanwhile the trench mortars kept up a steady bombardment of Hook Trench, and snipers picked off the enemy as he attempted to seek the safer shell-holes in the open.

During the next few days several deserters from the 5th Grenadier Regt. came in, and they, in common with other prisoners, persisted in stating that the enemy was contemplating a retirement. Patrols, however, always found Lanyard Trench and Hook fully garrisoned. The 167th Brigade had taken over the line from the 168th, and the 8th Middlesex attempted to rush both Lanyard and Hook ; this was not done in force, but was more in the nature of a surprise by strong patrols. They found the enemy too alert.

On the 19th something in the nature of an attack

in force was carried out. The 8th Middlesex made
a night attack, in conjunction with the 29th Division,
on Hook Trench and the support line behind it. The
Middlesex men gained the junction of Hook and Tool,
but were very " bunched " ; the 187th Brigade on
the left made no progress at all. It is probable that
the Middlesex were more to the left than they
imagined, as they were heavily bombed from both
flanks, and eventually forced to withdraw.

On the 20th May the weary troops of the 56th
Division were relieved by the 37th Division.

In these actions and in the battle on the 3rd May
the objectives were shallow and the enemy fully prepared to resist, with large reinforcements of men
and guns in the field. The enemy barrage was
considered the heaviest that had, as yet, been encountered. The positions attacked were well sited
and frequently masked, and there was also the com-
plication of night assaults at short notice. Brig.-Gen.
Freeth, in an interesting report of the battle on
the 3rd, says :

" . . . Owing to the darkness it was extremely
difficult for the assaulting troops to keep direction or
the correct distances between waves. The tendency
was for rear waves to push forward too fast for fear
of losing touch with the wave in front of them. Consequently, by the time the leading wave was approaching Tool Trench, all the rear waves had telescoped into
it. Even if Tool Trench had been taken, much delay
would have been caused in extricating and moving
forward waves allotted to the further objectives."

Anyone who has taken part in a night attack will
appreciate these difficulties. If it goes well it is very
well, but if not the confusion is appalling.

The casualties from the 29th April to 21st May were 79 officers and 2,022 other ranks.

The general situation was that on the 5th May the French had delivered their attack on the Chemin-des-Dames and achieved their object, but on the whole the French offensive was disappointing. On the British front, however, 19,500 prisoners and 257 guns had been captured, and the situation round Arras greatly improved. The spring offensive was at an end.

But fighting did not cease round Arras and over the width of the sixty square miles of regained country. The Messines attack in the north was in course of preparation, and the orders to the Fifth, Third, and First Armies were to continue operations, with the forces left to them, with the object of keeping the enemy in doubt as to whether the offensive would be continued. Objectives, of a limited nature, were to be selected, and importance given to such actions by combining with them feint attacks. They were successful in their object, but there was bitter with the sweet, as Sir Douglas Haig writes :

" These measures seem to have had considerable success, if any weight may be attached to the enemy's reports concerning them. They involved, however, the disadvantage that I frequently found myself unable to deny the German accounts of the bloody repulse of extensive British attacks which, in fact, never took place."

The attack on Messines was launched on the 7th June, and was a complete success. With the first crash of our concentrated artillery nineteen mines were exploded, and our troops swept forward all along the line. By the evening 7,200 prisoners, 67 guns,

94 trench mortars, and 294 machine guns had been captured.

The 56th Division indulged in a little well-earned rest. We read of sports and horse shows in the vicinity of Habarcq, of concerts given by the "Bow Bells" concert party (formed in 1916 at Souastre), and diaries have the welcome entries "troops resting" as the only event of the day. But this was not for long. Battalions were soon back in the line, though much reduced in strength. For the first time we find, in spite of reinforcements, that the average strength of battalions fell to just over eight hundred.

The 169th Brigade lost Capt. Newnham, who went to the New Zealand Division as G.S.O.2. He instituted a form of official diary which is a delight to read—concise, but with occasional reflections of a dry, humorous nature. Capt. Carden Roe, from the 29th Division, took his place as Brigade Major.

During the 9th, 10th, and 11th of June the division relieved the 61st Division in the line. The position was the same—Tool Trench from the copse, on the left, to Cavalry Farm, but it was extended to Wancourt Tower on the right.

The front now held measured 2,700 yards. Wancourt Tower was on the summit of the high spur which runs parallel to the Cojeul River on the south bank. The line can, then, be visualised stretching across the valley, with right and left flanks of the division on the high ground on either side of the river. From the right good observation was obtained over the enemy lines on the left of the divisional front, and from the copse, on the left of the line, similar observation could be had over the enemy on the right.

The 3rd Division was on the left of the 56th, and

on the 14th June, at 7.30 a.m., the former launched an attack on Hook Trench. The attack was a complete success ; the division came level with the 56th and captured 175 prisoners.

The right of the 56th Division was held by the Queen's Westminster Rifles, and a few minutes after five o'clock in the evening sentries noticed enemy movement behind a wood (Bois du Vert) which was opposite the 3rd Division and on the left flank of the 56th. Careful watching revealed the massing of troops. A warning was sent over the telephone. The 76th Brigade, immediately on the left of the 56th Division, was informed, as was the artillery.

Killing human beings is not dear to the heart of Englishmen. Green troops would stand violent shelling, merely looking a bit tense about the face, but although they saw their comrades fall, shattered to pieces, or badly wounded, they would sometimes show a great disinclination to fire on Germans walking in the open behind the enemy lines. It seemed as though the idea was that the particular German in question was not trying to injure them—he might have been carrying a plank or a bag of rations—and so they would watch him and no one would attempt to shoot unless there was an old soldier with them. This frame of mind, however, did not last long.

But the evening of the 14th June was an occasion for glee. The Hun was going to attack and all was ready for him. At 5.30 the grey waves left the enemy trenches, and at once a storm of artillery, machine-gun, and rifle fire met them. The Queen's Westminster Rifles, of course, could not fire, but they watched the action with great joy, and kept Brigade and Divisional Headquarters informed of every

enemy move.   The attack was smashed up and, thanks
to the Queen's Westminster Rifles, the enemy was
chased out of sight by the artillery.

After this costly lesson the Germans tried a night
attack on the 16th at 2.30 a.m.   This time they
succeeded in entering two posts, but the 3rd Division
drove them out and the men of the 56th inflicted heavy
casualties from the flank.

Nothing more was done in this line beyond some
skirmishing round a post.   The division was relieved
on the 4th July and moved to the Le Cauroy area.

.   .   .   .   .

We have said very little about the Divisional
Artillery, but to follow them too closely in these
engagements would lead to confusion.   They supported the 56th Division during the battle of Arras—
in the original scheme—and when the division
moved on the 20th April the artillery remained where
it was.   Brig.-Gen. Elkington writes :

" The 56th Divisional Artillery remained in the line
in this sector, under different C.R.A.s and covering
different divisions, and were not under my command
again until the end of May, as I remained with the
56th Division and commanded the artillery covering
them.   All the divisional artilleries became much
mixed up, and very few of the C.R.A.s had their
own artillery under their own command. . . .

On the 24th May the division moved to the
Habarcq area, and remained there until the 9th June.
I established the R.A. Headquarters at Beaumetz,
so as to keep in touch with our artillery, who were
still in the line.   At the end of May I got four days'
leave and went to Paris with Hawkes, Jorgensen, and
Robinson, and we were joined there by Cols. Groves

and Lemon. We all had an excellent time, and enjoyed it immensely. . . . On the 5th July the 56th Divisional Artillery returned to my command, and we started to march to the Ypres area, and arrived at Oudezeele on the 13th July 1917. This was a very clean and comfortable village, and all ranks were well billeted. We remained there until the 28th July, a very pleasant and well-earned rest for both officers and men, beautiful weather, and many sports were organised for officers and men. Several fatigue parties had to be furnished to assist the heavy artillery in the supply of ammunition, and these had very hard work and some casualties. During the later part our trench mortar batteries, under Capt. Robinson, went into the line with the Guards Division, and had rather a strenuous time doing excellent work. On the 9th July I went home on ten days' leave, and I got married on the 12th July. . . ."

At one period of the war it was thought that the artillery had a " soft " time, but as the war progressed it was seen that the zone which included the lighter guns included also conditions which rendered the comfort of artillerymen scarcely more enviable than that of the infantry. We shall soon be able to throw a little more light on the work of this very gallant arm of the Service.

CHAPTER V

On the 2nd July a rearrangement of the front had placed the 56th Division in the VII Corps, and they remained at Le Cauroy under the orders of that Corps until the 23rd July, when they moved to Eperlecques, near St. Omer, and came under the Fifth Army.

But the division lost Gen. Hull. It was absolutely necessary that he should undergo a surgical operation, and the matter could not be postponed any longer, so he went back to England. He was looked upon as a friend as much as a commander, his striking personality had impressed itself on all ranks, and his tall figure was recognised from afar and welcomed whenever he visited the line or billets. The men saw in him a fearless commander who knew his business. We are indebted to Major Newnham for the following anecdote :

" After the 1st July show (1916), the 169th Brigade held the trenches in front of Fouquevillers. The trenches, though on top of a hill, were dreadful. My diary records ' all C.T.s thigh-deep in mud.' Gen. Hull doubted our statement, so on Sunday, the 9th July, when he came to Brigade Headquarters, I showed him the state of things. We went up the main C.T., and gradually the slime rose, first ankle, then knee, then thigh-deep. At length, where the C.T. ran in a hollow, I said, ' Now we get to a really

deep bit, sir!' He said, 'Well, I'm damned if
I'm going through it—I'm getting out!' And we
went over the top, though in full view from a large
part of the Boche positions, and walked back in the
open, too!'"

And the General was enthusiastic in praise of his
division.
"We were a happy family," he says. And "what
pleased me as much as their fighting qualities was
their good temper and cheerfulness under all circumstances," and the circumstances were at times
appallingly severe. He was himself always cheerful,
though his pet dog, an Irish greyhound named Roy,
has been described as "a miserable hound." He
encouraged his staff to play "bridge" whenever their
work permitted, as a means of taking their minds off
the war. All work and no play would have made
even a G.S.O.1 a dull boy, and relaxation was not
easy to find. He commanded the 4th Battalion
Middlesex Regt. at Mons, and was given command
of the 10th Brigade on the 17th November 1914.
When he first entered the army in 1887, he joined the
Royal Scots Fusiliers, and was transferred to the
Middlesex Regt. in 1912. We are sorry to say that
the "miserable hound," Roy, who had been with the
General since January 1916, cut a tendon and had
to be destroyed in Belgium, although he survived the
war.
Gen. Hull was not, however, lost to the division,
as he returned later. Meanwhile Gen. W. Douglas
Smith was given command.
Troops were being massed for the big offensive at
Ypres, and the Fifth Army Staff, under Sir Hubert
11

Gough, had been moved to take command of the greater part of the salient. Sir Herbert Plumer was still there, but on the southern side, and with a reduced army.

.   .   .   .   .

In July 1917 England reached the summit of her military power in France. There were 52 divisions from the Motherland, 4 from Canada, 5 from Australia, 1 from New Zealand. One might, therefore, expect a year of great results. And so it was, though not perhaps obviously apparent.

Writing of the year as a whole, Sir Douglas Haig says :

" The general conditions of the struggle this year have been very different from those contemplated at the conference of the Allied Commanders held in November 1916. The great general and simultaneous offensive then agreed on did not materialise. Russia, though some of her leaders made a fine effort at one period, not only failed to give the help expected of her, but even failed to prevent the enemy from transferring some forty divisions from her front in exchange for tired ones used up in the Western theatre, or from replacing losses in his divisions on this side by drafts of fresh and well-trained men drawn from divisions in the East.

The combined French and British offensive in the spring was launched before Italy could be ready ; and the splendid effort made by Italy at a later period was, unfortunately, followed by developments which resulted in a weakening of the Allied forces in this theatre before the conclusion of our offensive.

In these circumstances the task of the British and French armies has been a far heavier one throughout the year than was originally anticipated, and the enemy's means of meeting our attack have been far greater than either he or we could have expected."

It was a year of disappointment, but was not a year without achievement. We had failed against the Turk at Gaza, but had succeeded at Baghdad ; the French spring offensive had not succeeded, and our own could only be described as a steadying blow at the Germans ; Kerensky came on the scene in Russia in May, and no doubt did his best, but discipline had gone, and the offensive of Brussiloff and Korniloff, though it succeeded at first, was well in hand, so far as the Central Powers were concerned, in July. The East was the weak spot in our calculations, with Russia going to ruin and dragging Rumania with her. It was as well that Britain was at the crest of the power wave.

After all, battles have a further object than the mere killing of men. For quite a long while after the commencement of the war the Germans talked boastfully of their " will." The will to victory was going to crush the *moral* of their enemies. But although the Russian revolution caused great rejoicing, although the German High Command claimed a long list of victories, it seemed that German *moral* was somehow flagging, and their enemy's will to victory was as determined as ever.

Ludendorff admits that in the summer of 1917 the position of the Central Powers was better than that of the Entente, but that there were other causes for " our spiritual decline." He says that Field-Marshal Hindenburg wrote to the Emperor on the 27th June that " our greatest anxiety at this moment, however, is the decline of the national spirit. It must be

revived or we shall lose the war." There were speeches
in the Reichstag containing the despairing cry that
it was impossible to win the war. On the 7th July
Hindenburg and Ludendorff met members of the
Reichstag to discuss " our defensive attitude throughout the first half of 1917, the various failures near
Arras, in the Wytschæte salient, and in Galicia, where
we had not as yet attacked, the absence up to date of
any decisive result from the submarine war, and our
serious situation as regards food and raw mate-
rials. . . ." And finally, on the 25th July, General
Ludendorff wrote that " it is certain that the Independent Social Democrats are carrying on an agitation
in the army which is in the highest degree detrimental
to discipline."

And the allies of Germany were giving her a great
deal of trouble.

One can only ask what created this frame of mind ?
Even a Social Democrat must have the ground prepared before his doctrines can germinate and flourish ;
it must be fertilised with dissatisfaction and watered
with despair. The German and Austrian nations
were as one in their desire for war in August 1914,
and so strong that they had little difficulty in winning the Turkish and Bulgarian nations to their
cause. Then surely we may answer the question
by saying that it was the guns of the Allied artillery
and the rifles of the Allied infantry that caused the
" will " to falter, even when the position seemed most
favourable to the War Lord and his advisers. It
was a slow process, but a sure one.

One must admit disappointment to France and
Britain, as the leaders of the countries allied against
the Central Powers, but we cannot see the justice of

the German contention that their own position was good. In considering the events of this war, it is not easy to appreciate the mind of a man who says "the military situation was good, but the condition of the country behind the army was bad." Country and army surely hang together. The Germans never looked upon war as a clash of armies alone, but sought by every means in their power, by oppression, by slavery, by terror, to bend the non-combatant population to their will. It is a logical view. This war, at least, was waged by country against country, by nation against nation, and as a nation Germany was cracking, and her allies with her.

This was the state of affairs when the Battles of Ypres, 1917, after an artillery preparation which had been growing in volume for a month, opened with a stupendous crash on the 31st July—an official date.

From the very first the Second and Fifth British Armies, and the First French Army on the left, met with the fiercest resistance. The left of the Fifth Army and the First French Army gained the greatest success—the right of the Fifth Army and the Second Army did little more than capture the enemy first line of defence. Whatever the condition of the German people, the German Army seemed as strong as ever. And yet it was being nursed.

The system with which the Germans started the war was not one based on consideration for lives. Verdun and the Somme had shaken the very foundations of that system, and, if the German Army was still strong and good, German Commanders had already expressed anxiety as to the future conduct of their troops. Loss of lives and loss of *moral* had been responsible for a new method of defence. The

front line was to be held by few men and many
machine guns, and retirement before strong enemy
fire was advocated. The position was to be regained
by means of rapid counter-attack. Instead of holding
a " line," a zone was held. Defence in depth was the
policy.

This loosened method of defence lessened the
wastage of troops from artillery fire, and in addition
the system of " pill-boxes " was instituted. These
small reinforced concrete forts could withstand a
direct hit of all but the heaviest shell, and were
admirably adapted for the defence of a place like
Flanders, where dugouts were almost an impossibility.
In fact, the new German pamphlet, " The Defensive
Battle," was a distinct departure from the old
" Cannon Fodder " point of view. If the Reichstag
was openly saying that the war could not be won,
the High Command of the Army was wondering if it
would stand many more blows.

Men who fought at Ypres will say that they noticed
no loss of *moral* in the enemy, and with this we
agree ; we only wish to insist that there were indications which had not escaped the eyes of the German
Command. As to the hard, heart-breaking fighting
of the Battles of Ypres, 1917, it is only just to the
gallant French and British troops to point out once
more the many advantages that lay with their
enemies.

For over two years the Germans had held their
semicircle round the east of Ypres. The positions
they occupied, though only the summits of insigni-
ficant-looking " rises," not even worthy of the name
of " hills," overlooked the whole of the French and
British assembly area. Not a move escaped their

observers, who knew every inch of the ground. What
a place to prepare for an attack !

Books of reference will give the 31st July as the
opening date of the 1917 Battles of Ypres. It is
false. The 31st is the date of the assault—the battles
started with the first indications of the British intention to attack. Every new trench, every trace of new
digging, every new track taped out, every building,
every hamlet, every wood was bombarded by the
enemy with guns and aeroplanes, which became
extremely active at this period. As the concentration
of troops increased, all attempts at concealment were
abandoned, and camps were pitched in the open.
The whole area was a " target," and was well
described by a gunner who remarked, " Every time
a coconut ! " Observation, on the other hand, was
denied to us.

All this, bad in itself, the troops were able to face.
But the enemy had another advantage, being on the
defensive, and that was the condition of the ground
over which the attackers had to advance.

There is no place on the whole of the Western
Front which can be compared to this stretch of
Flanders. If an infantryman or an artilleryman
attempted to give an adequate account of the conditions, and the horrors which they occasioned, he
would not be believed. We will, therefore, give the
words of the Higher Command, with the one criticism
that they are not strong enough. Sir Douglas Haig
wrote :

" The weather had been threatening throughout
the day (31st July) and had rendered the work of the
aeroplanes very difficult from the commencement of

the battle. During the afternoon, while the fighting
was still in progress, rain fell, and fell steadily all
night. Thereafter for four days the rain continued
without cessation, and for several days after the
weather remained stormy and unsettled. The low-
lying clayey soil, torn by shells and sodden with rain,
turned into a succession of vast muddy pools. The
valleys of the choked and overflowing streams were
speedily transformed into long stretches of bog,
impassable except by a few well-defined tracks, which
became marks for the enemy's artillery. To leave
these tracks was to risk death by drowning, and in the
course of the subsequent fighting, on several occasions,
both men and pack animals were lost in this way. . . .
As had been the case in the Arras battle, this unavoidable delay in the development of our offensive was
of the greatest service to the enemy. Valuable time
was lost, the troops opposed to us were able to
recover from the disorganisation produced by our
first attack, and the enemy was given the opportunity
to bring up reinforcements."

The enemy view of the conditions is given by
Ludendorff :

" Enormous masses of ammunition, such as the
human mind had never imagined before the war, was
hurled upon the bodies of men who passed a miserable
existence scattered about in mud-filled shell-holes.
The horror of the shell-hole area of Verdun was
surpassed. It was no longer life at all. It was mere
unspeakable suffering. And through this world of
mud the attackers dragged themselves, slowly but
steadily, and in dense masses. Caught in the advance
zone by our hail of fire they often collapsed, and the
lonely man in the shell-hole breathed again. Then
the mass came on again. Rifle and machine gun
jammed with the mud. Man fought against man,

INVERNESS COPSE AND GLENCORSE WOOD, AUGUST 1917

and only too often the mass was successful. . . . And yet it must be admitted that certain units no longer triumphed over the demoralising effects of the defensive battle as they had done formerly."

Very naturally Ludendorff claims that statues in bronze should be erected to the German soldier for the suffering he experienced at Ypres. But his own picture of the attackers seems somehow to be worse than that of the defenders, if there are degrees of suffering.

On the 31st July the assault of the Fifth Army met with complete success on the left, where the crossing of the Steenbeke was secured. But on the right the II Corps was only partially successful. After over-running the first system of defence about Hooge and Sanctuary Wood, divisions were met with tremendous opposition, and eventually checked at Inverness Copse and Glencorse Wood.

On the 4th of August the 56th Division started to move from Eperlecques, and on the 6th Divisional Headquarters were at Reninghelst under the II Corps. Major-Gen. F. A. Dudgeon assumed command of the division on the 10th ; and on the 12th the division took over the line from Surbiton Villas to Westhoek, facing Glencorse Wood and Nonne Bosschen. But before this date the Divisional Artillery was in action.

.   .   .   .   .

We cannot do better than quote from Brig.-Gen. Elkington's most interesting diary :

" On the 2nd and 3rd of August the 56th Divisional Artillery relieved the 8th Divisional Artillery in the line, taking over their gun positions near Hooge. The artillery then experienced what I think was their worst time during the war. All the battery positions were shelled day and night, more in the nature of harassing fire with occasional counter-battery shoots. The ground was so wet that digging was impossible, and the men lived in holes in the ground covered with corrugated iron. The early dawn was the only time it was safe to get supplies and ammunition if casualties were to be avoided, and with all precautions most batteries lost 100 per cent. of their gun line strength in killed and wounded. The artillery supported operations on the 10th, 12th, 16th, and 25th August, and answered S.O.S. calls on most days ; also a very heavy day on the 24th of August, when the enemy counter-attacked in force. On the 16th and 17th the whole of the guns of D/280 were put out of action; enemy shell fire and exploding ammunition practically blew them to pieces, and except for the actual tubes of the three howitzers, nothing was found worth salving. On the 31st August the artillery came out of the line, and entrained south on the 1st September to rejoin the 56th Division, and all ranks hoped they had seen the last of the Ypres salient."

We can only add to this that the selection of gun positions was a matter of finding a place where the guns would not disappear in the mud and which was not already occupied by another battery.

The battle of the 16th is the one which concerns us. On that day the Fifth Army attacked from the north-west corner of Inverness Copse to the junction with the First French Army south of St. Janshoek [the Battle of Langemarck, 1917]. The French always attacked on the left.

The II Corps, on the right, attacked with the 56th and 8th Divisions. The objective was the same as that of the 31st July, a line drawn to include some

500 yards in depth of Polygon Wood, and so on to the north. But there is not much point in going over orders. Brig.-Gen. Freeth reports (with some bitterness it seems to us) : " Orders were received and issued so hurriedly that it was impossible for brigade and battalion staffs to keep pace with them. There was not time for the scheme of operations to be thoroughly explained to regimental officers, much less to the men." Indeed, the mass of documents is appalling, and, taken together with the facts, point to confusion of a most distressing nature.

It must be understood that Gen. Dudgeon was in no better case than Brig.-Gen. Freeth. On the 11th August the division had been ordered to take over the line from the 18th Division and portions of the 25th Division. On that same day the General attended a conference at Corps Headquarters and learnt that the 53rd Brigade of the 18th Division would remain in the line and come under his orders for the battle. He was called upon to attack on a front of 1,500 yards on a depth of 1,700 yards, with a defensive flank of 1,700 yards extending from the south-eastern corner of Stirling Castle to Black Watch Corner. On the 12th the 169th Brigade was ordered to undertake a small operation with the object of improving the line about Glencorse Wood, an undertaking which the 18th Division had failed to carry out. But the 169th Brigade met with strong opposition and also failed. On the 14th the enemy attacked the 167th Brigade, on the left of the line, and drove in some posts ; they were re-established. Later on that day, at a conference, the Brigadier-General commanding the 53rd Brigade represented that his brigade was not in a state to carry out the attack ordered owing to heavy casualties. The General then placed the 4th London Regt. under the orders of the 53rd Brigade and the trouble commenced—the Commanding Officer was wounded on his way to interview the Brigadier. The second in command had then to go and reconnoitre on the following day, which left his battalion less than twenty-four hours in which to make the necessary reconnaissance and preparation to get into position.

On the 15th instant, as the result of a conference with the Corps Commander and the G.O.C. 8th Division, the starting line was altered.

Owing to the date fixed for the attack, an interbattalion relief was necessary on the night 14/15th. In fact the ground was so bad that there were reliefs, or remains of reliefs, going on every night. It was not possible to undertake any patrolling to gain a knowledge of the ground, and in daylight the shelling was so constant and accurate that study of the country was most difficult.

The General writes :

" The darkness of the night, the boggy state of the ground, heavy shelling of all approaches, and the fact that the division was strange to the ground and had little opportunity for reconnaissance and preparation presented great difficulties in carrying out the assembly . . . but the difficulties were surmounted and the troops assembled in time, though there is no doubt that the state of the ground caused much fatigue."

So by 4 a.m. the 53rd Brigade, with the 7th Bedford, 6th Berkshire, and 4th London Regts. in line, was on the right. In the centre was the 169th Brigade with the 5th and 2nd London Regts. in line. On the left the 167th Brigade with the 8th Middlesex and 1st London Regts. in line.

At 4.45 a.m. on the 16th August the barrage opened and the assaulting troops clambered out of their mud holes. Red and green lights were fired from the enemy rear lines, but his barrage did not answer to these signals for some minutes. But the new enemy system of defence in depth and by means of concrete forts was to be met for the first time by the 56th Division. The barrage was good and, if anything, crept forward too slowly, but the concrete fort was immune from damage by shells from the lighter batteries, and the German machine-gunner was able to fire through our barrage.

The 7th Bedford Regt. was stopped at once by one of these forts on the north-west of Inverness Copse. The failure to capture this point reacted on the 4th London Regt., which suffered very heavy loss and was brought to a standstill to the north of the western side of the wood ; they managed to work their way forward and form a defensive flank along the southern edge of Glencorse Wood.

The 169th Brigade progressed well at first. The London Rifle Brigade and the 2nd London Regt. disposed of isolated parties with machine guns dotted about in shell holes on their front, but soon bumped into a marsh. The 2nd London Regt. edged to the right, pushing the London Rifle Brigade still farther away. And the same obstruction being met by the 167th Brigade, the 8th Middlesex edged to the left, to avoid the marsh, pushing the 1st London Regt. as they did so. There was then a big gap between the two Brigades very soon after the start.

The enemy resistance was found by the 169th
Brigade beyond the marsh in the centre of Glencorse
Wood. Here, along a sunken road, was a line of concrete forts, or pill-boxes. Hard fighting and heavy
casualties followed. The artillery was no longer
helpful, but Glencorse Wood was finally cleared. The
leading waves of the two battalions then went on and
reached Polygon Wood, but what happened to them
is not known. The second waves were checked at
Polygon Wood by heavy fire from the front and the
flanks, and before they could steady themselves were
thrown back by a counter-attack which was only
stopped by the Queen Victoria's Rifles, who were
coming up in support. Later in the day a second
and heavier counter-attack from the east and south
drove the whole of the brigade back to the original
front line.

The 167th Brigade, on the left, made better progress
than any of the others—for a time. The gap between
the 169th and 167th Brigades was never filled, so
that when the 8th Middlesex came across a second
lake of mud, four feet deep, about the north end of
Nonne Bosschen, their right flank was exposed.
And on the left the 1st London Regt. had been heavily
shelled before the start, so that when they did advance
the rear waves pressed on the leading wave until
all became mixed, and no one carried out the special
task of clearing the ground as it was won ; the position
was that, although the main weight of the attack
was carried forward to the left of the 8th Middlesex,
many enemy snipers were behind both battalions of
the 167th Brigade. There is also, on this flank, the
mystery of a company that disappeared. Although
it seems pretty clear that the waves bunched up

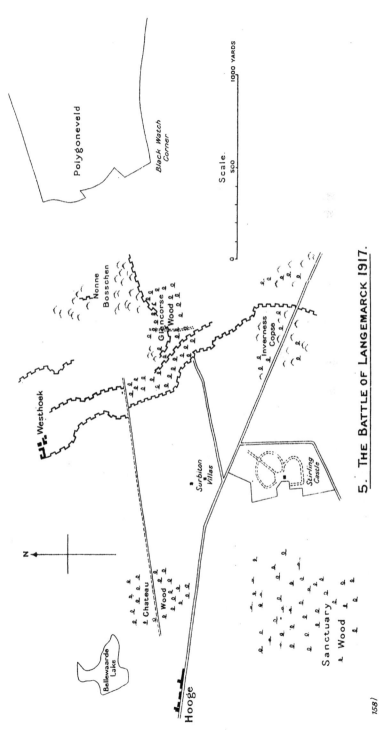

Polygoneveld

Black Watch
Corner

Nonne
Bosschen

Westhoek

Glencorse
Wood

Inverness
Copse

Surbiton
Villas

Stirling
Castle

N

Bellewaarde
Lake

Chateau
Wood

Sanctuary
Wood

Hooge

Scale.

0   500   1000 YARDS

5. THE BATTLE OF LANGEMARCK 1917.

158)

together, they must also have split; the third wave,
composed of the larger part of a company, was reported by its company commander, in writing sent
by runner, to be in a position north of Polygon Wood;
and no doubt he got there, but neither he nor his men
were heard of again. A thin wave of the 8th Division
reached this same line, but were immediately driven
back by a massed and carefully timed counter-attack.
But the attack of the 167th Brigade was completely
held up. At 7 a.m. the 8th Middlesex saw the troops
of the 169th Brigade falling back through Glencorse
Wood; they then took up a position to their rear,
their southern flank being refused so as to gain touch
with the 169th Brigade. The situation remained
unaltered through the afternoon.

About 3 p.m. the enemy was reported to be massing
opposite the 25th Brigade on the left of the 56th
Division, and shortly after to be attacking all along
the 167th Brigade front. In view of the barrier of
mud it is probable that he was only trying to re-
occupy the ground from which he had retired. But
our artillery had direct observation and heavy fire
was opened on him, and his troops dispersed.

About 5 p.m. the 167th Brigade again retired to a
more favourable position, which gave them a net
gain of 400 yards beyond their original line. They
were then in touch with the 25th Brigade, 8th Division.

All attacking battalions were withdrawn and the
line was held by the Queen Victoria's Rifles, the
Queen's Westminster Rifles, and the 7th Middlesex
Regt. The division was relieved the following night
by the 14th Division, and moved to Steenvoorde E.,
Ouderdom, Wippenhoek, the brigades being quartered
in that numerical order.

The total casualties from the 13th to the 17th August were 111 officers and 2,794 other ranks. The loss in senior officers was particularly heavy : Lieut.-Col. H. Campbell, Major V. A. Flower, Major J. E. L. Higgins, and Major M. R. Harris, all of the 13th London Regt. (Kensingtons); Lieut.-Col. R. R. Husey of the 5th London Regt. ; Lieut.-Col. J. P. Kellett of the 2nd London Regt. ; Lieut.-Col. P. L. Ingpen of the 8th Middlesex ; and Lieut.-Col. F. W. D. Bendall of the 7th Middlesex Regt. were all wounded.

Maybe the confusion was inevitable, but it makes a sorry story in which the great gallantry of the London Territorials stands forth like something clean and honest in the midst of slime and mud. Gen. Dudgeon gives us some of the causes of the failure to reach the desired objective.

" Insufficient time for preparation and explanation of the scheme of attack to those taking part, and insufficient time to study the terrain.

The portion of the 25th Division relieved by the 167th Brigade had only been in the line twenty-four hours previously, and could not assist much.

Lack of previous preparation. No dumps of any kind were taken over in the area, and there was insufficient time to form all those that were necessary.

Indifferent communications. Tracks east of Château Wood were non-existent, and the tapes were soon obliterated by the mud.

Difficulty of maintaining signal communication.

Fatigue of troops previous to the attack, owing to the bad weather.

The condition of the ground over which the attack took place. The bog at the source of the Hanebeck made a gap between the 169th and 167th Brigades, which laid their left and right flanks respectively open to counter-attack. It also caused great fatigue to the troops.

The nature of the hostile defences and new system of defence in depth. The enemy's counter-attacks were so timed as to strike the leading waves about the same time as they reached their objectives, when they were more or less disorganised, and had been unable to consolidate the ground gained.

The concentration of hostile guns opposite the front. The heavy shelling prevented the moving up of reinforcements, machine guns, and replenishment of ammunition."

It seems very certain that the British Staff was somewhat rattled by the German tactics in defence. Questions—long lists of them—were sent out, and reports asked for. The pill-box, it was agreed, disorganised our assaulting waves, although it did not stop them. But there is a limit to the possible advance of troops in a rush, and this had been calculated by the enemy, who placed his main forces so as to counter-attack the exhausted leading waves of attackers before they had time to consolidate, or even mop up the ground behind them. How was this to be overcome ?

All officers of the 56th Division seemed to agree on this question. The answer was, " Do not try to penetrate too deeply." Five hundred yards was a distance which troops could cover without exhaustion, and they would then be at such a distance from any troops assembled for counter-attack as would give them time to consolidate, bring up machine guns, and be ready for the counter-attack. Something of the sort was eventually done, so the experience of the 56th Division was of some service.

12

The attack was not renewed on this sector of the front until the 20th September, when the Second Army (Sir Herbert Plumer's command was extended to his left) captured Glencorse and the half of Polygon Wood.

The fighting in Flanders was carried on until November. The French launched a big attack at Verdun on the 20th August, which met with notable success. Ludendorff confesses to a feeling of despair. Concrete had failed him, and as to his troops, " At some points they no longer displayed the firmness which I, in common with the local commanders, had hoped for." By limiting the depth of penetration and breaking up the German counter-attacks with artillery fire the British troops were slowly eating their way through the defences in Flanders, in spite of having to wade through mud. Many were the consultations at German Headquarters. " Our defensive tactics had to be developed further, somehow or other." The wastage of troops had " exceeded all expectations." Seven divisions were sent to Italy. A countering blow was the best defence.

Sir Douglas Haig hoped that the phenomenal wet summer would be followed by a normal autumn, and continued his attacks through October. But the wet still continued, and important engagements, with large numbers of troops and tremendous expenditure of ammunition, only resulted in a " nibble " at the enemy territory.

The German-Austrian attack on Italy started on the 24th October, and resulted in the Italian Armies being driven back almost to the outskirts of Venice. This misfortune had the immediate effect of reducing the British Army on the Western Front by several

divisions, which were sent under the command of Sir
Herbert Plumer, and later of Lord Cavan, to help
our Italian Allies; it also determined Sir Douglas
Haig to continue his operations in Flanders. The
fierce battle for Passchendaele, in which the proud
divisions from Canada added to their immortal fame,
was fought, and operations in Flanders reached their
final stages about the middle of November.

For the effort expended, the gain in territory was
small, the number of prisoners was 24,065, the number
of guns captured (74) was insignificant. But the
balancing of results is a very delicate affair. During
the three and a half months of the offensive the
enemy had employed 78 divisions (18 of them had
been engaged a second or third time after having
rested and refitted). Deductions from such facts,
however, are a weak basis for argument. Sir Douglas
Haig wrote : " It is certain that the enemy's losses
considerably exceeded ours," but, apart from considerations of expediency, it is not clear how he
arrived at this startling conclusion.

To compare the number of prisoners we captured
with the number of bayonets which the Germans could
transfer from the Russian front is absurd. What
then have we left to show as a result for this costly
enterprise ? Only damage to that highly important
but very elusive thing which we call " enemy *moral.*"
The enemy charges us, perhaps with some truth,
with being clumsy soldiers with no imagination, but
he speaks with respect of the determination of the
British infantry, in a manner which suggests a
growing conviction that they could never be defeated.

.   .   .   .   .

An interesting figure was compiled by the II Corps

giving the amount of ammunition fired by the artillery of that corps from the 23rd June to 31st August —2,766,824 rounds with a total weight of 85,396 tons, delivered by 230 trains of 37 trucks and one of 29 trucks.

The battles of Ypres, 1917, are as follows : Battle of Pilckem Ridge, 31st July–2nd August; Battle of Langemarck, 16th–18th August; Battle of the Menin Road Ridge, 20th–25th September ; Battle of Polygon Wood, 26th September–3rd October ; Battle of Broodseinde, 4th October ; Battle of Poelcappelle, 9th October; First Battle of Passchendaele, 12th October; Second Battle of Passchendaele, 26th October–10th November.

BATTERY POSITION, ZOUAVE WOOD, HOOGE, AUGUST 1917

From a photograph taken by Lt. Wallis Muirhead, R.F.A.

CHAPTER VI

CAMBRAI

THE Divisional Headquarters opened at Reninghelst on the morning of the 18th August; brigades were quartered at Steenvoorde and Wippenhoek. These forward areas did not give uninterrupted rest; frequent and close attention was paid to them by aeroplanes, and during the following night two lorries were set on fire by bombs dropped by the night birds.

On the 22nd, 23rd, and 24th the division moved back, resting at Busseboom, and eventually arrived at the peaceful area of Eperleques. The 5th Cheshire Regt., however, remained in the battle area until the 29th. A further move started on the 30th, by train, to the ruined villages to the east and south of Bapaume, with Divisional Headquarters at Fremicourt.

Sports, horse-shows, and the Divisional Band now played a more prominent part in the life of the soldier, and we find the divisional canteen being enlarged—a greengrocery, eggs, and butter department being added, also a wholesale beer department. And, of course, there was training !

At the commencement of the war the British infantry were the greatest riflemen in the world. Then came a period when everyone was mad on throwing bombs, and the rifle was neglected. At the end of

the war one sighed in vain for a half, even a quarter
of the efficiency of the pre-war rifleman.

Training in 1917 was based on four weapons, and
the platoon. The platoon, we were told, was the
smallest unit comprising all the weapons with which
the infantry was armed. Exclusive of Headquarters,
twenty-eight other ranks was the minimum strength,
and when the platoon was below that strength the
necessary numbers would be obtained by the *temporary amalgamation of companies, platoons, or sections.*
We draw attention to these words because the order
was afterwards reversed.

The platoon was comprised of a rifle section, a
Lewis-gun section, a bomber section, and a rifle-
grenade section. The principles governing training
were based on these various weapons. The rifle and
bayonet were for assault, for repelling attack, or for
obtaining superiority of fire, and the training of this
section was considered of much importance. Each
man should be a marksman, first class with bayonet
and bomb, and a scout, in addition to being either a
Lewis-gunner or rifle grenadier. Bayonet fighting
was recommended to all sections, as it produced " lust
for blood."

The bomb was called the second weapon of all
N.C.O.s and men, and was to be used for dislodging
the enemy from behind cover or killing him below
ground. The section should study bombing attacks
and the duties of " moppers-up." These last individuals should work in pairs. They were to drop
into their objectives and work laterally outwards.
They killed the enemy met with in the trenches,
and they also guarded the entrances to dug-outs
and side trenches. They were not to penetrate down

dug-outs until the platoon they were working for arrived.

The rifle grenade was described as the howitzer of the infantry, and was used to dislodge the enemy from behind cover and to drive him below ground. The section was trained to a rifle-grenade barrage.

The Lewis gun was the weapon of opportunity. Its mobility and the small target it presented made it peculiarly suitable for working round an enemy's flank.

In each section sufficient ammunition was carried for immediate requirements. Every man (except bombers, signallers, scouts, runners, and Lewis gunners who carried 50 rounds) carried at least 120 rounds of rifle ammunition and 2 bombs. The Lewis-gun section carried 30 " drums." The bombers (with the exception of " throwers," who carried 5) carried at least 10 bombs each.

The men of the rifle-grenade section each carried at least six grenades. With this organisation training was carried out in trench-to-trench warfare and the enveloping of strong points.

In 1917 the strength of a platoon was not definitely laid down by the Higher Command. It was suggested that a suitable number for each section was nine— 1 non-commissioned officer and 8 men. But there was an order to leave 10 officers and 50 other ranks out of line for " reconstruction." They would not be available as reinforcements, but were, generally, specialists and good instructors, on whom the battalion could be rebuilt if casualties were heavy. Most units carried out the suggestion of 9 to a section, and any extra men, exclusive of the 50 for reconstruction, were used as reinforcements during the battle.

On arrival in the Third Army area (now under the command of General Byng, General Allenby having been given command in Egypt), the strength of the 56th Division was very low.

The four battalions of the 167th Brigade totalled altogether 63 officers and 1,754 other ranks ; the Machine Gun Company, 7 officers and 150 other ranks ; the Trench Mortar Battery, 5 officers and 50 other ranks.

The four battalions of the 168th Brigade totalled 94 officers and 2,802 other ranks ; the Machine Gun Company, 7 officers and 160 other ranks ; the Trench Mortar Battery, 5 officers and 90 other ranks.

The four battalions of the 169th Brigade totalled 61 officers and 1,921 other ranks ; the Machine Gun Company, 10 officers and 145 other ranks ; the Trench Mortar Battery, 2 officers and 75 other ranks.

It was therefore probable that when the period of rest was over the division would go into a quiet bit of the line.

All doubts as to the ultimate destination of the division were laid at rest on the 4th September, when the 168th Brigade relieved the 9th Brigade, 3rd Division, in the Lagnicourt section. The 169th Brigade relieved the 8th Brigade in the Louverval section on the 5th ; and the 167th Brigade relieved the 76th Brigade in the Morchies section on the 6th. The situation was quiet, and the weather fine and hot.

Patrolling, of an active nature, commenced at once, and on the 10th September the 167th Brigade secured a man of the 31st Reserve Infantry Regt. ; and on the same night the 168th Brigade secured two of the 86th Reserve Infantry Regt. Various enemy posts were visited from time to time, and occasionally

entered, but the gem of these small enterprises was
that of the Queen's Westminster Rifles. On the 29th
September 2/Lieut. W. H. Ormiston, with thirty men,
lay in wait in the middle of No Man's Land and successfully ambushed a patrol of fifteen Germans. Eleven
were killed and two brought in ; unfortunately, the
remaining two proved swift of foot and got away.
It was not done without a fight. Six of the Queen's
Westminsters were wounded. Both Corps and Army
Commanders sent their congratulations to this well-
known and gallant regiment, with the added message
that the identification was of great importance.
The prisoners were of the 414th Infantry Regt.

During this month six hundred gas projectors were
dug into the 56th Divisional Front.

During the month of October raids were attempted
by the London Scottish and the Kensingtons, but the
enemy were found alert and the parties failed to
enter the German line. The Kensingtons, however,
were successful in rescuing a British pilot whose
machine was brought down in No Man's Land, but
they had to fight for him.

The only incident of importance in the month of
October was a visit of ten days of Major-Gen. Bloxom,
U.S.A., with his chief of staff, with the object of
gaining experience.

The strength of the division remained about the
same.

On the 2nd November a document headed " IV
Corps, No. H.R.S. 17/48 " was received, into which
we must enter at some length.

The Third Army stretched from the little stream
of l'Omignon, which runs into the St. Quentin Canal
a few miles above that town, to Gavrelle, north of the

Scarpe. It was composed of the VII, III, IV, VI, and XVII Corps from right to left (and later, the V Corps). The III Corps had its right on 22 Ravine, between Villers-Guislain and Gonnelieu, and its left to the east of Trescault. Then came the IV Corps, with its left north of Lagnicourt, on a little stream called the Hirondelle. These two corps were facing the Hindenburg Line, and had in their immediate rear the battlefields of the Somme, and the country which the Germans had laid to waste in their retreat in the early spring.

At the time when our pursuing troops were brought to a standstill in front of this celebrated line, preparations were at once commenced for attack. Several actions had been fought on this sector before it settled down to a " quiet sector "; assembly trenches existed, and adequate shelter for brigade and battalion headquarters had been constructed. It was now chosen as a sector to be attacked.

At this time our Italian Allies were in serious difficulties, and seven German divisions were engaged in this theatre. And, although the movement of whole divisions had started from Russia without exchange from the Western Front, a mass of enemy troops were still pinned down in Flanders. It seemed as though a sudden surprise attack might benefit the Italian Armies and also improve the position on the Western Front. But there was the obvious difficulty of a lack of troops at Sir Douglas Haig's disposal; the Flanders adventure had been a most costly one for us, for practically the whole of the British Army had passed through the salient inferno Ypres. Finally it was decided that sufficient troops could be mustered to justify the attack, and as the French not only promised to engage the enemy's attention elsewhere, but actually set aside a large force of cavalry and infantry to help in the attack (they started to move on the 20th November), the order was given.

The scheme, as set forth in this document, was for the infantry to break through the German defensive system with the aid of Tanks on a front from Gonnelieu to Hermies, seize the crossings of the Canal de l'Escaut at Masnières and Marcoing, cut the last of the enemy's defences on the Beaurevoir-Masnières line, and pass the cavalry through the break thus made.

The cavalry were then to capture Cambrai and Bourlon Wood, cut all railway communications into Cambrai, and to occupy the crossings of the Sensée between Paillencourt and Palleul to the north of Cambrai. They would come up from Gouzeaucourt and Metz-en-Couture.

If this part of the plan was accomplished, the whole of the Third Army would participate in further operations to complete the surrounding of all the enemy forces in the Quéant salient. Presumably our Allies would have been called upon as well.

The III Corps, composed of the 20th, 6th, 12th, 29th Divisions, and 2nd and 3rd Brigades, Tank Corps (less three companies) would secure the canal crossings at Marcoing and Masnières, and form a flank from Gonnelieu through Bois Lateau, Creve-cœur, to a spot called la Belle Etoile a few miles south-east of Cambrai.

The IV Corps, composed of the 51st, 62nd, 36th, 56th Divisions, and 1st Brigade, Tank Corps, would attack with two divisions, on the left of the III Corps, and the right of the Canal du Nord, towards Flesquières and Graincourt.

The success of the whole plan depended on the capture of Masnières and Marcoing, at which point the cavalry would be passed through the break, and, as speed was the essence of the operation, in order to obtain liberty of movement before the enemy could organise either counter-attack or a fresh line of defence by bringing up fresh troops, the leading cavalry divisions would have to pass through on the afternoon or evening of zero day.

Meanwhile, the IV Corps would be pushing forward on the left, with the first object of establishing a line from Noyelles, along the Canal de l'Escaut, through Fontaines, and relieve the cavalry on Bourlon, or fight for that position, and join with the original front line in the Louverval sector.

Surprise was essential, so there would be no preliminary bombardment, and these instructions insisted that the greatest care should be taken not to divulge the presence of increased artillery to the enemy. Registration and calibration was to be carried out by order of the General Officer Commanding the Third Army Artillery.

One of the first tasks was to erect camouflage over all positions which would be occupied by the artillery. Then weatherproof cover for ammunition would be constructed. But little more than this could be done in the time at the disposal of the Army. In any case, the accumulation of ammunition would have to be spread over as long a period as possible, so as to minimise the increase of activity on the railways.

The action of the artillery would consist mainly in the formation of smoke screens and barrages, on the front and flanks of the attack (to cover the advance of the Tanks), and the neutralisation of hostile batteries, the bombardment of positions of assembly, rest billets, telephone routes, and known centres of communication and command. But the very nature of the operation precluded the careful registration of all batteries.

All the elaborate preparations of a trench-to-trench attack would be reduced to a minimum, and in many items must be done away with. Cover from weather would have to be provided for the full number of troops when concentrated, but no extensive scheme of hutting or new camps could be undertaken. In thick woods tents, suitably camouflaged, could be erected, and in thin woods wire netting must be stretched horizontally amongst the trees, about ten feet from the ground, and have twigs scattered on the top of it, thus making a sort of roof under which bivouacs could be pitched.

As to concentration, the idea was to complete the move of the artillery before the infantry was brought into the area, to have the extra infantry in the area as short a time as possible, and to bring up the Tanks at the very last moment.

Finally, No. 15 Squadron R.F.C. was ordered to note particularly whether any of the work being carried out was noticeable from the air.

The rôle of the 56th Division in all this was to make a demonstration on Z day and attract the attention of the enemy, and later on take part in the operation of rolling up the Hindenburg Line. When Bourlon Wood had been captured, the IV Corps would secure a line Rumancourt-Buissy-Inchy, which would cut off the German divisions in the Quéant salient and threaten with immediate capture their gun positions.

In this move two brigades of the 36th Division would take part on the east bank of the canal and one brigade on the west of the canal, starting from the Spoil Heap near Hermies and moving in the direction of Mœuvres and Inchy.

The 169th Brigade, which would be on the right of the 56th Divisional front, would be responsible for joining hands with the 109th Brigade, 36th Division, and with them attack in the direction of Tadpole Copse. In this attack Tanks were to be employed, but the number was never given.

Nothing amuses troops more than to deceive the enemy—and we say " amuse " advisedly, for though it is in the midst of a battle, with death and destruction going on all round them, men will be as keen as children in carrying out the scheme of make-believe, and if it succeeds will roar with laughter. Such a scheme was on foot for the 56th Division.

For the purpose of making the demonstration on the divisional front as realistic as possible, a number of dummy Tanks were to be made by the C.R.E., while brigades would amuse themselves by making dummy figures of men to act as supporting infantry. The Tanks were to be put out in No Man's Land during the night, and would be half hidden by the smoke barrage in the morning when the attack started; the figures would be pushed above the trenches as though infantry were just emerging. A motor-bicycle in the front-line trench was to imitate the noise of a Tank.

As might well be expected, excitement ran high in the division. The construction of dummy figures and dummy Tanks was taken in hand at once, and by the 19th November a dozen full-sized Tanks were ready, together with some two hundred and fifty figures to each brigade front.

On the 6th November wire-cutting was commenced by trench mortars in the neighbourhood of Quéant —250 rounds a day being fired—the Germans would probably think a raid was contemplated, which would account for any suspicious movements !

The time was short and, as preliminary preparation was to be cut down to a minimum, fatigues were not very arduous. There was a certain amount of work done on the roads near the front line, but the greatest care had to be exercised not to make improvements of an apparent nature. In the back areas, however, the strain was becoming intolerable. There were troops in every hole and corner. Tents were crammed full ; huts, ruins, any place where men could find a little shelter was used. And the weather was cold, and regulations about lights and fires were very stringent.

In the front line every precaution against accidents was taken. The attacking divisions occupied their positions in line, but the old troops remained in the outpost line in case the enemy should secure identification ; also patrols were ordered to avoid any possibility of capture.

On the 14th November the Corps ordered the 56th Division to hold the line with two brigades instead of three, so as to have a concentrated force ready to act in case of necessity. So on the night of the 18th the 167th Brigade extended its left and took over the frontage of the 168th Brigade, which concentrated in Fremicourt and Beugny, to the east of Bapaume.

On the night of the 19th the dummy Tanks were put in position about 300 yards from the front line.

At 2 a.m. on the 20th gas drums were projected into the German lines where the wire-cutting had taken place (Quéant), and at 6.20 a.m. the whole of the artillery on the Third Army front opened on the enemy lines with one stupendous crash.

In the 56th Division front line all was activity. The parties with the dummy figures moved them up and down in as lifelike a manner as they could, and other parties hurled smoke grenades so that the enemy might not see too clearly.

The " make-believe " attack was a great success. The Germans opened frantic and furious fire with machine-guns and artillery, and the dummy Tanks were shelled until mid-day !

By 9.15 a.m. the 36th Division (109th Brigade) had advanced along the west bank of the canal from the Spoil Heap to the Bapaume-Cambrai road, where the 169th Brigade joined up with it on the old German outpost line.

Meanwhile, great events had been taking place on the right. The III Corps, on which so much depended, advanced through the Hindenburg Line in grand style and, thanks to the rapid action of the 29th Division (General de Lisle), which was to wait until news arrived of the capture of the Hindenburg Support Line before advancing but attacked instead on observer reports, seized Marcoing and Masnières. The first bit of bad luck happened at Masnières, where the enemy had only partially destroyed the iron bridge over the Escault Canal. It might have been sufficiently strong for cavalry to cross over, or it might have been repaired to enable them to do so, but a Tank attempted to cross first and broke through it altogether. This unfortunate accident did not stop a squadron of

Canadian cavalry, who, with the dash usually associated with that arm, rode over a flimsy bridge across a lock on the Marcoing side of the town and attacked the enemy on Rumilly Ridge. It was probably troopers from this very gallant squadron who reached the outskirts of Cambrai.

Lieut.-Col. Johnston took the 2nd Hampshires across in a similar way and secured the crossing. But in Marcoing other troops of the 29th Division secured the bridge intact.

The III Corps had therefore done its job, but the IV Corps was not so fortunate. Havrincourt Wood had been of great service to the IV Corps in the assembly. The 51st and 62nd Divisions, with a fringe of the 36th Division in front of them until the last moment, had completed their concentration without a hitch. On the nights of the 16th, 17th, and 18th all the Tanks were moved into Havrincourt Wood, and except that a battery of 6-inch howitzers got into difficulties farther north, and that a lorry " ran into a train carrying Tanks," the whole concentration was carried out as desired. But, although we do not believe it made much difference, the enemy were aware of the attack. Unfortunately, some men were captured in a raid on the 36th Divisional front, and from the statements of prisoners they evidently divulged the fact that an attack was contemplated. The time and the extent of it, however, seems to have been a complete surprise to the Germans.

At zero hour the Tanks advanced, followed by the 51st and 62nd Divisions. There was in this sector some of the most formidable wire on the whole of the western front, but the Tanks crushed wide lanes through it and the troops advanced steadily. There

13

was some obstinate fighting in Havrincourt village and park, where parties of the enemy held out until the afternoon, but otherwise the Hindenburg front line was captured by 8 o'clock. A pause of two hours was allowed here to enable troops and Tanks to re-organise for the attack on the Hindenburg Support.

Once more the attack moved forward. The 62nd Division on the left met with little opposition, and that portion of the support line allotted to them was in their hands between 10 and 11 o'clock. But the 51st Division on the right met with resistance at the village of Flesquières. The infantry were prevented from advancing by machine guns and uncut wire, and the Tanks, which came up on the ridge, were at once put out of action by field guns, which had been pulled out of their pits on to the slopes to the north of the village. Six Tanks were to be seen here in a line, smashed to bits by a very gallant German Battery Commander, who, it was said, served and fired the guns himself, when his men had bolted.

The 51st Division could make no progress, but on their left the 62nd moved forward to Graincourt, and the 36th, still farther on the left, had moved along the canal to the Cambrai road. And on the right troops of the III Corps were well on towards Cantaign. The 51st Division made a second attempt with Tanks and again failed.

What follows is one of the mysteries of the Cambrai battle. A patrol of King Edward's Horse, operating with the 62nd Division, rode into Flesquières soon after mid-day from the direction of Graincourt. They reported only a few of the enemy there and do not appear to have suffered any casualties themselves. But the 1st Cavalry Division, which had been con-

centrated in the neighbourhood of Equancourt, had
been ordered at 8.25 a.m. to move forward with their
head on Metz, ready to advance. This they did.
About 11 o'clock they were ordered to push forward
through the Hindenburg Support Line, but found that
Flesquières was still in the hands of the enemy, and
they were unable to pass. About 2.30 p.m. they were
ordered to pass at least two regiments by Ribecourt
and Premy Chapel and work round Flesquières from
the north-east and assist the 51st Division in their
attack from the south. But they found they were
unable to carry out this co-operation on account of
the delay which had occurred, due to their first effort,
and also that Nine Wood was not clear of the enemy.
At 4 p.m. the Third Army ordered the cavalry to
push forward in full strength through Marcoing and
carry out the original plan of a break-through at that
point ; but darkness had come on and the order was
modified, one brigade being ordered to occupy Cantaign and cut off the enemy retreating from Flesquières.
Cantaign, however, was found to be too strongly held
for the cavalry to capture it, and therefore the leading
brigade remained at Noyelles for the night. It would
seem that the opportunity was missed.

As dusk fell, the 62nd and 36th Divisions were well
forward towards the Bourlon Ridge, the former just
short of Anneaux, and then forming a long flank
back east of Graincourt and to the west of Flesquières,
where they connected with the 51st Division. Farther
to the right of the IV Corps the III Corps had also
pushed well forward and made a similar flank facing
west, the ground between the two points of greatest
advance about Orival Wood being occupied by the
enemy's artillery. (Line C.)

Immediately after the capture of the Hindenburg system the redistribution of the artillery and machine guns began. The machine guns, which had been massed under corps control, reverted to their divisions. Four brigades of Field Artillery, one 60-pounder battery, and one, horsed, 6-inch Howitzer battery were placed under the orders of each of the 36th, 62nd, and 51st Divisions. But a fortunate circumstance arose : it was found difficult to get the heavy artillery across No Man's Land into the Flesquières salient, and the congestion there was such that the supply of ammunition would have been uncertain ; so it was decided to move the bulk of the artillery to the left, close to the old front line round about Demicourt, Hermies, and Morchies. In this position they assisted very materially in breaking up the great German attack on the 30th November.

During this first day the Queen Victoria's Rifles were on the right of the 169th Brigade, and worked along the German outpost line in touch with the 109th Brigade, who were clearing the Hindenburg Line, as far as the Cambrai road. The 2nd London Regt. was on the left of the Queen Victoria's Rifles.

It had been calculated that no large hostile reinforcements would be likely to reach the scene of action for forty-eight hours after the commencement of the attack, and Sir Douglas Haig had informed General Byng that the advance would be stopped after that time, unless the results then gained, and the general situation, justified its continuance. Although, as we have said, the movements of the Canadian Cavalry and King Edward's Horse would seem to suggest that the opportunity of passing other cavalry through had been missed, there remained one day when, given success, they could still be employed. The 51st and 62nd Divisions were therefore ordered to capture the Bourlon position, when the 1st Cavalry Division would follow up the attack and seize the passages of the Canal du Nord between Palleul and Sains-les-Marquion; and the 36th Division was to continue the advance on the west of the canal, and hold the two brigades on the eastern bank ready to push through and seize the canal, between Sains-les-Marquion and Mœuvres, as soon as Bourlon was taken. The 56th Division would be drawn farther into the operations on the left in the direction of Tadpole Copse.

When the day broke, Flesquières was found, by the 51st Division, to be unoccupied by the enemy; they therefore pushed on to the Marcoing-Graincourt road, capturing a number of guns in the valley which the enemy had not been able to remove in the night. The 1st Cavalry Division then advanced and took Cantaing, after some stiff fighting in which some of the 51st Division took part. On the left the 62nd Division captured Anneaux and Anneaux Chapel, after heavy fighting, and made more progress north of the Cambrai road, where they established themselves on the ridge west of Bourlon Wood, and also gained a further stretch of the Hindenburg Support Line. On the left of the 62nd the 36th Division advanced along the west bank of the canal, meeting increased opposition, and for a time held the south of the village of Mœuvres. On their left again the Queen Victoria's Rifles worked along the outpost line and captured a machine gun with its crew of seven. Resistance, however, was stiffening. The dividing line between the 109th and the 169th Brigades was the grid line to the west of Mœuvres, and any farther advance to the north would bring the 56th Division in contact with the Hindenburg Line itself. Meanwhile, in the centre of the battlefield, progress was not what had been hoped it would be. The 51st Division were to work round Bourlon Wood from the east, and join hands with the 62nd Division; but they met with such opposition as delayed their advance, and they did not capture Fontaine until late in the afternoon. The capture of Bourlon was not achieved. At nightfall the 51st Division was holding a line north of Cantaing forward to Fontaine, making a dangerous salient, and then in a westerly direction to the north of Anneaux, where, joining with the 62nd, the line was carried north of the Cambrai road, forming another salient north of the Sugar Factory. The 36th Division then carried on the line, which bent back towards the road near the canal bridge and then forward again to Mœuvres. Due west of Mœuvres the 56th Division held the line to the old British trenches. The Tanks, in diminished numbers, had assisted during the day, but no advance had been made without a struggle. (Line D.)

In the III Corps area there had been some heavy fighting during the day, which resulted in some improvement of our positions. Heavy counter-attacks were launched by the enemy, and much useful and gallant work was done by dismounted cavalry beating off these attacks. But the forty-eight hours had expired, and the high ground at Bourlon Village and Wood, as well as certain tactical features to the east and west of the wood, still remained in the enemy's hands. It seemed fairly clear that the surprise break-through and complete disorganisation of the enemy's back areas would not be accomplished.

Sir Douglas Haig had to decide whether to continue the offensive or take up a defensive attitude and rest content with what had been done.

" It was not possible, however, to let matters stand as they were. The positions captured by us north of Flesquières were completely commanded by the Bourlon Ridge, and unless the ridge were gained it would be impossible to hold them, except at excessive cost. If I decided not to go on, a withdrawal to the Flesquières ridge would be necessary, and would have to be carried out at once.

On the other hand, the enemy showed certain signs of an intention to withdraw. Craters had been formed at road junctions, and troops could be seen ready to move east. The possession of Bourlon Ridge would enable our troops to obtain observation over the ground to the north, which sloped gently down to the Sensée River. The enemy's defensive lines south of the Scarpe and the Sensée Rivers would thereby be turned, his communications exposed to the observed fire of our artillery, and his positions in this sector jeopardised. In short, so great was the importance of the ridge to the enemy that its loss would probably cause the abandonment by the Germans of their carefully prepared defence systems for a considerable distance to the north of it. . . .

It was to be remembered, however, that the hostile reinforcements coming up at this stage could at first be no more than enough to replace the enemy's losses ; and although the right of our advance had been definitely stayed, the enemy had not yet developed such strength about Bourlon as it seemed might not be overcome by the numbers at my disposal. As has already been pointed out, on the Cambrai side of the battlefield I had only aimed at securing a defensive flank to enable the advance to be pushed northwards and north-westwards, and this part of my task had been to a large extent achieved.

An additional and very important argument in favour of proceeding with my attack was supplied by the situation in Italy, upon which a continuance of pressure on the Cambrai front might reasonably be expected to exercise an important effect, no matter what measures of success attended my efforts. Moreover, two divisions previously under orders for Italy had on this day been placed at my disposal, and with this accession of strength the prospect of securing Bourlon seemed good.

After weighing these various considerations, therefore, I decided to continue the operations to gain the Bourlon position.

But in the morning, about 9.30 a.m., the enemy launched a heavy counter-attack on the 62nd Division west of Bourlon Wood which, although it did not succeed in driving them back, prevented any advance. And about 10.30 they attacked Fontaine from the north-west and east, and after heavy fighting drove the 51st Division out and clear of the village.

During the afternoon the Germans again attacked the 62nd Division, but were again repulsed, as they had been in the morning. On the left of the 62nd, the 36th were unable to gain ground on the east of the canal, and on the west bank entered Mœuvres for the second time, but after an hour or so were driven out. (Line E.)

On this day, the 22nd November, the 56th Division played a more important part. The 169th Brigade were still on the right of the division. The Queen Victoria's Rifles, in touch with the 109th Brigade, were holding a line of posts across No Man's Land and in the old German outpost line. The Queen's

Westminster Rifles were ordered to concentrate,
slightly to the north of the Cambrai road, and to
advance, in conjunction with the 109th Brigade, at
11 o'clock along the front trench of the Hindenburg
Line which runs to Tadpole Copse. They would also
work their way up the communication trenches to
the second line of the Hindenburg first system, and
clear both lines as far as Tadpole Copse. The London
Rifle Brigade were ordered to assemble in the captured Hindenburg Line south of the Cambrai road,
and follow the attack of the 109th Brigade to where
the Hindenburg system turned away from the canal
at Mœuvres (see Map) ; they would then follow
the Queen's Westminsters in two columns, one in the
first line and one in the second, and reinforce if
necessary. The 5,000 yards of British line up to the
Hirondelle River were held by the 167th Brigade.

The instructions were to carry out a determined
advance. The idea, of which this was the preliminary operation, was for the 36th Division to
move forward through Mœuvres and Inchy,, while
the 56th Division captured the Hindenburg Line up
to Quéant.

It was entirely a bombing fight, and was supported
by an artillery barrage, which lifted off Swan Lane at
11.30 a.m. and moved forward at the rate of fifty
yards every five minutes. The division, until the
night 21st/22nd, had been covered by the 281st Brigade
R.F.A. only—as was usual in these battles, the artillery
was switched about from one command to another—
but during the night the 280th Brigade R.F.A. had
moved to positions near Boursies and took part in
this attack.

It was hard and slow fighting, as is generally the

case in bombing fights. Colonel Glazier, of the Queen's Westminsters, writes :

" The barrage got some way ahead of our men, but owing to the uncertainty of the position of the troops it was impossible to bring it back. At 12.30 p.m. a runner came with a request for more bombs, and the news that our men had passed the Boursies-Mœuvres road and were using German bombs. . . . Bombs were sent forward; large quantities were taken forward by the Queen Victoria's Rifles."

News of progress was very slow in coming in, and the first definite information indicating success was obtained from observers, who reported at 2.40 p.m. that the enemy were shelling Tadpole Copse. Not until 5.30 was it known for certain that the copse was occupied by three companies of the Queen's Westminsters. They captured 3 officers, 70 men, and 3 machine guns.

The London Scottish had arrived at the old British front line about Louverval at mid-day with the object of relieving the Queen's Westminsters and carrying on the attack. They were informed that the attack would not be continued that day, and so formed a flank from the south of Tadpole Copse to the old British line, although for the moment they were unable to dislodge the enemy from a deep crater at the road junctions some two hundred yards south-west of the copse. At dawn they relieved the forward companies of the Queen's Westminsters and made ready for the morning attack.

Most useful work was also done during the night by the 416th Field Coy. R.E., who constructed a bridge over the canal at the Cambrai road, although the

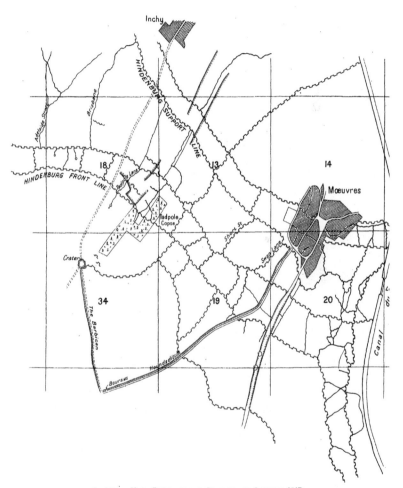

Inchy

HINDENBURG SUPPORT LINE

Adelaide St.

Brigade

HINDENBURG FRONT LINE

18

13

14

Mœuvres

Tadpole Lane

Tadpole Copse

Short St.

Snag Lane

Crater

The Barbican

34

19

20

Canal du N.

Houndsditch

Bourtive

6. LOCAL MAP. FRONT OF THE DIVISION AT CAMBRAI 1917.

enemy kept up a persistent shelling of the road, and particularly of the point of intersection with the canal. The 512th Coy. R.E. at the same time made good the road from Boursies to the canal.

So the only progress made by the IV Corps on the 22nd was the capture of Tadpole Copse by the Queen's Westminsters, an important gain as it occupies the high ground to the west of Mœuvres. But it became apparent that the enemy was rapidly massing strong forces to stay our farther advance.

The 40th Division passed into the Corps command and was sent to relieve the 62nd. The Corps orders that evening were for the advance to continue on the 23rd, with the assistance of Tanks, the chief objective being Bourlon village. The 51st Division was to attack it from the east and the 40th from the south-west ; but when it became known that the 51st Division had been driven out of Fontaine, their task was modified to the recapture of that village. The 36th and 56th Divisions were to continue the advance up the canal, and roll up the Hindenburg Support Line.

All through the night there had been much shell fire on the 56th Divisional front. Two counter-attacks had been successfully repulsed. Owing to darkness and the congested state of the trenches, the London Scottish were late in getting into their assembly positions, but as they were not to move until an hour and a half after zero (6.30 a.m.), which time was occupied by bombardment of the enemy positions, it did not matter.

" It was then found," Colonel Jackson writes, " that the 169th Brigade had not reached Tadpole Lane, but the communication trench running from front to

support trench on the north-west side of Tadpole
Copse, and that a fairly deep valley existed between
this communication trench and the Inchy-Louverval
road. The Germans could thus directly enfilade the
front and support trenches with rifle and machine-gun
fire from the other side of the valley, where they had
built strong blocks and loopholes during the night.
The battalion was thus held up at this point until 2.30
p.m. By this time " D " Company had, with the assistance of the Stokes Mortars (169th), been able to cross
the valley, face the block on the other side, and cross
the Inchy road, thus surrounding the enemy still
holding the block in the front line opposite " B " Company. Ten officers, 69 other ranks, 6 machine guns,
and 1 trench mortar—all of the 20th German Division."

It would appear that the German counter-attacks
during the night had gained some ground. The valley
alluded to by Colonel Jackson is not shown clearly
on the British maps and is only indicated by the very
unsatisfactory sign of " banks." An imaginative
person might have traced the re-entrant starting in
square 7 right up to these banks, but it was not
always wise to be too imaginative with the British
map ; at any rate the shape of the ground seems
to have been a surprise.

By 4.30 p.m. the battalion had reached its objective,
Adelaide street, and was immediately strongly counter-
attacked. The supply of bombs failed—it is extraordinary how many bombs can be thrown on such
occasions—and the support line was lost as far as
the Inchy road, but the front line was held. In this
counter-attack the London Scottish were reinforced
by two companies of the 4th London Regt. They
were ordered to consolidate.

The operations on the rest of the Corps front during

the day resulted in fierce fighting through Bourlon Wood, and the capture of Bourlon village by the 40th Division, and a tremendous struggle for Fontaine into which the 51st Division never really penetrated. Repeated and heavy counter-attacks forced the 40th Division out of Bourlon village to the north edge of Bourlon Wood. The 36th Division had captured and again been forced out of Mœuvres, and had not been able to make much progress on the east bank of the canal, a failure which caused the position of the 40th Division to become a somewhat isolated one. The gallant 51st Division, which had been used in such ruthless fashion, was relieved by the Guards Division and went back to Albert (Line F).

At 12.50 a.m. on the 24th the Corps issued orders for the ground gained to be held at all costs. The 40th Division were to consolidate their position and attack Bourlon village with the assistance of twelve Tanks at noon. The Guards Division were to consolidate the line taken over from the 51st, and the 36th and 56th Divisions to continue their clearing of the Hindenburg Line. But, as we have said, the order applying to the 56th Division was subsequently cancelled.

The 168th Brigade, which was now in the centre of the division, took over a stretch of the old British front line from the 167th on the left; the forward position of the 169th was still in the Hindenburg Line on the right. The main strength of the division was concentrated, of course, about the Hindenburg Line to the west of Mœuvres, while in the old British line it was strung out and thin. But the division as a whole was strengthened on the 24th by the addition of one brigade of Royal Horse Artillery.

At three o'clock in the afternoon the enemy again attacked under a very severe barrage, and the London Scottish lost their hold on the second line of the first German system, to the north of Tadpole Copse, but not without a strong fight. The enemy came down all communication trenches at once, while small parties of snipers advanced from shell-hole to shell-hole over the open. The attack was pressed so closely that the supply of bombs could not be maintained, and the London Scottish men had eventually to retire across the open. The front line, however, was still held to a point opposite Adelaide Street.

On the night of the 24th the division passed from the IV Corps to the VI Corps. But although the 56th Division passed from the IV Corps we must not lose sight of the doings of that corps, which continued to press towards the north, with the 56th Division on its flank. During the day many attacks and counter-attacks took place, and in the end the 40th Division retook the village of Bourlon.

By the morning of the 25th the London Scottish had been relieved by the Rangers (12th London), in view of an attack to regain the stretch of Hindenburg Line lost on the previous day.

The 4th London Regt. were in position on the right and the Rangers (12th) on the left. The 4th Londons, holding the bit of the Second Line north of Tadpole Copse, were to bomb straight ahead while the Rangers, who were in the First Line, would bomb up the communication trenches to the Second Line and join hands with the 4th Londons. The attack started at 1 p.m. and progressed very satisfactorily for a while; but the fighting was very hard and the men very tired. The 4th London at one time reached the

Inchy road, but their arrival there seems to have coincided with a particularly violent effort of the enemy which caused the Rangers to call for protective artillery fire; the artillery responded and the 4th London, being in the zone of fire, had to retire. The attack, which lasted until the evening, ended with a small gain, but left the Germans in possession of the banks about the valley north-west of the copse.

On the 25th the 40th Division was driven out of Bourlon village, but retained the ridge running through Bourlon Wood. They were relieved by the 62nd during the night. Three dismounted battalions of the 2nd Cavalry Division were placed at the disposal of the IV Corps, and did good work during the next three days in Bourlon Wood.

Bomb-fighting was carried on through the night about Tadpole Copse. We have casually mentioned that the men were tired, and on the 26th Gen. Dudgeon represented to the Corps that he considered his division was too extended. It had captured and was holding about one mile of the Hindenburg system, and, until Mœuvres was captured, his right flank was in danger, while his left flank, on Tadpole Copse spur, was not only exposed but being constantly attacked. Two brigades were involved in the fighting about the Hindenburg system, and, in addition, were holding a flank 2,000 yards long connecting up to the old British front line. The remaining brigade was holding 5,500 yards of British line, and had also to supply one battalion each night to work in the captured position. There was therefore no divisional reserve, nor could any reliefs be arranged for the troops who had been fighting. The VI Corps placed one battalion of the 3rd Division (on the left) at the disposal of the 167th Brigade, and this enabled the 8th Middlesex Regt. to be placed at the disposal of the 168th Brigade, which eased the situation in the Hindenburg system.

A heavy attack on the 27th was repulsed by the Rangers and the Kensingtons, and on the following two days there is nothing more to record than heavy shelling.

The 26th had been a quiet day for the IV Corps. Certain reliefs were carried out. The 36th Division was replaced by the 2nd Division ; the 1st Cavalry Division, which had taken part in the fighting up to this time, was ordered to return to its own corps ; and the 47th Division was ordered into the battle area east of the canal.

On the 27th, after a night of storm and snow, the Guards and 62nd Divisions attacked Fontaine and Bourlon villages. Though both divisions entered their objectives, the positions were not held. The resources of the Army were considered to be almost exhausted at this stage, which was probably the reason for using only three battalions of the Guards Division for this operation.

The 59th Division was placed at the disposal of the IV Corps and relieved the Guards on the next day, while the 47th Division relieved the weary 62nd. And the Tanks were completely withdrawn.

The battle had therefore petered out, leaving a most unsatisfactory state of affairs about Bourlon Wood and village ; the situation opposite Fontaine was also not good. It will have been noticed that, after the first rush, the fighting was done by the IV Corps against the northern side of the salient which had been created, and the III Corps held an extended

flank which, at the junction with the VII Corps on
their right, was somewhat thin.

On the face of it it seems as though the mind of
the Third Army Staff was concentrated on the doings
of the IV Corps and the enemy opposite them. The
Bourlon position had a mesmerising effect, and even
though the III Corps was suddenly warned by the
Army to expect an attack on the 29th, no very great
preparation for such an event seems to have been
made. The divisions did all they could. The 12th
Division on the right of the Corps moved the two
battalions in divisional reserve nearer the line, and
organised all reinforcements and the 10 per cent.
personnel, left out of the line, into a battalion about
850 strong. Other divisions issued a warning to
troops in the line. The 55th, on the left of the VII
Corps and next to the 12th, sent out a long order :

"Certain indications during the day point to the
possibility of the enemy making an attack against
our front. All troops will be warned to be specially
on the alert in trenches and all posts. Special patrols
will be sent out at 4 a.m. to watch for enemy movement. Artillery will open fire on the enemy front
line, commencing at 5 a.m. The most likely places for
concentration to be selected by brigadier-generals
commanding infantry brigades in consultation with
group commanders. In case of enemy attack all
posts and trenches will be held to the last at all costs,
and there will be no retirement from any line to
another line. The action of troops available for
counter-attack will be considered now. All machine
guns will be warned to be specially on the look-out
for S.O.S. signals. From 5 a.m. 29th inst., 1/4th North
Lancs. will be ready to move at half-hour's notice
from receipt of orders. Remainder of 164th Brigade

14

will be ready to move at one hour's notice from the same time."

On the other hand, the Guards and 62nd Divisions had already started to move out of the salient.

Nothing happened on the 29th, but on the 30th the enemy launched a big attack on the III and IV Corps with the intention of pinching off the salient and capturing all the troops in the area.

The enemy broke through the III Corps, the weight of his attack being directed at the junction of the 55th and 12th Divisions. General H. B. Scott, commanding the 12th Division, says :

"I do not consider that the troops in the front system were in any way surprised. In fact, far from it, as on some portions there was a heavy bombardment and the Divisional Artillery had opened fire on S.O.S. lines at 6.30 a.m. Also on the evening of the 29th November warning had been sent to all infantry brigades and the C.R.A. that an attack was possible on the eastern flank.

In my opinion, the troops in the centre of the 12th Division were pushed back by the force of numbers. The question of the flanks being turned is another one for which I have no evidence to show what actually happened to bring about those situations. From all accounts the flanks of the division were turned before the troops vacated the Banteaux Spur and Lateau Wood. This is verified by those in the vicinity of those places.

The enemy had great facilities in assembling unknown to us in Banteaux, in the factory, and in the wood. Undoubtedly these were the places he used. The main attacks were, I consider, made along the Banteaux Ravine, keeping south of the Banteaux Spur; up the ravine from Banteaux to

R23c (in the direction of la Vacquerie) and from the
factory and wood (in the valley north of Banteaux)
towards the western edge of Bonavis Ridge.
I am confident that the enemy suffered heavy losses.
Undoubtedly he attacked in force, and some must
have been caught by the artillery and machine-gun
barrage during the assembly and the initial stages of
his advance. Besides this, there was much close
fighting and many counter-attacks."

The gallant 29th Division held on to Masnières
like grim death, and the enemy never moved them
an inch, but he advanced as far as Gouzeaucourt and
was threatening Metz, through which lay the only
good road to the IV Corps.

It is not quite clear whether this was the main
German attack or not. About six divisions seem to
have been used, but, judging by the length of the
attack and its ferocity, the big effort is indicated on
the other side, the northern side of the salient.

On the north side of the salient the divisions ran :
the 59th, the 47th (London Territorials), the 2nd,
and the 56th. On the 56th Divisional front the
brigades holding the captured Hindenburg system
were disposed as follows :

The Queen's Westminster Rifles on the right and
the 2nd London Regt. on the left of the 169th Brigade
front in the Hindenburg Line, the London Rifle
Brigade and Queen Victoria's Rifles being in the old
British line behind them.

The 168th Brigade, reinforced by one battalion,
came next in the Hindenburg Line, with the 8th
Middlesex (attached) on the right and the London
Scottish on the left, and the 4th London Regt. holding
the defensive flank back to the old British front line.

The Kensingtons were in support in the old British front line, and the Rangers were at Beugny.

The 167th Brigade had been relieved by the 3rd Division, and had marched back to Fremicourt.

At about 10 o'clock in the morning the 2nd Division, who were astride the canal holding the ground won by the 36th Division, reported a heavy concentration of the enemy on the east of Quarry Wood, between the wood and the canal, and just behind Mœuvres, also a division entering Mœuvres itself. But before this mass of troops was reported, the London Scottish, 8th Middlesex, and Queen's Westminster Rifles had noticed unusual happenings in the enemy lines.

The enemy had started registration by aeroplane, which caused other observers than sentries to be on the watch. And then it was seen that the Germans were wearing steel helmets instead of the usual soft caps. The aerial activity increased, and soon heavy enemy fire was opened between Mœuvres and Bourlon. The registration on the 56th Divisional front was followed by slow, steady bombardment, which increased, until about a quarter to ten a heavy barrage crashed down on the whole front. It was obvious that an attack was impending, and the S.O.S. rockets were sent up.

The enemy barrage, which consisted of light howitzers, field guns, and trench mortars, was particularly heavy on the blocks in the captured communication trenches. Gradually the German guns lifted, and at 10.15 a.m. the enemy swarmed forward to the attack.

A glance at the map will show the precarious position, not only of the 56th Division and neighbouring

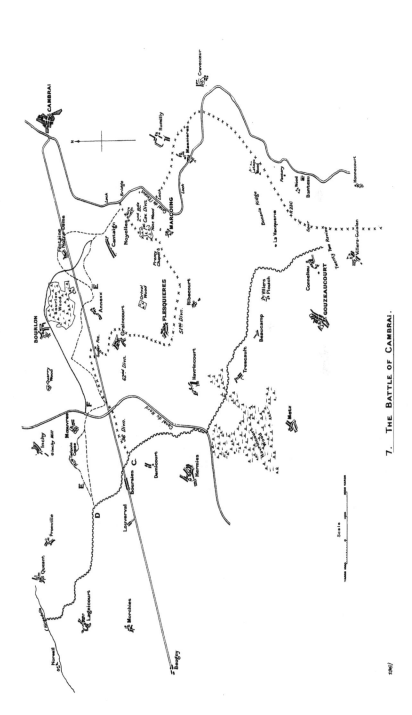

7. THE BATTLE OF CAMBRAI.

units, but of the whole of the Third Army troops engaged in the salient. South of the salient the Germans were through our lines, and if they broke through in the north an unparalleled disaster would be inflicted on the British Army. The Germans tried hard. During the day no less than five set attacks were launched, the heaviest with eleven lines of infantry advancing in succession to the assault. We wish to emphasise the position of the IV and III Corps and the general situation in the salient, for if the 56th Division failed to stand fast (and we know they could not be called fresh troops) the fate of the two Corps was sealed. On no portion of the front attacked could the Germans hope to gain a greater success than on the part held by the 56th Division.

The intricate nature of the Hindenburg Line, although it afforded the attackers cover for assembly close up to the troops of the 56th Division, had its disadvantages. Small bodies of defenders could inflict incalculable loss and, though surrounded, could break up the attack so that it only trickled through feebly ; but, of course, they must be good men.

The 56th proved themselves once more to be good men. The German storming parties were most cleverly supported by their trench mortars and field artillery. A deluge of shells descended on the posts holding the blocks in the communication trenches, and the enemy infantry supplemented the bombardment with rifle grenades. The artillery lifted slowly, and as it moved so the infantry, assembled at the other side of the blocks, leapt out on the parapet and attempted to rush the defending post. At the same time other infantry advanced over the open from the main trenches.

With such a short distance between opposing troops
one might well suppose that this form of attack would
succeed. It was sudden, it was confusing, inasmuch
as Germans appeared everywhere. But the men of
the 56th Division showed the most astonishing, the
most praiseworthy calmness. The training of the
division in the new organisation, with platoons composed of rifle, bombing, rifle grenadier, and Lewis-gun
sections, combined with the coolness of the men now
bore fruit. Volleys from the rifle grenadier sections
shook the Germans as they emerged from their
trenches; the riflemen picked off individuals who were
getting too close ; Lewis guns, sited to sweep enemy
avenues of approach, sent streams of bullets into the
mass of the enemy ; and where the Germans succeeded
in reaching the trenches they had to deal with the
bombers.

In the tremendous battle that followed, the Stokes
mortar batteries supported their comrades in exem-
plary fashion. The most striking individual work
of all that was done by these batteries was that
carried out by Corporal Macintosh, of the 168th Battery. This corporal had done extraordinarily good
work on the 24th, but on this occasion he surpassed
his previous record. Captain Crawford writes of
his utter disregard for his personal safety, of his
standing exposed, not only to the fire of artillery
and trench mortars, but the more deadly sniper,
calmly directing the fire of his gun where it was most
urgently needed. And what of Private Woods ?

" Private Woods had been forced to withdraw his
gun from its original position, and in doing so he
lost the stand. He took up a new position with

another gun, and carried on firing incessantly; and later, when the stand of his gun was giving way through excessive firing, continued to use the primary ammunition on the enemy whilst holding the barrel of the gun between his legs."

The Germans attacked with the greatest determination, and pressed forward with a multitude of men. Posts all along the front line were gradually surrounded, but the grim, steadfast fierceness of the men of the 56th Division was doing its work. The enemy losses were appalling. The losses of the 56th Division were great, and where gaps occurred the enemy slipped through. They appeared in the front line (the support line of the Hindenburg front system), on the right, in the centre, on the left. Hard fighting had reached the second line of the Queen's Westminsters and the 2nd Londons. Col. Pank, of the 8th Middlesex, was in his headquarter dug-out, situated in the support line (German front line), when he was told the enemy was in the front line ; he ordered his runners, signallers, everybody to man the trench outside, and, leading the way himself, clambered out of one entrance to the dug-out while the Germans threw bombs down the other. Col. Pank slipped down the communication trench which ran to the old German outpost line, and gathering together the first men he could find of his support company, with a supply of bombs led them back to attack.

The London Scottish were on the extreme left, holding the old German front line through Tadpole Copse and across the Inchy road, and therefore a continuation of the 8th Middlesex second line. Col. Jackson was suddenly startled by finding the enemy in his line. But the fierce attack led

by Col. Pank shook the enemy, and though the
London Scottish had their hands fairly full on their
front and left flank, they dealt with the party in their
trench. Col. Pank then cleared the whole of his
section of the old German front line. This was the
point of deepest penetration by the enemy, and was
reached somewhere about one o'clock.

We must point out that dug-outs in this line were far
from comfortable quarters. Their positions were
naturally known to the Germans and they were continually bombarded with enormous trench mortars,
said to be 12-inch. In the expressive language of
the Cockney, they were "bumped" from morning
to night. To get some idea of the effect of these
engines on those in the dug-outs, we need only say
that each explosion extinguished all the candles and
left the occupants in darkness.

The Kensingtons had been sent up to Barbican,
the sunken road in No Man's Land, as reinforcements,
but in view of the uncertainty of the position they
were ordered to remain there.

One cannot hope to give a detailed account of
attack and counter-attack in this mass of trenches.
Every hour brought a new situation, now in our
favour, now against us. The Queen's Westminsters
and the 2nd Londons had suffered severe casualties.
Everywhere the line stood firm in the old German
front line. Two companies of the London Rifle
Brigade had reinforced the Queen's Westminsters,
and three companies of the Queen Victoria's Rifles
had gone to the 2nd Londons. Practically the whole
of the 169th Brigade was engaged, and gradually
they wore down the German attack.

The message " Am holding on—hard pressed " came

by pigeon and runner with distressing frequency. The Rangers were put under the orders of the 169th Brigade. The remaining battalions of the 167th Brigade and the 5th Cheshires were marching towards the battle. The S.O.S. was signalled by the London Scottish at 4 p.m. At 6 p.m. fierce bombing was still going on in all trenches forward.

The position was that the 169th and 168th Brigades held the old German front line with blocks in all the communication trenches running to the second line. The Queen's Westminsters (in touch with the 2nd Division on the right), 2nd London, and 8th Middlesex, on whom the greatest weight of the attack had fallen, had lost the old German second line; the London Scottish, faced with the flank of the German attack, but nevertheless a hotly pressed attack, had lost no ground.

On this day the Divisional Artillery had fired on S.O.S. lines continuously from soon after ten in the morning until six at night. A number of fleeting targets and enemy batteries were also engaged with good results. The Germans attempted to press forward with their batteries; in fact, they believed they were going to break through, and the batteries could be seen galloping into action. On one occasion, about 1 p.m., a brigade of three German 77-mm. batteries raced into the open, and were engaged so swiftly by the 280th Brigade R.F.A. that only one battery was able to get off a round before being knocked out. As usual the 56th Divisional Artillery supported the gallantry of the infantry with equal gallantry and determination.

The German counter-battery fire had increased rapidly every day from the commencement of the operations, gas being used chiefly at night. But at no time did it reach anything like the same intensity as was experienced on the Ypres front, or even on the Somme. Hostile aircraft were very active, flying low over the front line and battery positions during the latter part of the battle ; and on two or three occasions they hindered batteries in the open by machine-gunning their crews when they were firing on S.O.S. lines.

On the right of the 56th Division, and on the west side of the canal, the 6th Brigade (2nd Division) stood firmly in line with the 56th. The attack on the east of the canal fell on the 99th Brigade of the 2nd Division and the 140th Brigade of the 47th Division, holding the crest of the ridge running from Bourlon Wood to the Bapaume-Cambrai road. The attack came on, time after time, only to be hurled back by the fire of the guns and the machine guns, and the fine fighting of the infantry. Full-strength attacks were delivered at 9.30 a.m., 11.25 a.m., and at 2.30 p.m., but the enemy gained nothing more than a few advanced posts, and an advance of about 300 yards near Bourlon Wood.

The situation in the morning had been a precarious one, indeed the greatest anxiety prevailed throughout the day. The Guards Division had stopped the German rush on the south side of the salient during the early afternoon, but if the 56th, 2nd, and 47th Divisions had not stood firm on the northern side, the Third Army would have suffered a heavy defeat. There were some frantic telegrams sent at times. At 10.30 a.m. the 2nd, 47th, 59th, and 62nd Artillery were ordered to be prepared to move their guns from the Graincourt Valley, and to have their teams up in

readiness, but these same guns did fearful execution.
The 47th Division reported at 11.35 a.m. : " Waves
attacking over crest F21 (Fontaine) held up by our
barrage, which is very accurate.   Our guns have
broken up concentration on E16 (west of Bourlon
Wood).   Dense waves moving along crest E to W.
Our guns apparently drawing them."

But the relief felt by the General Staff found
expression in a booklet entitled *The Story of a Great
Fight.   (Being an account of the operations of the 47th,
2nd, and 56th Divisions in the neighbourhood of Bourlon
Wood and Mœuvres, on the 30th November, 1917.*)
We can only give extracts which concern us :

" The 56th Division had been in line prior to the
British attack of the 20th November, in which its
right brigade had taken part, and since that date had
captured and held about a mile of the Hindenburg
Line west of Mœuvres, including Tadpole Copse.
Almost constant fighting had taken place in this area
since our attack, and the division, which at one time
had been holding a front of 11,000 yards, had already
been subjected to a very severe strain. . . . The story
of the subsequent fighting on the Bourlon-Mœuvres
front is one so brimful of heroism that it deserves to
take its place in English history for all time.   The
most determined attacks of four German divisions,
with three other German divisions in support, were
utterly crushed by the unconquerable resistance of
the three British divisions in line.   The 30th November, 1917, will be a proud day in the lives of all those
splendid British soldiers who, by their single-hearted
devotion to duty, prevented what would have become
a serious situation had they given way. . . . At 9.20 a.m.
the enemy had been seen advancing from the north
towards the Canal du Nord, and subsequently attack

after attack was delivered by him on both sides of the canal against the 6th and 169th Infantry Brigades. South of Mœuvres the enemy succeeded in gaining an entry, but was driven back by a bombing attack after heavy fighting. . . . From Mœuvres westward to Tadpole Copse a desperate struggle was taking place for the possession of the Hindenburg Line, in the course of which the enemy at one time reached the Battalion Headquarters of the 8th Middlesex Regt., attached to the 168th Brigade, 56th Division. Here the German infantry were stopped by the gallant defence of the officer commanding the battalion, who, with the assistance of his headquarters staff, held off the enemy with bombs until further help was organised and the trench regained. Though much reduced in strength by the fighting of the preceding days, and hard-pressed by superior forces, the troops of the 168th and 169th Brigades beat off all attacks. Queen's Westminsters, London Scottish, and the men of the 1/2nd Bn. London Regt. and 1/8th Bn. Middlesex Regt. vied with one another in the valour of their resistance. . . . At the end of this day of high courage and glorious achievement, except for a few advanced positions, some of which were afterwards regained, our line had been maintained intact. The men who had come triumphantly through this mighty contest felt, and rightly felt, that they had won a great victory, in which the enemy had come against them in full strength and had been defeated with losses at which even the victors stood aghast."

The survivors will at least agree that when General Headquarters took the trouble to print anything of this sort it had been well earned.

During the night of the 30th November reliefs took place. On the 169th Brigade front the London Rifle Brigade relieved the Queen's Westminsters and the 3rd London (attached) relieved the 2nd London. On the 168th Brigade front the Rangers relieved the London Scottish and the 1st London the 8th Middlesex. The Queen's Westminsters and the 2nd London, being the most worn troops, were sent into the divisional reserve at Louverval, while the rest occupied the old British line. The reliefs were not complete until 5 a.m. on the 1st December.

At about 3.30 p.m. the enemy commenced a heavy bombardment of the trenches held in the Hindenburg Line and the S.O.S. went up. From movement noticed beforehand on the north-west of Tadpole Copse it seemed likely that he would attack again, but the attempt, if it was to be made, was crushed by the artillery.

On the night of the 1st December the 51st Division started to relieve the 56th, but, so as not to involve the 51st Division until the following night, the front line was not relieved before the night of the 2nd December.

Gen. Dudgeon makes some interesting remarks on the battle :

" Although up to Z day the rôle of the division was to attack with Tanks over the open, the fighting which developed was almost entirely trench fighting with bombs. No shortage of bombs occurred, but the men employed at the divisional dump (eleven men) worked day and night detonating, and at one time the Divisional Artillery Column echélon had to be drawn on.

It was found that pigeon messages were very slow, probably owing to the season of the year. Trench wireless sets were used with success from positions within 200 yards of the enemy, being erected only at night and dismantled by day. The reliable method of communication was by runner from the captured trenches to our old line, viz. over about 2,300 yards of No Man's Land, and a series of relay posts was arranged. The 168th Brigade, with the help of, on an average, two companies 1/5th Cheshire Regt. and one battalion 167th Brigade (occasional help), dug a communication trench . . . (about 1,500 yards). This trench, being rather in line with the Inchy road, was somewhat subject to shell fire. 169th Brigade also, with the help of one company of Pioneers and one Field Company, dug a trench . . . (1,300 yards), which was less shelled. The Barbican and Houndsditch provided some shelter, but in most cases reinforcements and supplies had to go over the open in full view of Mœuvres, from which it was impossible to obtain concealment."

During these operations the 56 machine guns in the division (two companies of 16 guns and two companies of 12 guns) were used as follows : With each infantry brigade, 8 guns; in Divisional Pool, 32 guns. The 32 guns of the pool were employed on the 20th inst. in barrage work outside the divisional area to cover the attack of the 36th and 62nd Divisions. They returned to divisional control on the night of the 20th November. On the 21st and subsequent days the headquarters of the Divisional Pool were in a central position in Beaumetz. . . . On subsequent days the guns in the pool were used for protection of the flank (a maximum of 10 guns were employed on this) ; protective barrage on the Hindenburg Line and on the Hindenburg Support ; machine-gun defence behind the infantry.

We have mentioned the word " mystery " with

regard to the battle of Cambrai and the handling of
the cavalry. Though they fought on foot with the
best at Bourlon Wood and Villers Guislan, there
seems to have been some hesitation on the first day
of the battle. It is, however, debatable whether they
could have done much. Of the other mysteries the
success of the Germans on the southern side of the
salient is one. Early in the proceedings General Sir
O'D. Snow, commanding the VII Corps, is reported
to have placed his fingers on a map at the point of
Twenty-two Ravine, and said, " If I were a German,
I should attack there " ! No attempt was ever made
to reinforce divisions before the German counter-
attack, although the Army was aware that one was
threatened. And this brings us to another mystery.
Sir Douglas Haig repeats several times in his dispatch
a suggestion that he had a very limited number of
troops at his command. But we know that he had
the offer of French troops. He closes his account of
the fighting on the 30th November by recording—

" my obligation to the Commander-in-Chief of the
French Armies for the prompt way in which he placed
French troops within reach for employment in case of
need at the unfettered discretion of the Third Army
Commander. Part of the artillery of this force
actually came into action, rendering valuable service ;
and though the remainder of the troops were not
called upon, the knowledge that they were available
should occasion arise was a great assistance."

One naturally asks the question : " What would
have happened if French troops had been used even
as late as the 21st November ? " If they were still
too far away, there were undoubtedly British divisions

quite close up and quite fresh which could have been used to press the first great advantage gained, and the French would still have been in hand as a reserve. Casualties from the 20th November to the 3rd December were 9 officers killed, 202 other ranks killed, 43 officers and 1,003 other ranks wounded, 17 officers and 352 other ranks missing.

CHAPTER VII

THE GERMAN OFFENSIVE

THE FIRST BATTLE OF ARRAS, 1918

TELEGRAMS of congratulation on the action at Cambrai came from Corps and Army Headquarters; Sir Douglas Haig also sent a wire. But there was no question of rest for the 56th Division. The strength of battalions on the 1st December was:

		Officers.	Other ranks.
7th Middlesex	. . . .	41	760
8th ,,	. . . .	35	571
1st London	. . . .	43	740
3rd ,,	. . . .	37	813
4th ,,	. . . .	32	622
12th ,,	. . . .	28	754
13th ,,	. . . .	36	850
14th ,,	. . . .	42	949
2nd ,,	. . . .	32	529
5th ,,	. . . .	40	730
9th ,,	. . . .	31	789
16th ,,	. . . .	30	592

On the 3rd the division, less artillery, moved by tactical trains to the area behind Arras; Divisional Headquarters were at Fosseux; the 167th Brigade in the Montenescourt-Gouves-Wanquentin area; the 168th in the Warlus-Simencourt area; the 169th in the Bernaville-Dainville area. The next day the division moved into the XIII Corps area with Divi-

15   209

sional Headquarters in camp near Roclincourt. Gen. Dudgeon went to see the new line on the 6th, and on the 7th the relief of the 31st Division started.

The line taken over was between Gavrelle and Oppy: Gavrelle was held by us and Oppy by the Germans.

The enemy was very quiet and the weather not too bad for the time of year. There was, of course, rain, and it was very cold; a short time after the division took over the line it began to snow. Battalions had about a week in the front line, a week in support, and then in camp for a week. The great feature of this line was Arras, for at Arras many comforts could be purchased to alleviate the life of the soldier.

Identification was obtained by the 168th Brigade—a prisoner from the 7th Reserve Infantry Regt., 5th Reserve Division. There were one or two bickerings between patrols, but nothing of importance. And so Christmas Day was passed with the division still in line.

On the 26th December General Swift, U.S.A., and his Chief of Staff joined the division for a week, to study British methods.

On the 9th January the 62nd Division took over the line from the 56th.

.   .   ..   .   .

The outstanding events of the year 1917 must be carried in the mind so that the new situation can be appreciated. In the month of February the Germans had started an unrestricted U-boat campaign and America had broken off diplomatic relations with her. War was not declared between these two countries until April, and as an immediate consequence it influenced the plans of the Entente and Central

Powers according to the time which, in the judgment of either, it would be possible for America to make her strength felt.

The Entente Powers looked upon America as a reserve upon which they could count in twelve months' time, or slightly over. They were free to undertake large operations with ambitious objects, provided they did not either break their armies, or so reduce them in strength as to render their resisting power unequal to any sudden German attack.

On the other hand, the Central Powers had to do something before the American troops arrived and gave the balance of power definitely to the Entente.

Although American action in the future was the deciding factor, the formation of plans could not rest entirely on such a direct calculation. At first it seemed that the Entente had no reason to think that the abdication of the Tsar would mean the defection of Russia ; and the Central Powers could only hope to delay the American Armies by their U-boats. But the Russian debacle began with her defeat in Galicia in the latter part of July, and it soon became evident to the Entente that they would, before the American forces could be used, have to fight for their existence. They had, it is true, brought the Central Powers' offensive in Italy, which had threatened to cause a disaster, to a standstill, but the Bolshevist *coup d'état* in Russia in November had brought visions of an overwhelming mass of German troops moving to the west. December, January, and February were gloomy months of speculation which culminated in a state of nervous apprehension in March.

During the first half of the year the Central Powers had not much to congratulate themselves upon.

Baghdad was captured in March. The battles of
Arras in April and of Messines in June were sudden
and definite blows which shook them, and though the
Ypres battles in 1917 were a most costly affair to the
British, the German losses had been sufficiently heavy
to create consternation. Well might Ludendorff utter
a cry of elation when events in Russia opened prospects of an early release of the German armies on
that front! He no longer believed in the assurance
of the German Navy that the U-boats would neutralise
American effort, but he saw a chance of victory before
the fatal date of effective American intervention.

He and the Field-Marshal Hindenburg must have
known that they would have to make the last fatal
throw and that there was barely time to rattle the
dice. Austria was done, worn out, exhausted. It
was doubtful whether she could stand against the
Italians. Allenby, under whom the 56th Division
had fought in April, had gone to Egypt in June, and
by December had captured Jerusalem ; and Turkey,
at the end of her tether, lay at his mercy : events in
this theatre of war might move so fast as to bring
disaster from that direction on the Central Powers.
The Bulgarians were not trusted. And there were
signs that the German Army itself had lost its arrogant
spirit.

Hindenburg could count on a preponderance of
numbers on the Western Front, but desertions were
appalling in number. Tens of thousands, we are
told, crossed the frontiers into neutral countries, and
a great many more stayed at home, " tacitly tolerated
by their fellow-citizens and completely unmolested
by the authorities."

The movement of troops from east to west was

carried out rapidly. By the New Year the Germans had a majority of thirty divisions over the Entente on the Western Front. The plan was to attack with fifty to sixty divisions under massed artillery, varying between twenty and thirty batteries to each kilometre of front attacked, and a multitude of trench mortars as well.

Meanwhile American troops were arriving and training in the back areas.

. . . . .

The 56th Divisional Artillery had remained in the Mœuvres sector. Brig.-Gen. Elkington and his headquarters had, however, moved with the infantry, and we quote from the Brigadier's diary :

" The headquarters of the division and the R.A. were established in huts in Victory Camp, and I took over command of the R.A. covering the division on the 8th [December]. On the 17th and 18th the 56th Divisional Artillery returned to the division and took over in the line. This part of the front was at the time a very quiet one, but much harassing fire was done and a certain amount of enemy counter-battery work was done on the battery positions. Work was begun on rear lines and rear battery positions. Very cold weather was experienced in December.

We remained in this sector with headquarters at Victory Camp, which consisted of Nissen huts and was the coldest and bleakest spot I encountered—it was a desperately cold winter. From the 1st to the 3rd January an American General and his staff officers were attached to the division and went round battery positions and saw some shooting. On the 5th January the 62nd Divisional Infantry relieved the 56th Divisional Infantry, and on the 7th and 8th the R.A. of the 62nd Division came and looked over the batteries in the line.

On the 9th January the 62nd Divisional Artillery relieved the 56th Divisional Artillery and I handed over to the C.R.A., our batteries going back to the area round Berles for rest and training, the infantry having moved to the Villers-Chatel area. The R.A. Headquarters was established for the first four days at Bertincourt, and afterwards at the château at Berles, a very comfortable billet owned by a French Count who was very hospitable and glad to see us and did everything he could to make us comfortable. Inspection and training of batteries took place, but this was greatly hampered by the bad and severe weather."

Training of the infantry was, owing to the weather, not very ardent during the divisional rest from the 9th January to the 11th February. But it was a welcome rest.

British strength on the Western Front was now on the downward grade. From January divisions were cut down to nine battalions, and from the 30th of that month we must say good-bye to the 1st Battalion of the Rangers, the 1st Battalion of the Queen Victoria's Rifles, and the 1/3rd London Regt. The headquarters and transport of these battalions joined the 58th Division and were incorporated in the 2nd Battalions of their respective regiments. The 56th Division retained a certain number of the men, who were split up as follows : Queen Victoria's Rifles, 5 officers and 150 other ranks to the 13th London (Kensingtons), 12 officers and 250 other ranks to the 16th London (Queen's Westminster Rifles), 4 officers and 76 other ranks to the 4th London ; the Rangers sent 8 officers and 300 other ranks to the London Rifle Brigade; while the rest passed out of the Division (7 officers and 230 other ranks to the 1/23rd London, and

12 officers and 200 other ranks to the 2nd Battalion Rangers); the 1/3rd London sent 11 officers and 250 other ranks to the 1/1st London, 11 officers and 250 other ranks to the 1/2 London, and 2 officers and 34 other ranks to the 1/4 London (12 officers and 214 other ranks out of the division to their 2nd Battalion). So far as the infantry were concerned, the forty-seven divisions on the Western Front in March 1918 were reduced by a quarter—this is exclusive of the Canadian and Australian divisions, which retained their original strength, and includes the 41st Division, which returned from Italy on the 2nd March.

The relief of the 62nd Division by the 56th started on the 8th February, and on the 11th Gen. Dudgeon took over command of the line.

Meanwhile "the wind was whistling through the châteaux of the Higher Command ! " The severe cold and the snow at Christmas and the commencement of the New Year was followed by a thaw and a lot of rain. The result was that most of the trenches fell in. A period of feverish activity followed ; engineers and pioneers were working every night, and the infantry had to provide as many men as was possible. Gradually the defences were reconstructed and new ones added. All this activity, mingled with orders and provisions for retirement, was greeted by the troops with characteristic jeers.

We do not wish to contribute to the general abuse which was levelled at the heads of the " Staff " or " Red Tabs "—the arrangements made on this front at least were justified by the results—but we desire to give as far as we can the feeling of the private soldier and regimental officer.

Arrangements for retreat shock the troops in much

the same way as a coarse expression might shock a drawing-room full of ladies. They are offended. They ask the question : " What's the idea ? " And although they could not enumerate the difficulties of a gradual retirement, they seem to " sense " the fearful responsibility that is being thrust upon them. And the very nature of the situation caused orders to be given which suggested uncertainty and indecision. The private soldier's point of view was simple : he wanted to be given orders to fight on a certain spot, but to change the spot where he should fight annoyed him.

The system which was adopted to meet the onslaught of the Germans was to spread the defence over a wide belt of country. The front-line system was not to be held ; it was to be occupied by outposts whose duty was to watch the enemy and retire on the next line if he attacked. The fight itself was to take place in what was called the " battle zone " ; and behind was yet another line through which the enemy must pass before our defence was broken. If the Germans penetrated these lines, they might be said to have broken our first system of defence.

Behind the 56th Division were other defences on which it might fall back, but we are only concerned with the first system.

As to the general distribution of forces to meet the German offensive, one-half of the British strength was devoted to protecting the Channel ports, and the rest was thinly dispersed over the remaining front. It must be remembered that additional front amounting to 28 miles had been taken over by the British in January, and that Sir Douglas Haig was now responsible for 125 miles. In view of this length of line and the extreme importance of the Channel ports, the general disposition of troops would seem to have been wise.

The Germans claim to have effected a surprise in March 1918—a contention which is scarcely justified. In his interesting, lengthy, but somewhat vague account of the assembly of the great attacking force, Ludendorff says that ammunition dumps had been increased all along the British front, that movement of troops was carried out at night, but that German aviators sent up to report could see signs of concentration on the area chosen for attack which the blind English were *unable to perceive!* This is not accurate, but one must admit that the German concentration and preparation were superbly done.

We knew that a general movement of troops from east to west had been started in November, and that roads and railways were being improved, artillery increased, and ammunition accumulated all along the front from Flanders to the Oise, and by the end of February indications became apparent that the attack would be on the Third and Fifth Armies.

On the 19th March the Intelligence Department reported to Sir Douglas Haig that the enemy preparations on the Arras-St. Quentin front were complete and that the attack would probably be launched on the 20th or 21st.

Ludendorff assumes that "nor did the enemy discover anything by other means . . . otherwise his defensive measures would have been more effective and his reserves would have arrived more quickly." In this his claim of surprise might seem to be justified, although the charge can be met by a statement of the considerations which influenced Sir Douglas Haig through this anxious period; he could give up no ground in the northern portion of the British area where the Channel ports were threatened, and he knew that the ground was exceptionally dry and that preparations for an attack had been almost completed from the direction of Menin; the same applied to the centre, behind which lay the collieries of northern France, and important tactical features covering his lateral communications; in the south, in the Somme area, ground could be given up to a certain extent without serious consequences.

The dispositions of British troops according to the above considerations had an effect on the Germans, for Ludendorff tells us that when deciding on the front to be attacked he was faced with strong forces about Ypres, that the condition of the centre (the Lys Valley) would not admit an attack before April (which was late in view of the Americans), that an attack in the direction of Verdun would lead into very hilly country, and that in making his final decisions he was influenced by the time factor and the " weakness of the enemy."

During the early part of 1918 the whole of the British force in forward areas was concerned with the problem of defence. It was not a cheerful period. Closely typewritten sheets of paper flew about in all directions, giving instructions, making amendments to previous instructions, calling for suggestions, and ever warning commanders against attack. The Cheshire Regt. and the Engineers of the 56th Division worked night and day at improving rear lines and constructing alternative ones; fatigue parties were called for from battalions both in and out of the line; machine gunners and trench-mortar experts moved restlessly from point to point, selecting possible emplacements for their guns, and the artillery did the same farther back.

The men in the line were always the coolest in the whole of the army, but the officers were gradually being worked up to a state of feverish anxiety and a certain amount of bewilderment.

On the 9th March the Kensingtons carried out a smart and successful raid, killing about 20 and capturing 4 Germans. The prisoners stated that the German offensive was imminent. Orders were issued for battle positions to be manned at 5 a.m. as from the 13th.

Another raid by the London Rifle Brigade on the 16th was hung up in a mass of uncut wire, but 2/Lieut. Kite Powell hacked his way through and, followed by four men, managed to enter the German line and kill half a dozen of them. They secured no prisoner; still, the information that the enemy front line was strongly held and that they were very alert was of value.

Aeroplane activity was very great from the 18th onwards, and a great deal of individual movement was seen behind the enemy lines. Harassing fire by the 56th Divisional Artillery was increased, and with a good percentage of gas shells. The enemy seemed to give a great deal of attention to our wire with his trench mortars during the increasing bursts of artillery fire.

On the 21st March, with one tremendous crash, the great battle opened on a front of 44 miles, the artillery bombardment including the front held by the 56th Division. But the attack was launched farther south between La Fère and Croiselles.

No less than 68 German divisions took part in the battle on the first day, many more than the whole of the British Army contained. The training, carried out in some cases behind the Russian front, had been so complete as to include the practising of infantry behind an actual, live barrage. The result was admirable. Swarms of men, followed resolutely and closely by artillery, broke through the Fifth and the right of the Third Armies, which were composed of a total force of 29 infantry divisions and 3 cavalry divisions.

The German 17th Army, composed of 24 divisions, attacked north of Cambrai; the 2nd Army, of 17 divisions, immediately south of Cambrai; and the 18th Army, of 27 divisions, carried the attack down to La Fère.

The 2nd and 18th German Armies made good progress against the British Fifth Army, but the resistance of our Third Army limited the enemy's success, so that the 17th German Army was not able to cut off the Flesquières salient, near Cambrai, as had been planned. But during the night of 22nd/23rd March the Fifth Army was back at Peronne, and there was a deep bulge in the Third Army towards Bapaume. On the 27th the German line ran through Albert and Montdidier. But the right of the German 17th Army was not too comfortable—Arras must be swept aside!

Behind Arras the wildest excitement prevailed. The word " panic," a humiliating word, can be applied. But, as we have said before, there was always a zone of calmness, and that zone was the forward zone. Had the London men of the 56th Division been able to see the scurrying motors and anxious faces of the

" soft job " men behind them, they would have been amazed. But the 56th Division just went on with the ordinary, somewhat strenuous routine which had been instituted at the commencement of the year, strengthening the defences, putting out wire, arranging " blocks," constructing emplacements for machine guns and trench mortars. Being, however, on the flank of the XIII Corps, regimental officers were subjected to the annoyance of frequent changes of orders and plans.

On the 19th March an order was given for the 56th Division to alter the method of holding the line from a three-brigade front to a two-brigade front. Each of the two front-line brigades would have two battalions in line and one in reserve, and the division would have an entire brigade in reserve. The necessary moves were made on the night of 21st/22nd March.

An order was issued on the 20th that the division would be relieved by the 62nd Division, but this was cancelled on the 21st.   On the 22nd a further warning order was given that the division would be relieved by the 2nd Canadian Division, and this also was cancelled on the 23rd.

The situation of the Third Army, on the right of the 56th Division, brought a multitude of instructions. On the 22nd the XVII Corps had been ordered to withdraw to its third system on the south of the Scarpe, but to continue holding Monchy lightly. But north of the Scarpe the 4th Division, on the right of the 56th, would not move until Monchy had been captured by the enemy, in which case the 56th Division would adjust their line to run through Beatty Post, Bailleul Post, to le Point du Jour Post. General Matheson, commanding the 4th Division, did

not, however, intend to move unless definitely ordered
to do so, and if attacked would fight in three successive lines, the last bringing him to the Point du Jour
Post.

This last assurance of General Matheson was of a
nature to simplify the possible actions of officers of
the 56th Division, and was welcome. That the enemy
was going to do something was becoming evident.
At 5.30 p.m. on the 23rd he exploded a land mine
under the wire in front of Towy Post, and appeared
to be manning the line opposite the divisional front
thicker than usual. Harassing fire was turned on the
German trenches, and the reserve brigade was ordered
to stand to at 5 a.m. in future.

In the south the Germans were now approaching
Albert and Roye. All sorts of rumours were flying
about behind the lines. On the 24th the 169th
Brigade captured a wounded German, and he was
sent for examination in the early morning of the 25th.
He said that the 101st Reserve and 102nd Reserve
Regiments, belonging to the 219th and 23rd (Reserve)
Divisions, had occupied the Wotan Stellung, behind
the front line, on the night of the 24th. These
divisions had come from Riga, and would attack on
the 26th together with the 240th and 5th Bavarian
Reserve Divisions. They were to advance to a depth
of four kilometres with the right flank on Oppy, and
then swing round towards Vimy. The battalion
section of the 471st Regt. had already 60 trench
mortars in position, and 8 more trench mortar companies were to arrive on the night of the 25th. The
ammunition was already in the line. One may
imagine that Gen. Dudgeon's conference at 6.30 p.m.
was far from a dull affair.

The artillery were ordered to fire on chosen targets through the night, and patrolling was active. A great deal of movement had been seen throughout the day of men and light railways. Troops were seen detraining at Vitry. And that night there was an inter-battalion relief on the right, the Queen's Westminsters relieving the 2nd London. The party sent to relieve Gavrelle Post found it occupied by two dead men only—the remainder of the garrison had entirely disappeared. Signs of a struggle were there, but no one on either flank had reported the post being attacked, and, apparently, nothing unusual had been seen.

Gen. Dudgeon ordered both brigades to do their utmost to secure a German prisoner. Every effort was made, but the enemy was found more than ever on the alert, with parties lying out to catch patrols. It is curious that one patrol reported the enemy repairing their wire—it is probable that they were cutting it down.

The attack was coming, and Divisional Headquarters strained every nerve to direct, encourage, and advise for the struggle. Some of the orders are not too easy to understand, and one is of interest as an example of rumour being accepted as fact.

The artillery, of course, was very busy, and we find an instruction to cut German wire and to keep the gaps open ! And the order we refer to as being founded on rumour was as follows : " In view possible appearance enemy agents warn all ranks against use of word RETIRE. Any person using this word before or during an attack to be shot." This was, no doubt, based on a much-circulated statement that the Fifth Army debacle was largely due to German agents, dressed as British officers, giving the order to retire. We cannot believe in a swarm of disguised Germans.

It must, however, have been a very weighty consideration which induced the Higher Command to order an extension of divisional front on the 27th. General Sir H. de Lisle, better known as the commander of the 29th Division and now in command of the XIII Corps, was ordered to take over the line to the Souchez River, on his left. This meant that the 56th Division had to relieve the 3rd Canadian Division, on the left, at Tommy and Arleux Posts during the night of 27th/28th March. At the same time the division was again ordered to treat the front line as an outpost line, and to fight on the line between Ditch Post and Willerval South. But at the last moment the front line was ordered to be held as such so as to conform with the 4th Division on the right; the 56th Division was already so stretched out that this curious eleventh-hour change did not make much difference.

The Vimy Ridge lay behind the division, but the ground they fought on was not level. The 4th Division, on the right, was on high ground, and Gavrelle lay in a slight depression; the ground rose again towards Bailleul East Post, and fell once more in the direction of Oppy. The division was, however, on a forward slope which gave them good observation from a somewhat exposed position (see map contours).

The rearrangement of the line, which took place during the night, gave the Queen's Westminsters the right, holding Towy Post and Gavrelle Post with one company, while the other three companies held posts defending Naval Trench. The London Rifle Brigade held Mill, Bradford, and Bird Posts with two companies and one platoon, the remainder of the battalion holding posts on the Marine Trench line. The third battalion of the brigade, the 2nd London Regt., held the Ditch, Bailleul, and Bailleul East line. Behind them, in the Farbus line, was one company of the 5th Cheshire Regt., and in reserve the 169th Brigade held two companies of the 1st London Regt., attached from the 167th Brigade, and a detachment of the 176th Tunnelling Company, who were in the Point du Jour Post.

The 168th Brigade, on the left, held Beatty, Wood, and Oppy Posts with two companies of the 4th London Regt., and two in support on the line Duke Street; and Tommy and Arleux Posts with the Kensingtons, two companies in the front line and in support.

The actual distribution of troops on the left is not very clear, as the redistribution was not complete when, at 3 a.m. on the 28th March, the enemy opened a furious bombardment. We find a note that the London Rifle Brigade had not at that hour relieved Bailleul East Post, and that one company of the 1st Canadian Rifles were still holding Sugar Post. This latter company remained at Sugar Post throughout the battle, being placed, with that complete disregard of all, except the winning of the battle, which characterised the Canadians, under the orders of the 168th Brigade. But the London Scottish were also in this Sugar Post-Willerval line. In the Farbus line were two platoons of the 5th Cheshires, and behind them, in the Point du Jour-Ridge Post line, two companies of the 1st London Regt. and one and a half companies of the 5th Cheshires.

16

The two remaining battalions of the 167th Brigade and three field companies of Royal Engineers were in Divisional Reserve.

The opening of a modern battle is, with few exceptions, a matter of artillery. Brig.-Gen. Elkington's diary gives us some interesting facts :

" On the morning of the 28th March the 56th Division was holding a line south of Gavrelle to Arleux, a front of about 5,000 yards. To cover this front the field-guns under the command of the division consisted of the 56th Divisional Artillery and 9 guns of the 52nd Army (Field Artillery Brigade), or 45 18-pounders and 12 4·5 howitzers. Six 6-inch Newton mortars were in action in the first-line system, and three were covering the Bailleul-Willerval line (that is our main line of resistance). Of the former, only two were manned, as all the ammunition at the other mortars had been expended previously, in accordance with orders which, later on, were cancelled, but not before the ammunition had been expended.

Between 3 a.m. and 3.20 a.m. the Germans put down a heavy barrage of gas and H.E. shells of all calibres on the Bailleul-Willerval line and the support line. At 4 a.m. the barrage increased over the whole of the front-line system and our posts were heavily bombarded with trench mortars. From 6 a.m. the hostile barrage of all calibres was heavily concentrated on the front line, and continued to be intense on this area until 7.15 a.m.

During the above periods, that is from 3 a.m. until 7.15 a.m., our artillery was firing heavily on the enemy's front system of trenches, special concentrations being put down, in co-operation with the heavy artillery, on lines of organised shell-holes. It was considered at the time that these shell-holes were temporary trench-mortar emplacements, but from information given by prisoners after the attack, it appears likely that they were the assembly positions of the assaulting troops. From 6.45 a.m. onwards "counter preparation" was put into effect. At 7.15 a.m. the hostile barrage lifted from the front line to our support line, and the S.O.S. went up in the Gavrelle sector and was repeated almost immediately in the Oppy sector. Our S.O.S. was put down over the whole of the divisional front at the same time."

As may be imagined, the effect of this bombardment was terrible. The bulk of the forward posts were obliterated. But even such concentration as the Germans directed against the front line was not sufficient to destroy all life—it could not deal with the whole of the line. Towy Post and Wood Post had, during the last few days, been subjected to a great deal of enemy attention, and the posts had been moved—but even so the casualties were severe. One survivor came out of Mill Post and reported that the trenches had been "blotted out," and that the entrance to a big dug-out there was blown in and destroyed.

The Germans, advancing almost shoulder to shoulder, entered Gavrelle, which, as we know, was in a hollow. Although there was no living soul there to oppose them, the machine gunners had the place under indirect fire from fourteen guns, and the enemy losses were severe. But the first stages of the battle were centred round Towy and Wood Posts.

Capt. G. A. N. Lowndes, of the Queen's Westminsters, was in command of Towy Post, and with the lifting of the enemy barrage and the appearance of the first Germans there came from the post the crackling sound of rifle fire, joined, almost at once, by the rattle sound of Lewis guns, until the whole developed into what might be described as a roar. But the enemy was in Gavrelle and the undefended portions of the front line on either side of Towy Post. Once in the trenches, the storming troops could work slowly forward under some sort of cover. To the rifle fire of the defenders was soon added the crash of bombs. The enemy was confident; he worked slowly and surely round the post.

The glorious little band of Queen's Westminsters knew what was happening, but kept cool. Gradually they were forced into a small and cramped area; Lewis guns and rifles dealt with Germans in the open, clearing the ground round about and forcing the enemy to seek the safety of the battered trench; but the store of bombs was getting low.

Capt. Lowndes, ably supported by 2/Lieuts. L. W. Friend and J. C. B. Price, after hanging on to the last moment, directed his dwindling company to fight through the Germans in rear, using the remaining bombs, and swiftly, desperately, they broke through and reached Naval Trench and joined the rest of the battalion round headquarters.

But the Germans, coming through Mill Post, were already in Marine Trench, and Lieut.-Col. Glazier, commanding the Queen's Westminsters, passed a portion of his force into Thames Alley to form a flank.

Now trouble came from the right. The Lancashire Fusiliers, of the 4th Division, fell back on to the Ditch Post line, and the enemy entered Humid Trench. Col. Glazier swung back his right flank into Towy Alley, and held the Germans firmly. And then for a moment the fortunes of war turned against the Queen's Westminsters.

The 56th Divisional Artillery, aware that the enemy were in our lines, attempted to adjust their barrage in consultation with brigadiers. It was a most difficult task, for, needless to say, communication was almost non-existent. At the junction of Naval and Towy Trenches was a block, and in front of it the enemy was held, but the artillery, probably seeing the Germans in Humid and the end of Naval Trenches, put down their barrage too close and blew in our block. The German hordes quickly took advantage of this bit of luck and swarmed down Naval Trench, either killing or capturing the garrison up to the Gavrelle road.

About the same time the block on the left of the line, near Thames Valley, was forced by the enemy, and the whole of the Naval Line was in his hands. But the Queen's Westminsters, gallantly led by Col. Glazier, were still in front of the Germans on the line Keiller, Pelican, and Thames Posts. Every bit of the communication trenches which gave a good fire position, every dump-hole, even the shell-holes were manned, and, as the Germans advanced over the open, in reorganised lines, from Naval Trench, they were met with a fresh rattle and roar of rifle fire. The ground was covered with silent and groaning figures in the field-grey uniform, and the enemy had to resort once more to bombing.

Again the Queen's Westminsters gave up a little ground, but the enemy's effort was smashed. At 11 a.m. the position was : we held a block in Towy Alley, about 300 yards east of the Ditch-Bailleul East line, and Castleford Post, and the rest of the battalion had joined the 2nd London Regt. in the Bailleul-Willerval line.

The account given by the London Rifle Brigade on the left of the Queen's Westminsters is short, but in it one can read the desperate nature of the fighting and the gallant resistance which was put up. The relief of Bradford and Bird Posts was not completed until 3.30 a.m., when the bombardment which heralded the attack commenced. All forward and lateral communication was at once cut. Wire and posts defending the front line were wiped out. When the enemy infantry advanced, they simply walked into the front line, rushed the few men left at the blocks in Belvoir and Brough, and commenced bombing towards Naval Trench. The battalion was almost annihilated, and what was left joined the Queen's Westminsters in Thames Valley and became mixed up with them. The fighting strength of this battalion at the commencement of the battle was 23 officers and 564 other ranks ; it was reduced to 8 officers and about 60 other ranks.

The whole of the 169th Brigade now stood on the Bailleul-Willerval line and the enemy was held. Twice he attacked over the open, with aeroplanes flying low and pouring a hail of bullets on the defenders, while field guns were dragged by plunging horses and straining men across No Man's Land as far as Naval Trench, but each time he was defeated. The field guns fired no more than twenty rounds before being silenced by the 56th Divisional Artillery ; and though the enemy infantry had a novel method of advancing—they stood up, threw their rifles forward into a shell-hole, held up their hands, and advanced, only to drop by the side of their arms, which they immediately proceeded to use—they made no further progress.

The right of the 56th Division was, at 11 a.m., in touch with the 4th Division. A battalion of the 167th Brigade was placed under the orders of the 169th, and six machine guns were sent up to Point du Jour, and two field companies of the Engineers to Tongue and Blanch Posts, so that the right flank of the division seemed secure.

The 4th Londons, on the right of the 168th Brigade, put up a most gallant defence. Wood Post, held by 2 officers and 45 other ranks, had been moved before the bombardment and so was untouched. The full garrison was there to meet the enemy, who advanced in a solid line on the left of the wood, but came through the wood in groups of about ten men each, 40 yards or so apart, and followed by further groups of about thirty men each some 200 yards in rear.

The enemy was completely checked in the wood and on the left; but Beatty Post, on the right, which had been badly battered about by trench mortars, was occupied. The garrison, consisting at first of 3 officers and 84 other ranks, though much depleted when the assault was launched, was overwhelmed by sheer numbers, and only 1 officer and 6 men ever returned. The enemy then started to work round to the rear of Wood Post, but for over an hour this hard little band held out and repulsed the enemy.

Oppy Post was also smothered by artillery and trench mortars, and eventually overwhelmed by the storming infantry. Of the 2 officers and 48 other ranks forming the garrison, 1 officer and 5 other ranks were left.

Fifteen minutes after the assault was launched, the enemy was in the Earl Lane and Viscount Street, but were held for a time by the troops in Ouse Alley.

But so long as Wood Post held, the enemy did not make any great progress.

Major F. A. Phillips was in command of the forward fighting, and moved about encouraging his men, who were inflicting heavy casualties on the enemy whenever an attempt was made to advance over the open. But Wood Post fell back just before 9 o'clock, and soon after the enemy began to force their way up Ouse Alley from Viscount Street, in rear of the troops who were fighting so successfully in Marquis Trench. Major Phillips promptly attacked over the open with about twenty details from headquarters, and drove them back.

The enemy had built up heavy rifle fire from Oppy Wood, although he was suffering severely there from our artillery fire, and attacked the left of the battalion many times over the open; but the Marquis line held, and at 11 o'clock the position was extraordinary. The 169th Brigade on the right was back in the Bailleul-Willerval line; and while the advance companies of the 4th London were still holding the Marquis line, the enemy was in Ouse Alley and bombing his way towards the Bailleul line, also he was advancing over the open south of Ouse Alley. The position then was very precarious, and the reserve company, which Colonel Marchmont had sent to get in touch with the forward troops and form a flank, was unable to reach the forward troops. Major Phillips decided to withdraw.

The withdrawal was witnessed by Colonel Marchmont from his headquarters :

" I watched it through my glasses. It was carried out in a very steady and orderly way, the men leaving in groups of about a dozen. Although exposed to a heavy fire from front and flanks, they made excellent use of the ground, and suffered very few casualties. . . . The men of the reserve company met the survivors returning and covered their retirement."

The Kensingtons on the left of the division were not attacked. Some fifty of the enemy approached Tommy Post, but were at once driven off with casualties. But the battalion gave invaluable aid to the 4th Londons, on the right, inflicting heavy losses by Lewis gun, rifle, and rifle grenade fire on the German support troops as they came up to the wood. About 11.30 a.m. the battalion was ordered to retire, in conjunction with the right of the 3rd Canadian Division, on the left, and so came into line with the rest of the division.

The intense anxiety at Brigade and Divisional Headquarters can best be imagined. For the first two hours of the battle little news could be gained from Battalion Headquarters as to the progress of the fight. The whole battlefield was enveloped in smoke, and interest was chiefly centred on the fine stand which was being made by the Queen's Westminsters at Towy Post, where a power buzzer was installed, and messages were received from the signallers even after the capture of the post. At one time, while the 4th Londons were still holding the front-line system, the enemy was attacking Bailleul East Post, held by the London Scottish, and had captured two machine guns with crews just in front of the post. A well-timed counter-attack from this gallant regiment drove the enemy back and released the guns and crews.

As the smoke cleared from the field, the Divisional Artillery took every advantage of their well-situated observation posts. But, though the struggle was going on before them, observers found that both sides were frequently so mixed up that they could give no help. Small bodies of our infantry could be seen clearly, fighting with Germans on all sides of them.

On the right the situation of the 4th Division was very obscure. The division was reported to have lost touch with its own brigades, while the lateral line between the 169th and 12th Brigades was also cut.

With the withdrawal of the 56th Division to the Bailleul-Willerval line the situation cleared. They were then in touch with the 4th Division, and the artillery was able to put down a protective barrage in front of this line. The 3rd Canadian Division gave valuable assistance with nine 18-pounders.

"From this time till about 3 p.m." (writes Brig.-Gen. Elkington), "many excellent targets in the open were engaged by both field and heavy artillery with great effect. Unfortunately, owing to the limited number of guns available, and that many had to be used for the immediate protection of our infantry, only a few could be used for the excellent targets in the open. At about 3.30 p.m. the enemy made a heavy attack against the Bailleul line, particularly on Bailleul East Post; this was completely shattered by a concentrated barrage and by rifle and machine-gun fire. With the exception of hostile bombing attacks up the communication trenches leading to the Bailleul line, the enemy made no further serious effort to attack. All battery positions were heavily shelled throughout the day by all calibres of ordnance, the shelling being

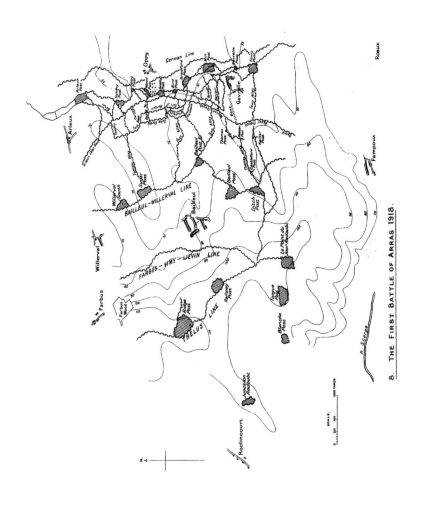

8. THE FIRST BATTLE OF ARRAS 1918.

more of the nature of area shoots than definite counter-battery work. As a result, from dawn on the 28th to dawn on the 29th twelve 18-pounders were destroyed or put out of action by enemy shell-fire. In addition two 18-pounders in position as an enfilade section near Arleux, facing south-east, had to be destroyed and abandoned when our line was withdrawn to the Bailleul line. This section engaged many targets with observation from the vicinity of the guns, and was fought until our infantry withdrew through it. The detachments then retired after damaging the guns, burning the dug-outs, and removing dial sights and breach blocks. All the six 6-inch mortars in the front line were lost to the enemy, and no news was available as to the fate of the officers and detachments of the two that were manned (they were afterwards found to have been made prisoners). . . . During the night of the 28th/29th, with the exception of two batteries, all the Divisional Artillery was withdrawn to positions at an average of about 3,600 yards to our new front, this move being carried out by single batteries in turns. . . . The ammunition expended from the early morning of the 28th to the early morning of the 29th by the 56th Divisional Artillery alone was : 23,000 rounds of 18-pounder and 8,000 rounds of 4·5 howitzer. . . . As a result of an urgent request to the Corps on the afternoon of the 28th for new guns to replace the damaged ones, six new ones were sent up—these turned out to be 15-pounders, for which we had no ammunition. . . . The Germans in their official communiqué reported that the 56th Division had been annihilated ! ''

The German attack was definitely crushed in the morning, but during the afternoon a number of half-hearted and tentative attacks were made. The situation, however, became more quiet about 6 p.m., and the 169th Brigade was relieved by the 167th, with the 5th Canadian Mounted Rifles in support at Point du Jour.

During the night the engineers were employed in blocking and filling-in the communication trenches in front of the new line, and patrolling was actively carried out. The Kensingtons penetrated into Arleux Loop South, Kent Road, and the junction of Tommy and Baron, which seems to show that the enemy were dazed.

On the 29th, except for some demonstrations at the bombing blocks, the enemy made no move. There were many reports that he was massing for further attacks, but it became evident that he was relieving his storming troops. As night fell, the first platoons of the 4th Canadian Division started to relieve, and during the night the 167th Brigade moved back to Villers au Bois, the 168th to Mont St. Eloi, and the 169th to Ecoivres.

On the 30th General Dudgeon visited the First Army Headquarters, where he was congratulated by His Majesty the King.

There is little doubt that the enemy hoped to achieve great results by this new stroke, and that its failure was a serious set-back. Five divisions attacked the 4th and 56th Divisions north of the Scarpe and, according to captured documents, when the line Vimy-Bailleul-St. Laurent-Blangy had been won, three special divisions were to attack and capture the Vimy Ridge on the following day. South of the Scarpe eleven divisions were launched, with the object of capturing Arras and carrying the attack as far south as Bucquoy. The German official list (published 1919) gives eleven divisions attacking north

and south of the Scarpe, one division at Neuville
Vitasse, and one at Moyenneville—thirteen in all. It
makes no mention of an attack south of Moyenneville.
But the eleven which attacked on the Scarpe were
beaten by the four British divisions which held that
line—the 4th and 56th on the north, and the 3rd
and 15th on the south.

From this date onward the great German offensive
began to decline, and ended in the Somme area with
a final effort to separate the French and British
Armies on the 4th and 5th April, by an attack on
the north and south of the Somme. "It was an
established fact," says Ludendorff, "that the enemy's
resistance was beyond our strength." Strategically
the Germans had not won what the events of the
23rd, 24th, and 25th March had led them to hope
for—the failure to take Amiens was a great disappointment.

The total casualties of the division were 55 officers
and 1,433 other ranks—not excessive, considering the
weight of the attack and the immortal triumph gained
by the 56th Division. The importance of this battle
is so great that we give the comments of the two
brigadiers.

Brig.-Gen. Coke says that during the six weeks his
brigade had been in the line, the Cheshire Regt. had
worked splendidly, and had put up double apron
belts of wire where they would be most effective—
the Naval-Marine line was protected by five belts of
wire—and this stood the bombardment well enough
to be a serious obstacle. When the smoke, which
had enveloped the field at the commencement of
the battle, had cleared, excellent observation was
obtainable, and the divisional observers and artillery

observers did splendid work. The enemy batteries, which came into action in the open during the afternoon, were brought up under cover of smoke, and started to fire point-blank at the Bailleul line, but the Divisional Artillery silenced them in a few minutes. There was no shortage of ammunition or bombs. The system of keeping a plentiful supply in deep dug-outs proved sound.

" All concerned are convinced that the enemy losses were extremely heavy in front of this brigade. The fullest use was made of Lewis guns and rifles, and every attempt of the enemy to advance on the Bailleul line over the open was checked by these means. The fire-bays constructed along Towy Alley proved specially valuable, and very considerable losses were inflicted on the enemy from them during our withdrawal to the Bailleul line.

Many officers testify to the gallant way in which the Machine Gun Battalion served its guns to the last and to the good results of the machine-gun fire.

Our artillery inflicted the maximum amount of damage possible. The number of guns available for the brigade section was quite inadequate to cover effectively such a wide front. But the infantry testify to the heavy losses inflicted on the enemy owing to the quick way in which the group and battery commanders engaged each good target as soon as it was observed.

Gallant work was done by the 169th Light Trench Mortar Battery during the day. Three of the teams disappeared with the garrisons in the left sector. During the withdrawal, mortars were placed to cover Pelican and Bailleul Posts."

It was widely noticed by the men of this brigade that the enemy approached in a slow, dazed manner. The brigadier thinks that this may have been due to the great weight carried by the German infantry. who seem, amongst other things, to have carried a week's rations. The enemy advanced in three or four lines and almost shoulder to shoulder. Brig.-Gen. Loch sent in a frank and interesting paper, in which he points out :

" (a) The uselessness of locking up large garrisons in the front-line posts which are clearly known to the enemy and are within effective trench-mortar range. Front-line posts should be held lightly, and be used as observation posts and to keep the enemy patrols from approaching our main line of defence. They should be carefully concealed, need have no regular communication trenches, and should be frequently changed. The garrisons should be small and frequently relieved. If rushed and captured from time to time, little harm is done, provided the garrison have no identification marks. Deep dug-outs in such posts are a positive danger and should not be allowed ; shelters against the weather are ample. If heavily attacked, the rôle of such posts should be to put up the S.O.S. and withdraw. The sole exception to this rôle is in the case of posts whose whereabouts can be properly hidden from the enemy. Such posts can be strongly garrisoned and may have machine guns, as they will have to break up and delay an attack. The losses in the forward posts are sufficient commentary on the unsoundness of the (present) system.

(b) The value of changing the actual position of the garrison in any post—vide Wood Post.

(c) The grave danger of altering carefully thought-out dispositions at the eleventh hour. On the evening of the 27th inst. my dispositions, which had been most minutely worked out to meet the situation of an attack on my right flank at the junction with the left of the 169th Brigade, about Viscount Street, and covering Bradford and Mill Posts, had to be changed as the result of orders, and consequently this portion of the line (always weak) was rendered hopelessly incapable of withstanding a strong attack. It is recognised that larger questions were involved, and no doubt decided the redistribution, which was not complete before the attack developed.

(d) The uselessness of Stokes mortars in the actual front line. Such weapons can only open on their S.O.S. lines, and are very vulnerable from attacks on the flanks. The four forward guns only fired about 50 rounds before being surrounded. Had they been behind the main defensive line covering the communication trenches, and themselves covered by the infantry, they would have been far more valuable, and would not possibly have been overrun.

(e) The value of trench blocks was fully found out. Such blocks should be prepared ready against penetration laterally, so as to localise it.

(h) Previous rehearsals and thorough knowledge of overland routes are essential. To the fact that these points had received proper attention is attributable the successful delaying action of this brigade.

(i) Defensive flanks prepared as such are invaluable.

(j) Infantry and machine guns must establish closer liaison. . . . It should be recognised once and for all that all machine guns in a brigade sector must come under the senior machine-gun officer in that sector. . . . Nothing herein said, however, should be permitted to detract from the principle that the battalion commander can and should issue orders to the guns covering him if he considers the situation demands it. . . .

(k) Main forward communication trenches should never be traced to lead into strong points. . . . Such communication trenches are mere covering approaches to these strong points and afford easy access to the enemy. Our main battle zone should not be covered by a single trench, e.g. the Red Line (Bailleul), but should consist of at least three trenches with strong points so constructed as not to be apparent and obvious. As with garrisons of forward posts, so with garrisons of battle trenches, they should be constantly moved so as to avoid giving away the position actually held."

A captured German officer of the 152nd I.R., 41st Division, gave as the main causes of the failure of the attack (a) the intensity of the machine-gun barrage, which caused heavy casualties. His regiment lost 12 officers and the 16th I.R. lost 24 officers ; (b) watches did not appear to have been correctly synchronised. We have mentioned the service rendered by the Machine Gun Battalion, but, unfortunately, there is no record of Lieut.-Col. E. C. S. Jervis' dispositions. This gallant and able officer says that the " tender spots " in his defence were the low ridges running due east and west through Bradford Post, and from Mill Post, south of Belvoir Alley, and then west. The former could not be covered by machine-gun fire, the latter was. And we know that the enemy, having exterminated the garrison, were mown down, in and round Gavrelle, from the indirect fire of fourteen machine-guns.

Apart from the heavy artillery fire, which, in itself, caused heavy casualties, Colonel Jervis points out an interesting feature in this battle : the complete mastery of the air which the enemy had throughout the day, resulting in machine-guns being spotted and engaged by low-flying aeroplanes, which also directed the fire of specially detailed heavy artillery. Needless to say, machine-guns are very vulnerable

17

to this form of attack ; and we must also point out, having mentioned the capture of guns, that when once the enemy has penetrated the trench system machine-gunners have great difficulty in dealing with bombing attacks from the flanks. The Machine Gun Battalion, however, had a great opportunity in this battle, and took full advantage of it.

Brig.-Gen. Elkington expresses the opinion that this was the best action fought by the 56th Division. We do not go quite so far as this. It was more satisfactory to the troops, no doubt, but there is a great difference between defence and attack. A successful defence is more cheering to the infantry and artillery, inasmuch as they can more easily estimate the damage they do to the enemy ; but it would not be fair to say that this was better than the hard fighting at Gommecourt and south of Arras in April 1917, or indeed on the Somme in 1916 and Ypres in 1917. The fact remains, however, that the 56th Division had, by its stout defence, twice saved the situation, which had been imperilled by enemy successes elsewhere.

CHAPTER VIII

THE ADVANCE TO VICTORY

BATTLE OF ALBERT 1918—BATTLE OF THE SCARPE 1918

IT must not be thought that this first great German effort ended like Act I at a theatre, with a curtain dropping for fifteen minutes while the actors rested and changed their clothes, and the spectators found solace in nicotine or alcohol.

Troops in line, though they were not being attacked, probably worked harder than ever before and the nervous tension was as great as ever. All were conscious that the Germans might erupt again, and, as is usual in such times of stress, the weak-hearted were always ready to endow the enemy with miraculous powers of assembling, of covering himself with a cloak of invisibility. The rush had been stopped, but only by the sacrifice of a very considerable area of ground, and at the expense of many reserves; but a mass of enemy divisions was still concentrated on the Somme.

It was certain that the enemy would attack again, and it seemed probable that it would be about the centre of the British line, where his preparations were already complete. Indeed, the situation was more serious than it had ever been.

The British Army had used up all its reserves

in the fighting on the Somme, and in addition ten divisions had been withdrawn from the north and replaced with worn-out divisions, reinforced from England. The reasons for draining the north are given by Sir Douglas Haig as being that he could, under urgent necessity, give ground there to a limited extent, but a break-through in the centre, about Vimy, " would mean the realisation of the enemy's plans, which had been foiled by our defence of Arras on the 28th March, namely, the capture of Amiens and the separation of the bulk of the British Armies from the French and from those British forces acting under the direction of the latter." Therefore, in view of the preparations which had been made on that sector by the enemy, British forces could not be reduced.

Certain preparations for an attack north of the La Bassée Canal had been observed prior to the 21st March, and there were indications that the enemy was completing these early in April ; but the extent and force of the possible attack could not be gauged.

On the 7th April a heavy and prolonged bombardment with gas shell was opened by the Germans from Lens to Armentières. And at 4 o'clock in the morning of the 9th the bombardment was reopened with the greatest intensity. At 7 o'clock, again helped by a thick fog, the enemy attacked the left brigade of the Portuguese 2nd Division and broke into their trenches; a few minutes later the attack spread to the north and south. The attack included the left of the First Army and the right of the Second Army.

This great thrust in the direction of Hazebrouck was brought to a standstill between Merville and the Forêt de Nieppe, but the enemy penetrated beyond

Bailleul, and in the north took Kemmel Hill and forced a retirement from the Passchendaele Ridge.

This brings the general situation up to the end of April. But we must note that on the 14th Marshal Foch became the Allied Generalissimo.

The next German move was on the 27th May, north-west of Rheims, on the Aisne front. The 19th, 21st, 25th, and 50th British Divisions, which had taken part in both the Somme and the Lys Valley fighting, had been sent down to a quiet part of the French front; they were joined by the 8th Division, which had been in some of the hardest fighting on the Somme. These divisions constituted the IX Corps and were included in the Sixth French Army. The German attack fell on the IX Corps and the French Corps on their left, which was holding the Chemin des Dames; they were forced from their positions, and by the 30th May the enemy had reached the Marne. The attacks continued until the 6th June, when they culminated in two attempts on the Montagne de Bligny, but here they were held.

By this time the Allied reserves were being used wherever they were wanted. But it had been for the most part French reserves which had come to the aid of the British. At the beginning of July, however, Marshal Foch believed that the enemy was about to attack east and west of Rheims, and he moved the whole of his French troops (eight divisions) from Flanders, and in addition asked for four British divisions to relieve French troops on the Somme. A further four divisions were also sent down as a reserve behind the French front.

As the Marshal had foreseen, the enemy attacked on the 15th July, and, after making progress and crossing the Marne, was held by French, American, and Italian divisions.

On the 18th July the Marshal launched his great counter-offensive on the Château Thierry-Soissons front, and in this used the four British divisions he had held in reserve, and which constituted the XXII Corps. (The 56th Division entered this Corps later on.)

In view of the defeats inflicted up to the moment of the counter-offensive, it might well be supposed that the troops of the Entente were despondent. The Germans were surprised at M. Clemenceau stating that he would fight before Paris, that he would fight in Paris, and that he would fight behind Paris, and this same spirit certainly pervaded the 56th Division. With these great enemy successes throughout the months of March, April, May, and July in mind, the actions of the 56th Division during those months are perhaps the most significant and, in our opinion, the most gallant work they performed. There was no set battle. And a set battle is in some ways the easiest kind of attack for the infantry. The operations through those months were of a minor character, calling for a high level of courage and determination from small parties of men, parties so small that the success of the enterprise must depend on individual gallantry, as there was no mass to drag them along. At any time minor operations deserve more praise than is allotted to them, and at this time, in the face of a series of German victories, they are worthy of the highest admiration.

Divisional Headquarters were at a place called Acq, to the north-west of Arras, and the brigades in the neighbouring villages. Again the division was not

to know a lengthy period of rest, for on the 8th April
the 56th Division had relieved the 1st Canadian
Division and Gen. Dudgeon took over command
of the line. During the week of so-called rest,
brigades were called upon to provide anything
between 1,200 and 1,500 men each night for fatigues,
digging further lines of defence. " Bow Bells " were
active, and those who were not on fatigue joined in
many a chorus with a flavour and memory of London
Town.

The new front was south of the Scarpe and the
Arras-Douai railway, ground over which the division
had fought in the same month of the previous year.
The high ground of Monchy and Orange Hill, on this
side of the Scarpe, had been lost on the 28th, and
the line now ran through Fampoux, on the north of
the river, in front of Feuchy to Bois des Bœufs, to
the east of Tilloy, and so to Neuville Vitasse. Bois
des Bœufs was about the centre of the line held by
the division, which was thus astride of the Arras-
Cambrai road. The Corps was the XVII (Fergusson),
and had been part of the Third Army, but on the 8th
it was transferred to the First Army.

From the moment of taking over the line, patrols
were pursuing an aggressive policy. Many small
encounters took place in No Man's Land, the 56th
Division gradually gaining the ascendancy over the
enemy.

On the 19th, at 4.30 a.m., the 168th Brigade
carried out a most successful enterprise. The idea
was to advance the outpost line on the Tilloy-
Wancourt road, and was undertaken by the London
Scottish on the right, with one company and a
bombing section, and the 4th London Regt. on the

left, with one platoon and two bombing sections. The enemy were taken completely by surprise. One warrant officer and three other ranks were captured, together with nine machine guns and a Grenatenwerfer. The enemy line was held throughout the day, but the hostile artillery fire became stronger, the position was not particularly good, and towards the evening orders were given to evacuate it. While this was being done at dusk, the Germans launched a counter-attack and a lively scuffle ensued. The enemy was first beaten off, and then the retirement was effected.

A curious incident occurred during this brush with the enemy. The Germans, as usual, sent up a multitude of lights, and a combination of these appear to have presented to the artillery observers a cluster of lights such as our S.O.S. rocket contained at that moment. The S.O.S. barrage was accordingly put down, much to the surprise of the London Scottish.

The prisoners were of the 65th Infantry Regt., 185th Division.

On the 23rd April the 56th Division took over from the 15th Division the sector north of the Arras-Cambrai road, and held the whole of the XVII Corps front.

The enemy raided on the 24th, and occupied for a short period a gun-pit post. He was ejected and gained no identification, but two of his dead were found and proved to be of the 28th Infantry Regt., 185th Division. But the next night two prisoners were captured by a patrol on the extreme left of the line, near Broken Mill, belonging to the 14th Bavarian Regt., 16th Bavarian Division, which indicated a relief of the 185th Division.

Gen. Dudgeon, who had led the division through some very heavy fighting, fell ill on the 25th and was sent to hospital. His record with the division is a fine one. At the third battle of Ypres he had scarcely time to look round, knew no one in the division, and his position might be described as most unenviable; at the battle of Cambrai he was called upon to carry out a most difficult task; at Arras he went through a most anxious and trying period. At none of these places did he falter. The ordeals which were thrust upon him were heavy, but he brought the division through them triumphantly.

Brig.-Gen. Freeth assumed temporary command of the division, until Gen. Hull arrived on the 4th May.

No man had such power over the 56th Division as Gen. Hull. The wonderful pugnacious spirit they had shown in the Laventie-Richebourg line was roused to its highest pitch when, after a quiet ten days' study of the line, the General ordered a whole series of raids, which at last caused the Germans to erect a board, in their line, on which was chalked: " Please don't raid us any more ! "

On the 21st May the 8th Middlesex raided near the Tilloy-Wancourt road and captured four prisoners and a machine gun. They established the important fact that the 16th Bavarian Division had been relieved by the 214th, the prisoners being of the 50th Regt.

On the 27th patrols ran into strong parties of the enemy covering a large number of men engaged in wiring the enemy front. The next night a somewhat ambitious raid was made on a wide front of either side of the Tilloy-Wancourt road. On the left was

the 7th Middlesex, in three parties (one company in
all), on the right two platoons of the 1st London Regt.
The raid was a great success. Under an excellent
barrage, of which everyone spoke with the highest
praise, the raiders entered the enemy lines. They
found it packed with men north of the road. The
1st Londons claimed to have killed 40 south of the
road, and the 7th Middlesex appear to have spread
terror and devastation in their area.

The right party of Middlesex estimated that they
had killed 32 of the enemy and captured 1 machine
gun. The centre party first met the enemy in
shell-holes outside their wire, and quickly disposed
of them; they claimed 35 Germans killed, 1 prisoner,
and 1 machine gun. The left party counted the
damage they inflicted as no less than 60 killed. The
artillery had also done fearful execution. Although
many of the enemy were seen running away, the
total casualties inflicted by this raid were reckoned
to be 200. Making every allowance for exaggeration
—for it is extremely difficult to count dead men
during a raid—the facts remain that the raid was a
huge success and the casualties inflicted exceedingly
heavy.

No attempt was made to advance our outpost line
and our wounded were taken safely back. The total
casualties of the raiding parties were 2 officers killed
and 2 wounded, 2 other ranks killed and 49 wounded
—the wounds were mostly slight. The identification
procured was normal—50th Regt., 214th Division.

On the 30th May the Kensingtons sent out an
enterprising patrol which rushed an enemy post and
captured two more prisoners. Identification normal.

The month of June opened with a raid by the

Kensingtons near the Cambrai road. Many of the enemy were killed and 27 taken prisoners. The Germans did not show much fight on this occasion, but in most cases emerged from dug-outs with no rifles or equipment. They were again of the 50th Infantry Regt., 214th Division. The Kensingtons' casualties were 1 killed and 17 wounded.

On the 10th June the 7th Middlesex raided on the left of the line, near Broken Mill, and secured two prisoners of the 358th Infantry Regt., 214th Division.

One company of the London Rifle Brigade suddenly raided at 3 o'clock in the afternoon on the 12th June south of the Cambrai road. They advanced under cover of smoke and killed about 24 of the enemy and captured 1 machine gun. Their casualties were only 3 killed and 11 wounded, in spite of their daring. Identification normal.

Soon after this raid the Germans were seen to be active in their lines. Many officers were noticed examining our lines on the 24th June, and the next night a platoon of the 1st Londons and a platoon of the 8th Middlesex entered the enemy lines on the left and inflicted casualties, but failed to obtain identification. This was soon secured, however, by the London Rifle Brigade, who brought in a man of the 50th Infantry Regt. on the 3rd July.

The Queen's Westminsters sent a company over into some fortified gun-pits on the 8th July, and secured three prisoners of the 358th Regiment, 214th Division. They took over with them some heavy charges of ammonal, as it was known that a deep dug-out existed. As soon as the raiders reached the gun-pits the garrison, led by an officer, attempted to come out of the dug-out. The officer was promptly shot, though he missed the leading man of the Queen's Westminsters by a hair's-breadth, and a charge of the explosive was thrown down the dug-out. A terrific explosion completely destroyed that entrance. The raiders then found the second entrance and treated it in the same fashion. The prisoners stated that between fifty and sixty men were in the dug-out with two officers.

This ended the series of raids, and it would seem as though the 185th and 214th German Divisions had good cause to remember the 56th Division. But it is an exceedingly fine record, and speaks highly of the *moral* of the London men and the inspiring leadership of their General.

Gen. Hull handed over to the 2nd Canadian Division on the 15th July, and the division moved through Roellecourt to Villers Châtel.

Before leaving this period we must quote from Brig.-Gen. Elkington's diary :

" In addition to the 56th Divisional Artillery I had several other R.A. brigades under my command to assist in covering the front, namely the 29th, 277th, and 311th R.A. Brigades. During April and May Gen. Dudgeon suffered from severe rheumatism and had to give up command of the division. Major-Gen. Hull returned and took over command. Reconnaissances and selection of several back lines, in case of withdrawal being necessary on this front, were carried out, and all battery positions carefully marked and their observation posts selected, also their lines of retreat if necessary. Continual training in moving warfare was also carried out by means of skeleton drill with full staff. A polo ground was used near Dainville and play went on twice a week until the enemy elected to shell the ground, when it had to be stopped. During this period the artillery supported many successful raids by our infantry and the Canadians on our right. . . . The ' Bow Bells ' established themselves in a hut near our headquarters and gave many excellent shows to crowded houses. Towards the end of May Indian drivers were sent to us from the Divisional Ammunition Column to release the European personnel. These drivers did very well after they had been trained, but suffered rather from the cold during the winter. On the 15th July the 56th Divisional Infantry was relieved by the 2nd Canadian Division, and I remained in the line commanding the R.A. until the 21st July, when we were relieved."

Refitting and training were carried out, and after two weeks in the back area, which was not free from enemy attention in the nature of aeroplane bombs, the division started on the 31st July to relieve portions of the 1st Canadian Division in the Tilloy and Vitasse sections of the line. The Telegraph Sector was relieved during the night of the following day, and on the 2nd August Gen. Hull took over command of the line.

The weather generally was very good and the line quiet. The 167th Brigade obtained identification on the 4th showing that the 185th German Division had been relieved by the 39th Division. On the 8th the division projected gas on Neuville Vitasse, but otherwise everything was quiet.

On the 15th the 167th Brigade was relieved by the 44th Brigade, 15th Division, and moved by rail to Izel-les-Hameau area. On the 18th the 168th Brigade was relieved by the 46th Brigade and moved to Mazières area. And on the 18th the 169th Brigade went to Arras.

At that date there was a proposal that the XVII Corps should attack Orange Hill and Chapel Hill, and the 56th Division was to take part in this attack. Days, however, were spent in moving about. On the 20th Sir Douglas Haig visited Gen. Hull. The same day the 169th Brigade moved to Avesne-le-Comte area, and the 168th to Lignereuil. At mid-day on the 21st the 56th Division was transferred from the XVII Corps to the VI Corps, and the whole division moved to the Bavincourt area, when an entirely new scheme of attack came into being.

. . . . .

In his dispatch covering this period Sir Douglas Haig writes :

"The definite collapse of the ambitious offensive launched by the enemy on the 15th July, and the striking success of the Allied counter-offensive south of the Aisne, effected a complete change in the whole military situation."

This first big operation of Marshal Foch had inflicted heavy losses on the enemy. Ten divisions were broken up and the remnants used as reinforcements to others. The attempt to make the Entente Powers sue for peace before the arrival of the Americans had failed—not only were a million troops from the United States in France, but the English divisions had been largely made up to strength. Between May and June ten English divisions had been reduced to cadres—seven of these were reconstituted during July and August. And German General Headquarters had been forced to take momentous decisions. They had to withdraw from the salient between Rheims and Soissons, and

also abandon their idea of a new offensive in Flanders.
" By the beginning of August," says Ludendorff,
" we had suspended our attack and reverted to the
defensive on the whole front."
At a conference, held on the 23rd July, it was
arranged by Marshal Foch that the British, French,
and American Armies should each prepare plans for
a local offensive. The objectives on the British front
were the disengagement of Amiens and the freeing
of the Paris-Amiens railway by an attack on the
Albert-Montdidier front. The rôle of the French and
American Armies was to free other strategic railways
farther south and east.

There seems a suggestion in his dispatches that
the British Commander-in-Chief was somewhat per-
turbed by this decision. He had the safety of the
Channel ports and the danger of a fresh German
offensive in that direction ever in his mind, and we
know that it was Ludendorff's plan. There is an
indication that Sir Douglas Haig was urging a counter-
stroke in the north. " These different operations,"
he says, " had already been the subject of correspond-
ence between Marshal Foch and myself." Ultimately
he came to the conclusion that the tasks assigned to
the British forces east of Amiens should take prece-
dence " as being the most important and the most
likely to give large results."

The attack opened on the 8th August on a front
of over eleven miles from just south of the Amiens-
Roye road to Morlancourt. On the right was the
Canadian Corps, in the centre the Australian Corps,
and on the left the III Corps. The attack of the
First French Army was timed to take place an hour
later between Moreuil and the British right. By the

12th August 22,000 prisoners and over 400 guns had been captured, and the line had been advanced to a depth of twelve miles, to the old German positions in 1916.

The 8th August was the black day of the German Army in the history of this war, says Ludendorff.[1]

"The Emperor told me later that, after the failure of the July offensive and after the 8th August, he knew the war could no longer be won. The official report of the evening of the 8th announced briefly that the enemy had penetrated our line south of the Somme on a wide front. Early the following morning General von Cramon rang me up from Baden. He informed me that my report had caused great alarm in Vienna. I could not leave him in any doubt as to the serious view I took of the situation. Nevertheless he begged me to remember how detrimentally the blunt admission of defeat must affect our allies, who had placed all their hopes in Germany. This occurred again on the 2nd September.

The impression made on our Allies by the failure on the Western Front was great. The Emperor Charles announced his intention of coming to Spa in the middle of August."

The great salient the Germans had created towards Amiens was disappearing, and Sir Douglas Haig was faced with the old positions of the opening of the battle of the Somme in 1916. But there was a difference. The situation and his reasoning are succinctly related in his dispatch :

"In deciding to extend the attack northwards to the

[1] *My War Memories*, 1914—1918.

area between the Rivers Somme and Scarpe I was
influenced by the following considerations.

The enemy did not seem prepared to meet an
attack in this direction, and, owing to the success of
the Fourth Army, he occupied a salient the left flank
of which was already threatened from the south. A
further reason for my decision was that the ground
north of the Ancre River was not greatly damaged by
shell-fire, and was suitable for the use of Tanks. A
successful attack between Albert and Arras in a
south-easterly direction would turn the line of the
Somme south of Péronne, and give every promise of
producing far-reaching results. It would be a step
towards the strategic objective, St. Quentin-Cambrai.

This attack, moreover, would be rendered easier by
the fact that we now held the commanding plateau
south of Arras about Bucquoy and Ablainzeville,
which in the days of the old Somme fighting had lain
well behind the enemy's lines. In consequence we
were here either astride or to the east of the intricate
system of trench lines which in 1916 we had no choice
but to attack frontally, and enjoyed advantages of
observation which at that date had been denied us.

It was arranged that on the morning of the
21st August a limited attack should be launched
north of the Ancre to gain the general line of the Arras-
Albert railway, on which it was correctly assumed
that the enemy's main line of resistance was sited.
The day of the 22nd August would then be used to
get troops and guns into position on this front, and
to bring forward the left of the Fourth Army between
the Somme and the Ancre. The principal attack
would be delivered on the 23rd August by the Third
Army and the divisions of the Fourth Army north of
the Somme, the remainder of the Fourth Army
assisting by pushing forward south of the river to
cover the flank of the main operation. Thereafter,
if success attended our efforts, the whole of both

18

armies were to press forward with the greatest vigour and exploit to the full any advantage we might have gained.

.   .   .   .   .

It will be seen, therefore, that as the attack from Amiens advanced, it was being taken up by troops on the left. On the 21st August the IV Corps was engaged, with the 42nd, New Zealand, and 37th Divisions, and the VI Corps, with the 2nd and Guards Divisions. On the 23rd a series of strong assaults were delivered on practically the whole front of thirty-three miles from our junction with the French at Lihons.

As the attack spread to the north, so activity in Corps, Division, and Brigade Headquarters preceded actual movement of troops. A state of brain and nerve tension prevailed. There was, too, a change of plan, which is always one of the trials of the regimental soldier. It is as well to recapitulate some of the movements.

The relief in the line was completed on the 18th August, and on the 19th the 169th Brigade was sent to Arras to carry out preparations for an attack on Orange and Chapel Hills. Owing to the change of plan this brigade was sent back to the Avesnes-le-Comte area on the 21st, and on the same day the 168th Brigade marched from the Mazières area to Lignereuil. The 56th Division now came under the VI Corps (Haldane), and Gen. Hull at once visited Corps Headquarters, but did not succeed in gaining any exact information as to the rôle the division would play in the forthcoming operations. During the night 21st/22nd the division marched to the area Barly-St. Amand-Saulty-Bavincourt.

Early in the morning of the 22nd Gen. Hull was called to a conference at Corps Headquarters, where the operations for the next day were decided upon. He did not get back to Bavincourt until 10.30 a.m., when he held a conference and explained the operations to all concerned. Officers of all brigades were then sent off to reconnoitre ; and the 168th Brigade marched at 3.30 p.m. to Blairville, a distance of seven and a half miles.

Time was now getting on and the Corps Operation order had not been received. Gen. Hull, however, sent out his orders based on what had been said at the conference in the morning, and at 9 p.m. the 168th Brigade, with the 1st London Regt. attached, moved to the assembly area, a march of another four and a half miles, ready to attack on the left of the Guards Division. In the midst of all this movement and with only a short time at their disposal, officers had no opportunity of seeing the forward assembly areas or the objectives. They assembled in the dark and attacked in the morning, never having seen the ground before.

The artillery was no better off than the infantry.

" On the 21st August orders were received to join the VI Corps, and I went off to see the Corps R.A., who were a long way back, and also to see the 40th Division Artillery and the Guards Artillery and to try to reconnoitre the new front. On the evening of the 21st I received instructions from the R.A. VI Corps that all arrangements were at once to be made to put the 56th Artillery in action to cover the attack of the 56th Division on the morning of the 23rd, the divisional front being roughly from 500 yards north of Hamelincourt to just north of Boiry

Becquerelle. The Divisional Artillery, for purposes of the initial attack, consisted of six brigades R.F.A., as follows : (a) Guards Divisional Artillery, (b) 57th, (c) 56th. On the 21st August these brigades were as follows : (a) in action on the front, (b) in reserve near St. Pol, (c) in reserve at Simencourt and Berneville. Reconnaissance was carried out during the morning of the 22nd, and at 8 p.m. that evening the brigades moved off to occupy the positions selected, and ammunition to the extent of 400 rounds per gun had to be dumped at the same time. This involved an immense amount of work, but it was successfully carried out by the brigades of the 56th Divisional Artillery by 2 a.m. on the 23rd ; but the brigades of the 57th Divisional Artillery, though all guns were got into action, were delayed by heavy gas shelling, and were as a result unable to complete the gun-dumps by the opening of the barrage. At this time the artillery covering the division was organised as follows :

Right group :
   74th and 75th Brigades R.F.A. Guards Divisional Artillery, in action west of Boisleux-au-Mont.

Centre group :
   285th and 286th Brigades R.F.A. 57th Divisional Artillery, in action south-east of Boisleux-au-Mont.

Left group :
   280th and 281st Brigades R.F.A. 56th Divisional Artillery, in action south-west of Boisleux-au-Mont.

As far as the field artillery was concerned, the strength of the barrage was about one 18-pounder gun per 27 yards.

Affiliated Heavy Artillery group—two brigades R.G.A." [Gen. Elkington.]

The position from which the division attacked was a very strong one for defence. The Cojeul River has two branches. The northern branch, running from the high ground by Adinfer Wood, passes to the north of Boisleux-St. Marc and Boiry Becquerelle. The southern branch, running across the front of the division, is underground between Hamelincourt and Boyelles, where it comes to the surface and joins the main stream south of Henin.

The left flank of the division rested on Cojeul (north). There was, therefore, a wide field of vision in front of them, with the one exception of the spur which shoots out between the two branches of the river to the north of Boyelles, and which afforded the enemy a concealed position on that portion of the front. The general run of the valley was across the direction of the 56th Division attack, and Croisilles and St. Leger were over the ridge on the far side of the valley. Beyond these villages the Hindenburg Line ran roughly from Arras in a south-easterly direction, obliquely across the line of attack.

The first objective of the 168th Brigade, which was to make the attack, was the blue line—that is, the two villages of Boyelles and Boiry Becquerelle ; and the brigade would then push out a fringe of posts in front. Twenty-one Tanks (two companies, 11th Battalion Tank Corps) were to help in this attack.

As the battalions of the 168th Brigade marched to their positions, the Germans used gas freely and respirators had to be worn. Fortunately the night was light, but even so progress was slow, and such light as there was did not help officers, when they had placed their men in position, to see very much of what sort of a place it was they would attack in the

morning. It seemed that the enemy was very alert,
as he fired a great deal with machine guns and light
trench mortars during the night.

At 4.55 a.m. in the murky light of dawn the
barrage, which had opened at 4 a.m. at Gommecourt
on the right of the VI Corps, crashed down in front
of the 56th Division. The Kensingtons, on the right,
north of Hamelincourt, the 4th Londons in the
centre, and the London Scottish on the left advanced
to the assault twelve minutes later. The Tanks
cleared the way for the Kensingtons very effectively,
only a few small parties of the enemy showing much
fight. The battalion, however, was worried by
machine-gun fire from the left, and it was seen that
the 4th Londons were meeting with more determined
opposition. Two platoons of the Kensingtons were,
therefore, sent to assist by attacking Boyelles from
the south. By 6 o'clock the Kensingtons had
reached their objective.

The 4th Londons had the village of Boyelles and
the curious circular Marc system in front of them.
The ruins of the village could be seen from the
right, but Marc system was blind. Actually the
ground between our front-line trench and the enemy
line was level, but it dropped suddenly from the
German line and was helped by a sunken road, so
that there was plenty of shelter from the barrage.
The left of the 4th Londons was held up in front of
this place. For some reason no Tank attacked the
forward Marc system, and until a platoon enfiladed
the sunken road from the south, and the London
Scottish threatened from the north, the garrison
held up the advance and inflicted heavy casualties.
When the troops pressed in from the flanks, how-

ever, the Germans, 2 officers and 80 men, surrendered.

Much the same thing happened to the right company of the 4th Londons in the village of Boyelles. But here four Tanks came on the scene, and again the garrison surrendered with eleven machine guns. Six light, heavy, and medium trench mortars were captured in the banks on the north of the stream.

The London Scottish on the left met with opposition from Boiry Becquerelle, but carried out a smart enveloping movement, closing on the village from the flanks, and eventually getting behind it. Over 100 prisoners and 8 machine guns were taken by this well-known battalion.

All the first objective was then in our hands.

At 9.15 a.m. the 168th Brigade was ordered to continue the advance so as to conform with the 2nd Guards Brigade on the right. The brigade was to gain touch with the Guards at Bank Copse on the east side of the railway curve into St. Leger. But this order had to be transmitted by runner and distances were great ; it did not reach the centre battalion until 11.15 a.m.

The Kensingtons started their advance at 1.30 p.m., and almost at once met with strong machine-gun and artillery fire. The advance was held up on the Ervillers-Boyelles road, and much confused fighting ensued. Two platoons managed to get round the opposition and joined the Guards, with whom they attacked the railway bank to the west of Bank Copse. The remainder of the battalion was apparently fighting in small groups and was much scattered. The commanding officer, Lieut.-Col. R. S. F. Shaw, went forward to try to clear up the situation and was killed by a sniper. The position on this battalion front was not certain until 9.30 p.m., when it was ascertained that they were on the line of the Ervillers-Boyelles road.

The 4th Londons did not advance until 4.30 p.m. They attacked in widely extended formation and casualties were very light. There was opposition from five enemy machine guns, but these were outflanked and overcome. The line of Boyelles Reserve was reached and patrols pushed out 500 yards beyond without encountering any of the enemy.

The London Scottish attacked at the same time as the 4th Londons and encountered strong opposition at Boiry Work, at the northern end of Boyelles Reserve. For one hour the London Scottish worked slowly to get round this position, but before they closed in the garrison surrendered—86 prisoners. They were then in line with the 4th Londons and their posts pushed out some 500 yards in advance.

In spite of the hurried orders it had been a successful day for the 56th Division. The Kensingtons had had the worst time, but they captured in all 167 prisoners, while the 4th Londons had 243, and the London Scottish 253.

Commenting on the attack, Brig.-Gen. Loch says that the chief difficulty was the short notice given, and the fact that the brigade was billeted in a much scattered area made the rapid issue of orders impossible. It was also impossible to reconnoitre the ground, and the approach march was made in exceptionally hot weather. There had been no preparation of the front prior to the attack, and signal communications were poor. Visual signalling was of little value, owing to the dust and the heavy state of the atmosphere, and reliance had to be placed, as it invariably was, on runners who worked well, but as the distances were ever increasing it was a slow method.

" The Tanks," he says, "were most valuable, although through various causes they, in some cases, arrived late in the assembly areas. Their greater speed enabled them to catch up the infantry, and by working forward and then to a flank they evidently much demoralised the enemy and caused them to surrender more freely than usual."

The machine guns, which since the beginning of March had been formed into a battalion, were controlled by Lieut.-Col. Jervis, who was with the Brigade Headquarters, and were echéloned in depth, the forward line advancing with the assaulting infantry.

The enemy was in considerable strength, as is shown by the number of prisoners, 663, and the 59 machine guns and 18 trench mortars which were captured.

Other divisions of the VI and IV Corps were equally successful, and the Germans holding the defences to the south, about Thiepval (which had caused us such efforts to win in 1916), were in a precarious position. The attack was pressed without giving the enemy breathing-space, and he was becoming disorganised and showing signs of confusion.

But in writing of this great and last advance we are conscious that a division, which until this moment had always appeared to be a large and important unit in any operations, was being swamped by the numbers set in motion. One of five or six is such a much bigger proportion than one of fifty-seven or fifty-eight. And the French, American, and Belgian Armies were moving too.

During the night the London Scottish were placed under the orders of the 167th Brigade, which relieved the Kensingtons and 4th London Regiment. The 169th Brigade moved to the Basseux area and, in the morning of the 24th, to the Purple Line behind Boisleux-au-Mont.

The 167th Brigade were ordered to attack the next day, the 24th, with Summit Trench as their first objective, refusing their left flank so as to join with the 52nd Division on the northern boundary. The second objective was Fooley Reserve-Hill Switch-Cross Switch, with the object of enveloping Croisilles from the north, while the Guards Division carried out a similar operation from the south. Twelve Tanks and one company of the Machine Gun Battalion were to assist.

At 7 a.m. the barrage opened on the enemy front-line posts, and, after ten minutes, crept forward, at the rate of 100 yards in four minutes, followed by the infantry. The whole of the brigade, of course, attacked—the 8th Middlesex being on the right, the 7th Middlesex in the centre, and the 1st London Regiment on the left. The Guards Division also attacked on the right, and the 52nd on the left.

The 8th Middlesex reached their objective in Summit Trench and Ledger Reserve about 10 o'clock. Opposition was not of a fierce nature and took the form of " patchy " machine-gun fire and rifle fire. Small parties of men kept working forward and could be seen, with Tanks, in and about Summit Trench by 8.30 a.m. The 7th Middlesex and 1st Londons

advanced in a similar fashion and with the same
opposition.

But news came from the Corps which, for the
moment, checked the advance. From prisoners'
statements it was learned that three fresh divisions
had arrived in Bullecourt and Hendicourt, and the
56th Division was ordered to make preparations
to meet a counter-attack. The 169th Brigade was
ordered forward behind Boyelles, and the 167th
Brigade was told to occupy Croisilles " by peaceful
penetration." Meanwhile the right brigade of the
52nd Division, which was attacking Henin Hill,
had been compelled to withdraw and was echéloned
on the forward slopes to the left rear of the 56th
Division.

Patrols began to probe the country before them,
and at 1.30 p.m. the situation was . the 8th Middlesex
had one company on the western side of Croisilles
with patrols on the outskirts of the village, two
companies in Summit Trench and that end of Leger
Reserve, and one company in Boyelles Reserve.
The 7th Middlesex had two companies in Summit
Trench, with patrols in front, and support and reserve
companies in depth in rear. The 1st Londons had
two companies in Summit Trench, in touch with the
52nd Division, and support and reserve companies
in rear.

Reports tended to show that Croisilles had been
evacuated, and after a consultation with Brig.-Gen.
Freeth, Gen. Hull ordered the Brigade to attack
and establish itself in the Hindenburg Support Line
between Hump Lane and River Road (Sensée River).
Six Tanks were to be used, and the 52nd Division
was to attack on the left.

Attempts made by the 8th Middlesex to enter
Croisilles were not successful, and at zero hour,
7.30 p.m., the village was still in the hands of the
enemy. The attack was met with determined and very
heavy machine-gun and artillery fire, and failed
to gain any ground. Only one Tank came into
action, and that was met with gas which rendered
it useless. Croisilles Trench had been reached by
troops, but found to be only 2 feet deep at the most,
and quite useless as a reorganising point for further
advance. This trench had unfortunately been
shown as an organised and deep defensive work.
Brig.-Gen. Freeth, therefore, ordered Summit Trench
to be held as the line of resistance.

The days' fighting had resulted in an appreciable
gain, but the enemy's resistance was increasing.
The Corps ordered an attack on the Hindenburg
Support the following day, without the help of Tanks,
and Gen. Hull had to point out that the resistance
was not only very strong, as he had proved that
day, but that the' Hindenburg system was very
heavily wired. Tanks would have dealt with this
wire had they been available. The Corps then modified the order and instructed the General to capture
Croisilles and obtain a footing in Sensée Avenue,
to the north-east, so as to conform with the 52nd
Division, who were to attack on the left.

During the night the front-line battalions were
heavily shelled with gas, which forced them to wear
gas-masks, in one case for six hours. Patrols, however, went out, and their reports coincided with
that of the Guards Division on the right, that
Croisilles was full of machine guns. Also the 52nd

Division on the left reported that the Hindenburg
Line was very strongly held. It was decided to
bombard the village while patrols would try to gain
ground.

But the 25th August was a negative day. Some
posts were established in front of the main line, but
the village itself was too strongly held and the
bombardment, apparently, failed to dislodge the
enemy.

Meanwhile the 169th Brigade reconnoitred the
position with a view of attacking and enveloping
Croisilles from the north and capturing the Hindenburg Line.

At 8 a.m. the 56th and 52nd Divisions had been
moved from the command of the VI Corps to that
of the XVII Corps, and it was decided that the
167th Brigade should attack on the 26th and establish
itself on the line of the shallow Croisilles Trench
and Fooley Reserve. Roughly the XVII Corps
faced the Hindenburg Line, which swung round the
left flank of the 56th Division, and on this flank the
52nd Division were to advance on the Hindenburg
Line in conjunction with the attack of the 167th
Brigade. Farther north the Canadian Corps were
to assault the actual Hindenburg Line, and if they
were successful the 52nd Division would continue
to push down the system and roll it up in a south-
easterly direction.

The attack of the 167th Brigade took place at 3 a.m.,
and was nowhere successful. The wire was still uncut
(there were in some spots five belts of it), and the
machine guns in Croisilles poured a devastating hail
of bullets on the assaulting troops. But to the north
the Canadian Corps had been successful and had

pierced the Hindenburg system. The 52nd Division had thrust one battalion into the celebrated line, and was progressing towards Henin Hill.

During the afternoon the 52nd Division reported the line from the Cojeul River to Henin Hill clear of the enemy, and the 167th Brigade was then relieved at 6 o'clock by the 169th.

The battalions in line from the right were the Queen's Westminsters, the London Rifle Brigade, and the 2nd Londons. On taking over, the 2nd Londons attempted to clear the situation on the left by a " stealth " raid with two platoons. The experiment was bad, as the platoons were almost wiped out by machine guns.

The battle was continued the following day, the 27th, at 9.30 a.m. The task was to keep in touch with the 52nd Division and sweep round the north of the village. The Queen's Westminsters, therefore, stood fast while the London Rifle Brigade and the 2nd Londons executed a wheel to the right. This was successful in reaching Farmers' Avenue and Sensée Avenue, while, on the left, the 52nd Division reached Fontaine Croisilles and established themselves to the east of that village. A glance at the map will show how the Hindenburg Line was being rolled up, how desperate was the case of the Germans opposite the 56th Division, and how necessary it was for them to concentrate their fiercest resistance against the advance of the 56th Division. The day was noteworthy for the good work done by the 2nd Londons in what was the nearest approach to open warfare which had as yet been attempted.

Croisilles was the obstacle which stood in our way. The Guards Division attacked on the right of it, and after an initial success was counter-attacked so severely that they fell back on Leger Reserve, and left a gap on the right of the Queen's Westminsters, which was filled by two platoons of the latter regiment. Farther to the south troops were fighting on the Somme battlefield of the month of September 1916—still some way from the Hindenburg Line. But, as has been pointed out, the whole of the old Somme positions were being turned from the north.

During the afternoon the 168th Brigade took over the frontage held by the right and centre battalions of the 169th Brigade. These two battalions were then able to enter the Hindenburg system which had been captured by the 52nd Division, and move along it towards the Sensée River, where they would start the attack. The 2nd Londons meanwhile cleared their front of some small parties of the enemy and crossed the Sensée to Nelly Avenue, part of an outpost line to the main defences. The division then stood fast under orders to attack the Bullecourt area the next day.

During the night dispositions were altered. The 167th Brigade took over the right of the Divisional front, with the 8th Middlesex, to the west of Croisilles, and the 168th Brigade moved in position to support the 169th in the attack along the Hindenburg Line. Also, the 168th Brigade was to protect the flank of the 169th, if the village was not taken, and "mop up" generally behind the attacking troops.

The first objective for the 169th Brigade was given as Queen's Lane-Jove Lane; the second was the trenches south-east of Bullecourt.

Patrols of the 8th Middlesex attempted to enter Croisilles several times during the night, but were always met with machine-gun fire. In the morning of the 28th, however, an aeroplane reported the village empty, but at 8.30 a.m. patrols of the 8th Middlesex found only the western portion of the village clear. The whole battalion then advanced, and after some lively fighting occupied the village.

The 52nd Division, which had been relieved by the 57th Division, passed through the troops in the line and joined in the general attack of the 56th Division at 12.30 p.m. The action that followed is one of the utmost confusion. The Queen's Westminsters, who led the attack, started from the line Nelly Avenue. The Germans on the right, in Guardian Reserve, held out, and the 167th Brigade found sufficient of the enemy to hold them up on the railway south-east of Croisilles. But two companies of the Queen's Westminsters and part of the 2nd Londons lost direction, and seem to have become inextricably mixed with troops of the 57th Division somewhere to the north of Hendicourt.

Apparently trouble started on the previous day (27th), when the Queen's Westminsters and part of the London Rifle Brigade were relieved by the London Scottish in front of Croisilles. The two former battalions had to march to a flank to get into the Hindenburg Line, and were severely shelled in doing so. On arriving at the Hindenburg Line, progress to their positions of assembly was seriously impeded by the 52nd Division, who, at that moment, were also assembling to attack on the following day. Col. Savill, who was commanding the Queen's Westminsters, says that his men arrived " dead beat " at Nelly Avenue and Burg Support, having been on the move all night. He gives as the cause of the loss of direction the heavy machine-gun fire which his troops met from the right on emerging from the trenches, but a glance at the map suggests another and more probable reason. He was unable to assemble his battalion on a front conforming with the general line of advance. The right of his leading companies was in Nelly Avenue, and the left in Burg Support with orders " to swing round at right angles to the Hindenburg system."

It was pointed out at the battle of the Somme that the complicated manœuvre of changing direction at the commencement of an assault should be avoided. It is probable that the commanding officer had no other alternative, but the lesson is once more demonstrated. To the difficult task imposed upon them must be added the further embarrassment of never having seen the ground. True that the attack did not start until 12.30 p.m., but it was extremely difficult to fix landmarks owing to the country being so overgrown with long grass and weeds, and in any case there was rising ground between Burg Support and Bullecourt, so that the few hours from dawn to the attack were of little benefit.

The change of front by the left of the attacking force was further complicated by the thick wire between the trenches of the Hindenburg System. Before any manœuvre of the sort could be undertaken, these belts of wire had to be passed, and by the time this had been accomplished, all idea of direction had fled.

The London Rifle Brigade, in close support to the Queen's Westminsters, had three companies in line, the fourth company being in support on the right and Battalion Headquarters on the left. The left

19

and centre companies followed the Queen's Westminsters—even in field practice this would probably
occur.

The 2nd London Regt. was already reduced to
11 officers and 193 other ranks, and assembled in
King's Avenue. The two left companies followed
the Queen's Westminsters, while the two right
companies fought down Tunnel Trench.

Col. Savill, believing his battalion to be more or
less on their way to Bullecourt, moved with his
headquarters down Burg Support and very soon
encountered the enemy. He was joined by the headquarters of the London Rifle Brigade and the 2nd
London Regt. It was thought that the " mopping-
up " had been badly done, and a message was sent
for reinforcements while the staff details tried to
bomb their way forward.

Soon after the attack opened, therefore, the 169th
Brigade was trying to capture Bullecourt with two
companies of the London Rifle Brigade on the right,
three battalion headquarter staffs and a few scattered
men of the Queen's Westminsters in the centre, and
two companies of the 2nd London Regt. (not a
hundred men) on the left. The right, which was the
strongest part of the total force, was definitely held
up by a strong enemy garrison in Guardian, and in
other parts of the front the enemy resistance was too
strong to be overcome by so weak a force.

Eventually a company of the 4th London Regt.
was sent up Burg Support, and by 5 p.m. progress
had been made as far as the Hump. But on the
right the enemy, who were being continually reinforced
by troops falling back from the attack of the 167th
Brigade through Croisilles, still held Guardian

Reserve. "Guardian Reserve," writes Brig.-Gen. Coke, "was a thorn in the side of the brigade until 6 p.m." Not only was the advance severely harassed from this place, but no track for carrying ammunition, etc., was available until it had been captured. By 6 p.m., however, the London Rifle Brigade, reinforced by two companies of the Kensingtons and the 168th Trench Mortar Battery, drove the greater part of the remaining Germans to surrender.

The advance continued on the right as far as Pelican Avenue, but in the centre the Knuckle was not cleared until 5 a.m. on the 29th. The situation all through the afternoon and night of the 28th August was most complicated, the 2nd London, London Rifle Brigade, 4th London, and Kensington Regts. being involved in a series of separate operations dealing with scattered machine-gun nests, disposed in trenches and in broken ground.

During the afternoon the 168th Brigade had been ordered to move to Leg Lane and get in touch with the 167th Brigade, also to be prepared to move into Pelican Avenue with the object of attacking Bulle- court early in the morning of the 29th. But, owing to the state of affairs in the main Hindenburg System, this was impossible, and troops were moved into position in daylight on the 29th.

Meanwhile, all those troops who had gone careering about on the left had become mixed up with the 172nd Brigade in the neighbourhood of Cemetery Avenue to the north of Hendicourt. They had suffered a number of casualties, and the remaining captain of the Queen's Westminsters had returned wounded during the afternoon, and had reported to the 169th Brigade that he and the force of which he

assumed command had occupied Pelican Lane. This
will give some idea of the difficulties which confronted
Brig.-Gen. Coke.

The attack was resumed in strength at 1 p.m. on
the 29th. The 168th Brigade were in Pelican Avenue,
with the Kensingtons on the right and the London
Scottish on the left, right and left support being the
4th and 1st London Regts.

Pelican Lane appears to have been held by small
parties of the enemy, and the 169th Brigade assembled
in the trenches north-west of that place. But the
missing companies, with the exception of the 2nd
London Regt., had not returned. The London Rifle
Brigade led the attack with two companies, having
in close support 40 men of the Queen's Westminsters
(which were all that could be found), and behind them
the 2nd Londons, with a total strength of 7 officers
and 95 other ranks.

The objective for the division was the trench
system east of Bullecourt and south of Riencourt.
At the very start of the attack the Kensingtons were
held up at Station Redoubt ; but the London Scottish
made good progress on the left, and by 2.15 p.m. were
through Bullecourt. The weak 169th Brigade made
progress as far as Saddler Lane and the sunken road
on the left of the village. And the 57th Division
reported that they had captured Riencourt and were
through Hendicourt.

Tank Avenue was strongly held by the enemy and
successfully arrested any further advance in the
centre ; and on the flanks the first check was not
overcome. And so the line remained with the
London Scottish bulged out round Bullecourt, and
the Kensingtons bringing the right flank back to

Station Redoubt, and the 169th Brigade the left flank to Saddler Lane. The right of the division was in touch with the 3rd Division, but the position of the 57th was obscure.

The 167th Brigade then relieved the whole of the divisional front, and the night passed in comparative quietness.

At about 5 a.m. on the 30th the enemy counter-attacked the line Hendicourt-Bullecourt-Ecoust in strength, and drove the 167th Brigade out of Bullecourt to the line Pelican Lane and Pelican Avenue. At the same time the 3rd Division on the right was driven out of Ecoust, and on the left the 57th Division lost Riencourt and fell back on the Bullecourt Hendecourt road, the enemy securing the factory on that road.

The 167th Brigade at once attempted to regain Bullecourt; but the enemy forces in Bullecourt received such strong support from the Station Redoubt that all efforts failed. Gen. Hull arranged for a bombardment of the Station Redoubt by the heavy artillery.

Orders from the Corps fixed the 31st August for a renewal of the attack in conjunction with the VI Corps on the left. And so the 168th Brigade was once more ordered to take Bullecourt and the Station Redoubt, relieving the 167th Brigade on that portion of the front. A company of the latter brigade would then take up a position on the left of the 168th Brigade and attack the factory. The objective was Tank Support with the left flank thrown back to the factory.

The relief took place, and all preparations were completed. At 5.15 a.m. on the 31st the brigade advanced under a creeping barrage, with the London Scottish on the right, the 4th London Regt. in the centre, and the 7th Middlesex on the left.

The London Scottish carried the Station Redoubt, and attacked Bullecourt Avenue at 8 o'clock, obtaining touch with the 4th Londons. But the latter regiment was held up in front of Bullecourt; and on the left the 7th Middlesex were unable to capture the factory. A company of the Kensingtons was sent up on the left, and by 10.15 a.m. the factory was captured, and touch obtained with the 171st Brigade of the division on that flank. Meanwhile, the London Scottish had captured Bullecourt Avenue.

At 1 o'clock an artillery observer reported the enemy advancing over the open and assembling in Tank Avenue and Support. All field guns and the heavy artillery was concentrated on this target, and no counter-attack developed. But the plans were modified to the capture of the village only.

Two companies of the Kensingtons were sent up as reinforcements, and bombing from the flanks was carried on round the village. By the time it was dark only the eastern portion was not cleared up; and the enemy remained in Gordon Reserve.

The 56th Division was then relieved by the 52nd, and marched out of the line to rest about Boyelles. The captures during these operations were :

29 officers, 1,047 other ranks.

2 77-mm. guns and 1 8-inch howitzer.

200 machine guns and over 50 trench mortars.

The casualties of the division were :

123 officers and 2,381 other ranks.

The hard-working but cheery artillery remained in the line. All through the battle they had pushed

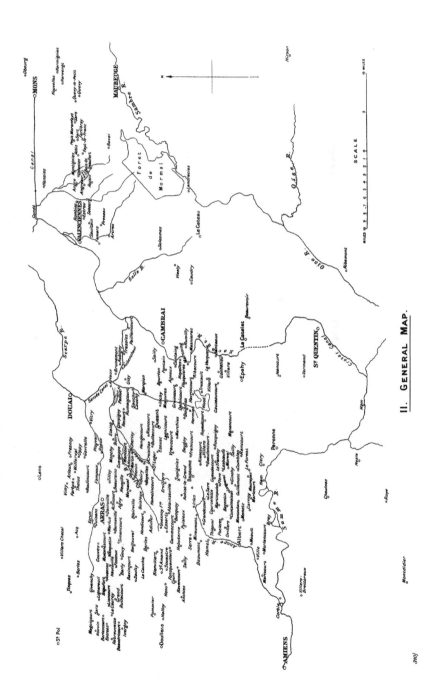

II. GENERAL MAP.

forward close behind the infantry. On the 25th August the Guards Artillery had returned to their own division, and as a consequence the 56th Divisional front had been covered by the 57th Divisional Artillery on the right and their own artillery on the left. At this time the 13th and 22nd Brigades of the Royal Garrison Artillery had been affiliated with the 56th Divisional Artillery. The enemy paid the closest attention to our artillery, bombarding the battery positions incessantly with high-explosive and gas shells.

On the 29th, early in the morning, all brigades of artillery advanced to the outskirts of Croisilles. In the previous fighting they had been 1,200 yards behind the infantry in Summit Trench. On this same day the 232nd Army Brigade R.F.A. was transferred to the 56th Division, and formed an independent group with S.O.S. lines superimposed. After the advance in the morning the 56th Divisional Artillery became the right group and the 57th the left group. And the next day the 40th Divisional Artillery replaced the 57th.

The artillery passed under the command of the 40th and then the 63rd Divisions, and eventually withdrew from the line on the 5th September, all ranks and horses having suffered severely from gas.

There was to be little rest.

It is interesting to note that the official report of the Battles Nomenclature Committee gives the Battle of Albert the dates 21st–23rd August and boundaries Road Chaulnes—Lamotte—Corbie—Warloy—Acheux —Souastre—Berles-au-Bois—Brétencourt—Héninel; and the Battle of the Scarpe 1918 the dates 26th–30th August and boundaries Noreuil (exclusive)—

St. Leger (exclusive)—Boisleux-au-Mont—Roclin-court—Bailleul—Oppy. The ground from the right of Boyelles (about the station) to Mercatel is therefore included in both battle fronts—the Battle of the Scarpe opening with the 167th Brigade attack on Croisilles Trench and Fooley Reserve—and places the 56th Division operating on the flank in each battle.

CHAPTER IX

THE ARMISTICE

WHEN once the great offensive had started there was no pause in the fighting. Divisions were relieved to reorganise. Sometimes they stood their ground, so that supplies could be brought up, and so that they might not shoot too far ahead of the base from which supplies were drawn. The turmoil of the front line was assuredly no greater than the turmoil in rear of the fighting troops. Activity, effort, unending toil, went on behind the line as well as in the line. As the troops drove the enemy in front of them, so engineers stood ready to rebuild the shattered railways and reconstruct the shell-battered roads. But the Army Service Corps could not stand still while the railways and roads were in the hands of the engineers. They had to struggle forward as best they could, and it is to their everlasting industry that the troops in the fighting areas were fed, clothed, supplied with ammunition, and, very frequently indeed, provided with water.

When the infantry of the 56th Division returned to Boyelles, the place was unrecognisable. The railway was through. Trains were in Boyelles, and lines of lorries stood, being loaded by a swarm of men. It was a cheering sight for the tired but happy division.

Meanwhile the advance continued, fiercely opposed,

but irresistible. On the right of Bullecourt the Fourth and Third Armies had, by the night of the 30th, reached a line from Cléry-sur-Somme, past the western edge of Marrières Wood to Combles, les Bœufs, Bancourt, Fremicourt, and Vraucourt. And, south of Péronne, Allied infantry had reached the left bank of the Somme from Nesle to the north. Farther south still, the French held Noyon. On the 1st September the Australians entered Péronne.

On the left of Bullecourt the First Army had advanced (we have already noted the advance of the Canadians) and were now on the high ground east of Cherisy and Hautcourt, and had captured Eterpigny. On the north of the Scarpe we had captured Plouvain. The Quéant-Drocourt line was now within assaulting distance.

This powerful line ran from the Hindenburg Line at Quéant to Drocourt, in the neighbourhood of Lens, and was attacked by the Canadian Corps and 4th Division, of the First Army, and the 52nd, 57th, and 63rd Divisions, of the Third Army, on the 2nd September. It was one of the greatest assaults of the war, and was completely successful.

As the 56th Division knew very well, the Germans had been contesting every inch of the ground. But now the enemy were in a most unfavourable position, and started to fall back on the whole of the Third Army front and on the right of the First Army. On the 3rd September the enemy was on the line of the Canal du Nord ; on the following day he commenced to withdraw from the east bank of the Somme, south of Péronne, and on the night of the 8th September was on the line Vermand, Epehy, Havrincourt, and so along the east bank of the canal.

Meanwhile the division rested, bathed, and reorganised. Divisional Headquarters were at Boisleux St. Marc, and on the 3rd September Sir Douglas Haig visited Gen. Hull and congratulated him on the good work done for the division.

On the 4th a warning order, followed by one of confirmation, was received that the division would move to the Quéant-Pronville area in readiness to relieve the 63rd Division in the line on the 5th. But at mid-day on the 5th this order was cancelled. Meanwhile the 167th and 169th Brigades had already moved to the new area, and so had a useless march back again.

On the same day Gen. Hull was informed that his division would be transferred to the XXII Corps and would relieve the 1st Division in the line, command to pass on the 9th.

Due north of Cambrai there is a very marshy tract of land. It was a feature, it will be remembered, in the scheme of attack on Cambrai in 1917. These ponds are fed by the Sensée and Cojeul Rivers, and the Canal du Nord is planned to run up, after passing Mœuvres, by Inchy-en-Artois, Marquion to a place called Palleul, where it cuts across this marsh and joins up with the Canal de l'Escaut and the Canal de la Sensée. This water covers a stretch of ground running well to the west, towards the Scarpe, and tails off near a village called Etaing. When the Canadians made their gallant and successful attack on the Quéant-Drocourt line, the left flank of the advance rested on the ponds and marshes of the Sensée, and this was the front which the 56th Division was to take over.

The line was well up to the water and extended

from a point about 500 yards north of Eterpigny, south of Etaing, south of Lecleuse, and joined with the Canadians 1,500 yards east of Récourt.

The relief of the 1st Division took place on the 6th, 7th, and 8th, command passing at 10 a.m. on the 9th September. The enemy was quiet, but the weather was bad, cold and showery.

On the 16th it was arranged that the 4th Division should relieve the 11th, on the left, and. that the 56th would extend the front held to their right, taking over from the 3rd Canadian Division. Battalions then engaged in a series of side-stepping reliefs to the right until, on the 25th, the right of the division was on the Arras-Cambrai road. On this day the only incident of note occurred when the enemy twice attempted to raid the London Scottish, and was, on each occasion, driven off with loss.

By this time preparations were complete for a further advance across the Canal du Nord on the 27th September. The crossing of the canal was to be forced by the Canadian Corps, when the 11th and 56th Divisions would relieve the left of the Canadians and attack due north along the eastern bank of the canal and towards the marshes of the Sensée. The 56th Division would be on the left—that is to say, they would advance along the canal bank. The 169th Brigade was given the task of attacking along the eastern bank, and the 168th was to clear up the western bank.

The great attack on the 27th September met with the fiercest opposition. It was obviously of vital importance to the enemy to maintain his front opposite St. Quentin and Cambrai. The advance of the British Armies was striking directly at the all-important lateral communications running through Maubeuge to Hirson and Mezières, by which alone the German forces on the Champagne front could be supplied and maintained. It had been decided that the Americans were to attack west of the Meuse in the direction of Mezières, the French west of the Argonne with the same general objectives, and the Belgians in the direction of Ghent. The British attack in the centre was where the enemy's defences were most highly organised, and if these were broken the threat directed at his vital communications would react on his defence elsewhere.

The British attack was, too, largely on the field of a former attack in 1917, but there was this difference : the Canadians had smashed through the Quéant-Drocourt system on the left. This would make the attack on the Bourlon Wood positions somewhat easier. But the whole system of defence round and about the Hindenburg Line varied in depth between 7,000 and 10,000 yards, and was a most formidable series of fortifications.

The First and Third Armies attacked with the IV, VI, XVII, and Canadian Corps, the operation of the 56th Division being on the extreme left and subsequent to the launching of the main attack. The problem on the left, which the 56th Division helped to solve, was that the northern portion of the canal was too formidable an obstacle to be crossed in the face of the enemy, and it was therefore necessary to force a passage on the narrow front about Mœuvres, and turn the line of the canal farther north by a divergent attack developed fan-wise from the point of crossing.

The morning broke wet and misty. The wind was

from the west, and carried the opening crash of the British barrage, at 5.30 a.m., well behind the German lines. But they did not need this sort of warning. For days they had watched the assembling of batteries, stores, a gigantic army behind the infantry, who were ever keeping a steady pressure on their advanced lines. Prepared as they were, however, nothing could stop the assaulting lines of Canadians. News came in to the 56th Division early that all was going well.

Enemy retaliation on the 56th Division was slight, and practically ceased by 5.40 a.m. But as the morning progressed it became apparent that the Canadians were meeting with strong opposition on the extreme left. They were timed to reach a line immediately south of Sauchy by mid-day, and the 169th Brigade was to carry on the attack from there at 2.48 p.m.

Brig.-Gen. Coke ordered the London Rifle Brigade to send a company, as soon as the barrage would permit, to establish posts on the east bank of the canal, and cover the Royal Engineers, who were to build a bridge about 1,000 yards north of the Arras-Cambrai road. A similar bridge was to be made some 300 yards south of the road. The northern bridge was to be complete by 11 a.m. and the southern one by mid-day. But the village of Marquion was on the east of the canal, and on the Arras-Cambrai road, and at 11.45 a.m. the village was still holding out, which made it impossible for the 169th Brigade to keep to the time-table and be in position for attack by 2.48 p.m. It was therefore decided to postpone the attack until 3.28 p.m.

Meanwhile, the Engineers (513th Coy. and 512th

Coy.) and Pioneers had gone forward to construct their bridges, and had found themselves opposed by hostile infantry. They, however, cleared the eastern bank and commenced to build. At mid-day it was reported that Marquion was clear, and the 2nd London Regt. started to cross about that time, followed by the Queen's Westminsters and the London Rifle Brigade. The advance of the 169th Brigade to the assembly positions completed the clearing of the ground behind the Canadians—the Queen's Westminsters capturing no less than 50 prisoners from fighting groups they met with before forming up.

At three o'clock the brigade was in position with the 2nd Londons on the right and the Queen's Westminsters on the left. The London Rifle Brigade had one company between the two branches of the River Agache clearing up the ground, and two companies in support of the 2nd Londons; the fourth company was engaged in covering the Engineers, who were making the northern bridge.

The attack swiftly reached and captured all the small copses, Kamwezi, Kiduna, and Cemetery, which yielded many prisoners, but the 2nd Londons were checked by machine-gun nests on the railway embankment south-west of Oisy. The 2nd Londons and the London Rifle Brigade attacked four times without success, and on the fifth the surviving enemy and their machine guns were captured.

The Queen's Westminsters met with the same sort of opposition. The swampy ground in the triangle where the Agache joins the canal was an effective obstacle behind which the enemy had placed machine guns, which swept the line of advance. But the

Queen's Westminsters worked cunningly round by
the banks of the Agache, and eventually surrounded
the Germans, capturing 1 officer and 22 other ranks
(21 dead bodies were counted in the post). By
7 p.m. the line of the railway south-west of Oisy was
held, and with the capture of a final machine-gun nest
defending the canal bridge east of Mill Copse, the
Queen's Westminsters reached the final objective of
the attack early in the morning of the 28th.

The task of advancing on the western bank of the
canal was given to the 168th Brigade, and was carried
out by the Kensingtons. For some way they
advanced in line with the Queen's Westminsters, but
were then held up by machine guns in Mill Copse.
The country was extremely difficult owing to water.
Mill Copse could only be approached by a narrow
pavé lane, which was flooded and much blocked by
fallen trees. At 6.30 p.m. the leading company was
about 500 yards south of the copse, and it was
decided not to attempt its capture by daylight, but
to wait for the moon. The advance was then continued at 2 a.m., and reached the final objective
without opposition.

The following day the 169th Brigade pushed on to
the marsh land east of Palleul, meeting with no
resistance, but securing a few prisoners. Altogether
this brigade captured over 400 prisoners and 34
machine guns.

The total captures of the division were : 12 officers,
501 other ranks, 45 machine guns, and 10 trench
mortars.

The 8th Middlesex (167th Brigade) then entered
the village of Palleul, after making a temporary
bridge over the blown-up causeway, and established

a bridgehead at Arleux, a village on the north of the marshes. The enemy made a small attack in this direction on the 29th, and drove in the bridgehead; they also shelled Palleul with mustard gas. But the German resistance was broken. Gouzeaucourt, Marcoing, Noyelles-sur-l'Escaut, Fontaine-Notre-Dame, and Sailly had been captured, together with over 10,000 prisoners and 200 guns. Consternation reigned at the headquarters of the Central Powers. The Austrian Peace Note made its appearance on the 15th September; Bulgaria surrendered on the 29th; and Damascus fell on the 20th. The German troops on the Western Front fought desperately and well, but they were being beaten, and frequently, on the British front, by inferior numbers.

The actual position held by the 56th Division was along the marshy ground on both banks of the canal. It included Palleul and the Bois de Quesnoy. But on the 30th the front was prolonged to the right, when the 168th Brigade took over from the 11th Division, up to a point on the eastern outskirts of Aubencheu. The enemy were very alert, and opened heavy machine-gun fire on the approach of patrols. And on the 6th they set fire to Aubenchaul. When the fires had died down, patrols established posts on the bank of the canal.

This burning business was carried on extensively. Fires, accompanied by explosions, were continually breaking out behind the enemy lines. On the 9th October the division was ordered to take over a further length of front and relieve the whole of the 11th Division, who had their right flank on the village of Fressies. The object was to free the 11th Division, so that they could follow the enemy, who

20

were evacuating the area between the Canal de
l'Escaut and the Sensée Canal, as the result of the
capture of Cambrai by the Canadian Corps. (Battle
of Cambrai 8th–9th October.)

During the day it was found that the enemy were
actually retiring on the 11th Division front, and the
56th Division was ordered to ascertain whether the
villages of Arleux, Aubigny-au-Bac, and Brunement
were still occupied. Both the 167th Brigade on the
left and the 168th on the right sent out patrols, which
were fired on and engaged by the enemy the moment
they crossed the canal. In Arleux quite an exciting
patrol action was fought, in which four of the enemy
were killed.

The relief of the 11th Division was completed by
six in the evening. Patrols found that the enemy
was still holding Fressies, and the 168th Brigade was
ordered to attack and capture that village.

The operation was carried out by the Kensingtons,
who stormed the village most successfully at 7 a.m.
on the 11th October. Two companies only attacked,
and the casualties were 1 killed and 9 wounded. On
the other hand, they captured 2 officers and 39 other
ranks. A most praiseworthy little action.

The enemy was now cleared from the south bank
of the canal along the whole of the divisional front.
The 11th Division, pressing forward, was still on the
right of the 56th, and on the left was the 1st Canadian
Division. Farther on the left was the VIII Corps,
and, on this same day, they captured Vitry-en-
Artois and drove the enemy back on Douai. On
receipt of this news the 56th Divisional Artillery was
ordered to keep the crossings of the canal from Arleux
northwards under fire, and the 167th Brigade were

instructed to push forward patrols and obtain a footing in Arleux if possible. This they were unable to do, in face of the machine-gun fire, and a most unfavourable approach.

In the evening the division passed to the command of the Canadian Corps. The 1st Canadian Division, on the left of the 56th, had been pushing forward on the north of the ponds and marshes for some days, and on the 12th they captured Arleux in the early hours of the morning. The 167th Brigade co-operated in clearing up the southern portion of the village and relieved all Canadian troops, so as to include Arleux in the divisional front.

Meanwhile, during the night 12th/13th October, the 169th Brigade relieved the 168th on the right. A clever and daring enterprise to capture Aubigny-au-Bac was then undertaken; in the words of Gen. Hull, "initiated and carried out entirely under the orders of the Brigadier-General commanding the 169th Infantry Brigade, who deserves great credit for the successful exploit."

The 169th Brigade held the right sector, with the London Rifle Brigade and the Queen's Westminsters in line, and as the front was very extended, Brig.-Gen. Coke decided to attempt the capture of the village with two companies of the 2nd London Regt.

The problem he had before him was to attack across the Canal de la Sensée, which was 70 feet wide and had no bridges. Strong German posts were stationed at two points, where bridges had formerly existed, about 1,200 yards apart, and he decided to cross between these two destroyed bridges.

Absolute silence was essential for the success of the

scheme. The 416th Field Coy. R.E. was ordered to
construct rafts to carry over an officers' patrol of the
Queen's Westminsters as soon as possible after dark,
and, after landing, the officers were to ascertain
whether a sufficiently large area, free of the enemy,
existed for the assembly of the attacking company.
If it was found that there was room for a company,
the engineers were to construct a floating footbridge
for them to cross.

The time for making reconnaissance and bringing
up material was very short. The men who were to
attack had to carry up the material. It was raining,
and the approach was over marshy ground. All the
men were wet to the skin before even the bridge was
started.

Lieut. Arnold, of the 416th Field Coy., had silence
and speed to consider, and also the amount of material
which could be brought up in any given time. He
decided he would not waste precious minutes over
rafts, but would proceed at once with the foot-bridge.
By three o'clock in the morning the bridge had been
constructed, and the patrol of Queen's Westminsters
went across. One cannot give higher praise to the
engineers than this : on landing, the patrol found
that they could not proceed more than ten paces in
any direction without being challenged by German
sentries—there appeared to be three posts in the
immediate vicinity of the bridge.

It seemed as though the enterprise must be abandoned. But as the enemy had not opened fire, the
brigadier ordered the patrol to try to rush the
posts without raising an alarm.

The bridge was, from its very nature, an unstable
affair, with no hand-rail, and, owing to the rain which

never ceased, a very slippery surface. The night, however, was very dark and the rain was perhaps a great advantage. A platoon of the 2nd Londons crossed over stealthily and quickly overpowered two Germans, which was all the enemy force they found. The remaining platoons of the attacking company now crossed over.

The assembly area was far from a good one, being intersected by two small streams, La Navie and La Petite Navie, of which nothing was known. The artillery barrage was arranged against the flank of the enemy position, creeping in a north-westerly direction. To follow it in an ordinary way was out of the question, as the country was cut up by many hedges and ditches. So platoons were directed to make their own way to various points as soon as the barrage started.

At 4.30 a.m. Capt. Sloan, who was in command of the company, had his men assembled, as well as he was able, in the blackness of early morning, when dawn is postponed by rain and thick, low-flying clouds. In silence they waited for zero, which was at 5.15 a.m.

The rest is a story of complete and absolute surprise. The attack came from the least threatened side of the enemy position. Two machine-gun teams tried to resist, but after several had been killed, the rest threw up their hands. Altogether about 160 prisoners were taken in the village.

Posts were established on the outskirts of the village, but it was not found possible to occupy the station, where the enemy was strong and thoroughly roused, and so the momentary hope that Brunemont might also be surprised, vanished.

At 6 a.m. two platoons of the supporting company came up and were used to reinforce the posts already established.

The enemy now began to show fight. Two machine guns worked up close and gave Capt. Sloan a lot of trouble. They were engaged with rifle grenades and rushed successfully. The remaining portion of the support company was moved across the canal and into the village.

As the morning advanced and the light grew better, the infantry observation posts in Quesnoy Wood reported parties of the enemy moving towards Aubigny. These were quickly dispersed, with many casualties, by the artillery, who also put to flight the crews of several trench mortars which were giving some trouble.

About ten o'clock a heavy enemy barrage was put down on the village, together with a concentration of machine-gun fire. This lasted for half an hour, and was followed by a most determined attack, with a force estimated at a battalion, from the north, and a smaller force from Brunemont. In spite of heavy losses, the Germans pressed on and slowly outflanked one post after another, greatly aided by trench mortars. The 2nd Londons were pressed back to La Petite Navie stream, where a stand was made and the enemy prevented from bebauching from the village.

Being familiar with the ground, however, the enemy made full use of the hedges, and although the four Stokes mortars of the brigade battery, which supported the 2nd Londons, did exceedingly good work, it became advisable to fall back farther to the canal bank.

A bridgehead was maintained for some time, but at 5 p.m. all troops had returned to the southern bank. They brought with them three enemy machine guns, and threw ten others into the canal.

But in the early morning, when still dark, a patrol started to cross over the bridge with the object of establishing a post on the north bank. The enemy was so close that the end of the bridge was within bombing distance. This caused the men to " bunch," with the result that the bridge broke. Cpl. McPhie and Sapper Cox, of the 416th Field Coy. R.E., jumped into the water and held the cork floats, which supported the structure, together, getting their fingers badly trodden on by the patrol. But the patrol crossed before the two gallant men let go. Cpl. McPhie, realising the serious position of the men who had crossed to the north side, set about gathering material to repair and strengthen the bridge. Daylight came on apace, but the corporal never wavered in his intention. Having assembled what he wanted, in the nature of wood, he led the way with the curt remark to his men : " We've got to make a way for the patrol—it's a death-or-glory job."

The patrol on the north bank helped him to the best of their power, but they had the slenderest hold on that side of the canal. It was daylight, and enemy snipers were concealed in every hedge. The corporal started to work with bullets cracking like whips round his ears. He was shot in the head and fell in the water. Sapper Cox tried to pull him out, but Cpl. McPhie had sufficient strength to tell him to leave go, as he himself " was done." Sapper Cox persisted in his efforts. The enemy fire increased : the corporal was hit again and again; Sapper Cox had six bullets through him. The corporal was dead, and Cox let go of his body.

Then Sapper Hawkins ran to the bank and threw a rope to Cox. This wonderful man still had the strength to hold on to it while Hawkins drew him ashore.

Cox died two days later !

McPhie was awarded the Victoria Cross.

.   .   .   .   .

In this very fine enterprise 3 officers and 87 other ranks formed the attacking party. Altogether 6 officers and 165 other ranks passed over the canal. But this small force captured 4 officers and 203 other ranks. The casualties suffered by the whole of the 2nd Londons during the day were 3 officers and 140 other ranks.

Until the 169th Brigade handed over to the 10th Canadian Infantry Brigade, on the 14th October, they held the bridgehead and patrolled the north bank of the canal. But on the 15th the Germans succeeded in rushing the bridgehead, although they failed to get any identification.

On relief the 169th Brigade moved back to Sauchy-Cauchy, and the 168th, who were in reserve, entrained for Arras. On the 15th the 167th Brigade was relieved by the 11th Canadian Brigade and moved to Rumancourt. On the 16th the whole division was in the outskirts of Arras with headquarters at Etrun (except the artillery).

All through these weeks of fighting a great strain had been imposed on the Royal Army Service Corps and the Divisional Ammunition Column. The roads were bad and fearfully congested, and the distances

10. BATTLE OF THE CANAL DU NORD.

were great and continually changing. When the great advance commenced railhead was at a place called Tincques ; on the 23rd August it changed to Gouy-en-Artois ; on the 27th to Beaumetz ; on the 31st to Boisleux-au-Mont. On the 8th September it was at Arras and on the 11th October at Quéant. Not for one moment had supplies failed to be up to time. The work of this branch of the organisation was excellent, and the work of these units of supply should always be borne in mind in every account of actions fought and big advances made.

The artillery remained in the line until the 23rd October, and then rested in the neighbourhood of Cambrai until the 31st October.

. . . . .

The whole of the Hindenburg Line passed into our possession during the early part of October, and a wide gap was driven through such systems of defence as existed behind it. The threat at the enemy's communications was now direct. There were no further prepared positions between the First, Third, and Fourth Armies and Maubeuge.

In Flanders the Second Army, the Belgian Army, and some French divisions, the whole force under the King of the Belgians, had attacked on the 28th September, and were advancing rapidly through Belgium.

Between the Second Army, the right of the Flanders force, and the First Army, the left of the main British attacking force, was the Fifth Army under Gen. Birdwood. This army was in front of the Lys salient, which was thus left between the northern and southern attacks with the perilous prospect of

being cut off. On the 2nd October the enemy started
an extensive withdrawal on the Fifth Army front.
Meanwhile the Belgian coast was cleared. Ostend
fell on the 17th October, and a few days later the
left flank of the Allied forces rested on the Dutch
frontier. The Fourth, Third, and First Armies still
pushed on towards Maubeuge, and by the end of the
month the Forêt de Mormal had been reached.

The enemy was thoroughly beaten in the field.
Though he blew up the railways and roads as he fled,
he was becoming embarrassed by his own rearguards
pressing on his heels as they were driven precipitately
before the Allied infantry ; and the position of his
armies revealed certain and overwhelming disaster.

.   .   .   .   .

On the 27th October Austria sued for peace.
On the 28th the Italians crossed the Piave.
On the 29th the Serbians reached the Danube.
On the 30th October Turkey was granted an
armistice.

The Central Powers lay gasping on the ground.

.   .   .   .   .

The 56th Division meanwhile led a quiet life,
training and resting round Etrun and Arras. Organisation of battalions was overhauled in accordance
with a pamphlet numbered O.B./1919 and issued by
the General Staff. It was designed to deal with the
decreasing strength of battalions, but, as it supposed
a greater number of men than were in many cases
available, it was troublesome.

The outstanding points were that platoons would
now be composed of two rifle and two Lewis-gun

sections ; that a platoon, so long as it contained two sections of three men each, was not to be amalgamated with any other platoon ; and that not more than six men and one non-commissioned officer to each section should be taken into action.

" The fighting efficiency of the section," says the pamphlet, " is of primary importance, and every endeavour must be made to strengthen the sections, if necessary, by the recall of employed men and men at courses, or even by withdrawing men from the administrative portions of battalion and company headquarters, which must in an emergency be temporarily reduced. After the requirements of the fighting portion for reconstruction have been met (50 other ranks), if the battalion is up to its full establishment, a balance of 208 men will remain for the administrative portion (90) and for reinforcements. This balance will include men undergoing courses of instruction, men on leave and in rest camps, men sick but not evacuated, and men on army, corps, divisional, or brigade employ. These latter must be reduced to the lowest figure possible, and will in no case exceed 30 men per battalion."

The order against the amalgamation of platoons applied also to sections, but was not invariably carried out by company commanders. It had become a universal practice to detail six men and one non-commissioned officer to each post. With double sentries this gave each man one hour on and two hours off—anything less than these numbers threw a big strain on the men ; and so long as the company commander had sufficient men for an adequate number of sentry posts, he made them up of that number.

The details of a battalion as arranged by this pamphlet are interesting :

	Fighting position.		Administrative position.		Reconstruction (not for reinforcement.		Supplies for reinforcement.		Total.	
	Off.	O.R.	Off.	O.R.	Off.	O.R.	Off.	O.R.	Off.	O.R.
Battalion Headquarters . .	5	70	2	66	2	8	—	27	9	171
4 Company Headquarters . .	4	74	—	24	4	10	—	—	8	110
Attached from platoons . .	—	2	—	—	—	—	—	—		
16 Platoon Headquarters . .	12	38	—	4	4	8	—	—		
Section commanders acting as platoon sergeants . .	—	10	—	—	—	—	—	—	16	64
N.C.O.s for reconstruction . .	—	—	—	—	—	8	—	—		
64 sections . .	—	448	—	—	—	16	—	91	—	555
Total .	1	642	2	90	10	50	—	118	33	900

It will be seen that 732 other ranks were required to fill the fighting and administrative minimum. The ration strength of battalions from the 1st August and on the first of each month to the date of the armistice was :

	August.		September.		October.		November.	
	Off.	O.R.	O.	O.R.	Off.	O.R.	Off.	O.R.
7th Middlesex .	39	950	35	678	43	865	43	863
8th ,, . .	40	948	38	787	41	864	39	813
1st Londons . .	40	931	27	613	40	657	40	712
4th ,, . .	42	898	32	710	37	705	38	721
13th ,, . .	38	925	24	685	41	691	46	649
14th ,, . .	43	925	30	548	31	622	34	705
2nd ,, . .	37	891	27	599	31	717	35	601
5th ,, . .	35	989	25	669	32	603	33	631
16th ,, . .	42	959	27	577	31	560	29	612

But these figures must be read with a reservation. In spite of all efforts, men always disappeared. No battalion or company commander ever had the men who were on the ration strength. Guards, fatigue parties, sudden demands for men from higher commands, dozens of reasons could be given for the evaporation of strength. Probably two-thirds only of these men were really available for fighting. In those days a general when inspecting companies had no difficulty in finding fault if he wished to do so.

During the rest Gen. Hull discussed the subjects of organisation and training with the officers of each of his brigades.

But in the evening officers and men could be cheered by " Bow Bells," which were to be heard at the theatre in Arras and the cinema at Haut Avesnes.

On the 31st the division moved into XXII Corps Reserve with headquarters at Basseville, and on the 1st November was ordered to relieve the 49th Division during the night 2nd/3rd.

On the 31st October the line immediately south of Valenciennes rested on the 4th Canadian Division, from the Canal de l'Escaut to the outskirts of the village of Famars, the 49th Division, on the high ground west of the River Rondelle, the 4th Division, astride the river and to the east of Artres, and then the 61st Division.

The 4th and 49th Divisions of the XXII Corps attacked on the 2nd November with the object of capturing the two villages of Preseau and Saultain, but only the first was taken, and the 49th Division held the Preseau-Valenciennes road.

The 56th Division was now plunged into real open fighting. Their objectives were no longer trench lines, but tactical features, such as spurs, rivers, woods, and villages. An examination of Gen. Hull's operation orders reveals the new nature of the fighting. The 169th Brigade was given the right and the 168th the left. The objective of the XXII Corps, which was attacking with the 11th Division on the right and the 56th on the left, was given as the " general line of the Aunelle River left bank." The Canadian Corps would cover the left flank of the 56th Division by the capture of Estreux. The division would be covered by six brigades of field artillery.

On attaining the high ground on the left of the Aunelle River, patrols would be pushed out, " since if there is any sign of enemy retreat the G.O.C. intends to push on mounted troops to secure the crossing of the Petite Aunelle River and will order the leading brigades to support them." The mounted troops referred to were two squadrons of Australian Light Horse.

Each of the attacking brigades had at the disposal of the Brigadier a battery of field artillery, also two sections (8 guns) of the M.G. Battalion.

As the front to be covered by the 56th Division was very extensive, the 146th Brigade, of the 49th Division, remained in line on the left, and was to advance until squeezed out by the converging advance of the 56th and Canadian Divisions.

On the night 2nd/3rd November the 169th and 168th Brigades relieved the right of the 49th Division on the Preseux-Valenciennes road without incident. Soon after 8 a.m. on the 3rd, patrols reported that the enemy had retired. The two brigades advanced and occupied Saultain, which was full of civilians, before mid-day. The cavalry and a company of

New Zealand Cyclists were then ordered to push forward and secure the crossings of the River Aunelle. The line of the left bank of the river was reached at 6 p.m., where machine-gun fire was encountered. The brigades remained on that line for the night.

The advance was resumed at dawn on the 4th, when the Queen's Westminster Rifles crossed the River Aunelle and captured the village of Sebourg ; there was some half-hearted opposition from about thirty of the enemy who were rounded up, but when they attempted to advance east of the village they came under intense machine-gun and rifle fire from the high ground. Attempt to turn the enemy flank met with no success, and as there was no artillery barrage arranged, Brig.-Gen. Coke contented himself by holding the road to the east of the village.

The 168th Brigade on the left were also held up by the enemy on the high ground. The 4th London Regt. led the attack and took the hamlet of Sebourt-quiaux (slightly north of Sebourg), only to find that they were not only faced with the enemy on the high ground to the east, but that heavy enfilade fire was being directed on them from the village of Rombies, on the western bank of the river, and on the Canadian Corps front. The 4th London Regt. took up a position to the east of Sebourtquiaux and astride the river, and so remained for the night. (Battle of the Sambre.)

This attack had been made without artillery preparation, but the position of the artillery is well described by Brig.-Gen. Elkington in a short report drawn up at the end of the operations. He says the barrage put down on the 1st November had been a very heavy one, and that the enemy never again waited for the full weight of the artillery to get into action.

" The problem for the artillery then became a matter of dealing with machine-gun nests, isolated guns, and small parties of the enemy who were delaying our advance and enabling the main body of the enemy to retire. The enemy blew up bridges and roads, whenever possible, to delay the advance of our guns. In these circumstances the following points were emphasised :

(1) The benefit of allotting artillery to each battalion commander in the front line. The battery commander, by remaining with the battalion commander and keeping good communication with his battery, could bring fire to bear at very short time on targets as they were encountered. In practice it was generally found that a full battery was too large a unit, and that four guns, or even a section, was of more use.

(2) When more than one artillery brigade was available for an infantry brigade, the necessity of keeping them écheloned in depth and maintaining all but one brigade on wheels. If resistance was encountered, the brigade, or brigades, on wheels in rear could be moved up to reinforce the artillery in the line to put down a barrage for an attack, or, if no resistance was encountered, a brigade in rear could advance through the artillery in action, which in turn could get on wheels as the advancing brigade came into action. This procedure enabled brigades to get occasional days' rests and obviated the danger of getting roads choked with advancing artillery.

(3) The necessity of impressing on infantry commanders that though at the commencement of an attack it is possible to support them with a great weight of artillery, it is not possible to push this mass of artillery forward when movement becomes rapid,

and that if they push forward rapidly, they are better served by a small mobile allotment of guns."

The rapidity of the advance was little short of marvellous, for one must remember that it did not depend on the ability of the infantry to march forward, but on the engineers behind them, who were reconstructing the roads and railways for the supply services. Lieut.-Col. Sutton, who was controlling the Quartermasters' Branch of the division, has a note in his diary :

" The enemy has done his demolition work most effectively. Craters are blown at road junctions and render roads impassable, especially in villages, where the rim of the crater comes in many cases up to the walls of the houses. Culverts are blown on main roads, and a particularly effective blockage is caused in one place by blowing a bridge across a road and stream, so that all the material fell across the road and in the river."

This demolition was the great feature of the advance. The infantry could always go across country, but guns and lorries were not always able to use these short cuts. The weather was unfavourable, as it rained practically every day. When craters were encountered, the leading vehicles could perhaps get round, by going off the road, but they had the effect of churning up the soft ground so that the crater soon became surrounded by an impassable bog. The engineers and 5th Cheshires worked like Trojans to fill up these terrific pits, or make a firm surface round them.

At this date railhead was at Aubigny-au-Bac, the scene of that great exploit of the 2nd London Regt.

21

And when one takes into account dates and distances, the achievement of those who were working behind the infantry must be ranked as one of the finest in the war. One cannot get a picture of the advance by considering the mere width of an army front. The infantry were the spearhead, the supplies the shaft, but the hand that grasped the whole weapon and drove it forward was that of the engineer, the pioneer, the man of the Labour Battalion. The effort of the army then must be considered in depth, from the scout to the base.

Under these circumstances communication between units became a matter of vital importance. The ordinary administrative routine of trench warfare required little modification, up to the point of the break through the Hindenburg Line—after that it became impossible. Brigade Headquarters were responsible for the distribution of rations, engineer material, ordnance, mails, and billeting. In the orders for advance the General Staff informed the Brigadier-General what units, or portion of divisional troops, including Divisional Artillery, would be under his tactical control, and these units, irrespective of their arm of the service, constituted the Brigade Group. The supply of ammunition, on the other hand, was worked by arms of the service and not by Brigade Groups. The channel of supply being the ordinary one—from the Divisional Ammunition Column to batteries, or Infantry Brigade Reserve, or Machine-gun Battalion Reserve.

The administrative instructions for the division point out,:

" The outstanding difficulty in all the administrative

services will be that of intercommunication between the troops and the échelons in rear which supply them. The system of interchange of orderlies between the forward and rear échelons has been found unsatisfactory, as if the two échelons both move at the same time, all touch is lost. Prior to the advance, therefore, the administrative staff of each brigade group will fix a ' meeting-point ' or ' rear report centre ' as far forward as possible on the probable line of advance. This point will serve as a rendezvous for all maintenance service. . . . The principle of intercommunication by means of a fixed report centre will also be adopted by Divisional Artillery and the Machine Gun Battalion for the purpose of ammunition supply."

This arrangement does not seem to have worked well for the artillery, as we find Brig.-Gen. Elkington reporting :

" For a time communication by orderly between units became the only feasible plan. Owing to the rapid movement these orderlies had the utmost difficulty in locating units. In this Divisional Artillery the system of using village churches as report centres was successfully tried, but, owing to the cessation of hostilities, the trial was not as exhaustive as could be wished. Notices showing change of location were simply stuck on the church doors or railings, and orderlies were instructed to at once proceed to the church for information on entering a village."

This modification of the original scheme would seem to be a useful one.

In spite of all these difficulties, the 56th Division was advancing. On the 5th November a barrage was arranged to cover troops attacking the high

ground to the east of the River Aunelle, as a preliminary to subsequent advance. The London Rifle
Brigade led the attack of the 169th Brigade at
5.30 a.m., and by 7.30 a.m. had captured the village
of Angreau. Here they were checked by the enemy,
who occupied the woods on both banks of the
Honnelle River. On their right the 11th Division
captured the village of Roisin, but on their left the
168th Brigade had not made such good progress.

Attacking, with the London Scottish on the right
and the Kensingtons on the left, the 168th Brigade
were much hampered by flank fire from Angre and the
ground to their left, which was still held by the enemy.
The situation was somewhat eased by the capture
of Rombies, by the 4th Canadian Division, and at
3 p.m. the artillery put down a rolling barrage,
behind which the Kensingtons, and the London
Scottish on their right, advanced to the outskirts of
Angre. The position for the night was on the high
ground west of the River Grande Honnelle.

The enemy had determined to defend the crossing
of the river, and had an excellent position on the
eastern bank, where they held the Bois de Beaufort
in strength. The advance was to be resumed at
5.30 a.m., but just before that hour the German
artillery put down a heavy barrage of gas-shells.
Undaunted, the 2nd Londons on the right and the
London Rifle Brigade on the left of the 169th Brigade
attacked in gas-masks and crossed the river. The
168th Brigade, attacking with the London Scottish
and Kensingtons in line, met at first with slight
resistance, but as soon as the river was reached they
were faced with a heavy barrage of artillery and
machine-gun fire. In spite of very accurate fire, they

succeeded in crossing the river to the north and south of Angre. The position in front of them was of considerable natural strength, but was turned by a clever move of the London Scottish from the south, which established them firmly on the east bank. The Kensingtons advanced to the high ground immediately east of the village of Angre, and here met a heavy counter-attack which drove them back to the west bank.

Meanwhile the 169th Brigade was engaged in heavy fighting. Only the northern portion of the Bois de Beaufort was included in the attack, and the enemy were found to be strongly situated on ground which dominated the western bank of the river. The attack was delivered with spirit, and the enemy driven back. The 2nd Londons had the wood in front of them, and the London Rifle Brigade shot ahead on the left, outside the wood. The enemy rallied and counter-attacked the forward troops, while at the same time a force of Germans debouched from the, wood on the right flank of the Rifle Brigade men, who were driven back to the west of the river. Some of the 2nd Londons were involved in this successful enemy counter-attack, but a party of forty— a large party in those days—held on to the position they had reached in the Bois de Beaufort until late in the afternoon, when, discovering what had happened on the left, and being almost entirely surrounded, they retired fighting to the western bank of the river.

The right brigade, therefore, remained on the west bank. The casualties had been heavy, amounting to 394.

The London Scottish had retained their hold of the east bank, and later in the afternoon the Ken-

singtons again succeeded in crossing the river, and
definitely established themselves to the east and in
touch with the London Scottish. The casualties of
the 168th Brigade during these operations were 207.
The prisoners captured by them were 111. The
prisoners captured by the 169th Brigade were 43.

The general destruction of roads, combined with
the vile weather, now began to cause anxiety. Horses
were used as much as possible—a horse can drag a
cart through places which would be impossible for a
motor lorry—and civilian wagons were pressed into
service, being used in conjunction with spare army
horses. This was all the more necessary as the
administrative branch of the division had the
additional responsibility of feeding civilians.

All the villages captured or occupied by the troops
were filled with civilians. So great was their emotion
on their release that they pressed whatever they had
in the nature of food and drink on the troops. The
coffee-pot of the French or Belgian housewife was
replenished with reckless disregard for " to-morrow."
And then as the country was regained, so the villagers
were cut off from the source which had provided
them with their limited supplies. With Germans in
retreat on one side and roads blown up on the other,
they were more isolated than they had ever been.
On the 6th November the 56th Division was rationing
16,000 civilians, and most of this work was being done
by the transport of the 168th and 169th Brigades.

The battle on the right of the division had progressed with almost unfailing success. The 11th
Division on their immediate right had met with the
same check on the River Honnelle, but farther south
the Army had forced their way through the great

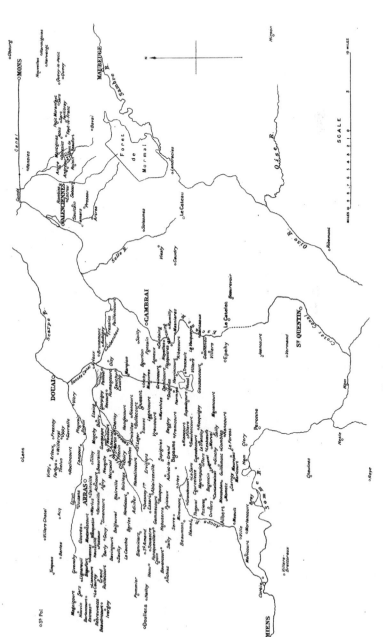

II. GENERAL MAP.

Forest of Mormal, and troops were well to the east of it. The German rearguards were only able, on especially favourable positions, to check the advance of a few divisions ; on the whole the rearguards were being thrown back on the main retreating force. The roads were packed with enemy troops and transport, and the real modern cavalry, the low-flying aeroplanes, swooped down on them, with bomb and machine gun spreading panic and causing the utmost confusion.

During the night 6th/7th November the 63rd Division was put into line on the front of the 168th Brigade, and the 169th was relieved by the 167th Brigade. The 56th Division was then on a single brigade front, with the 11th Division on the right and the 63rd on the left.

At dawn on the 7th patrols found that the enemy was still in front of them, and at 9 a.m. the brigade attacked with the 8th Middlesex on the right and the 7th Middlesex on the left. They swept on through the northern part of the wood, and by 10.30 a.m. the 7th Middlesex entered the village of Onnezies. The Petite Honnelles River was crossed, and the village of Montignies taken in the afternoon. But after the Bavai-Hensies Road was crossed, opposition stiffened, and both artillery and machine-gun fire became severe. A line of outposts held the east of the road for the night.

Explosions and fires, which were continually observed at night behind the enemy lines, were more numerous on the night of 7th/8th, and when the advance was continued at 8 a.m., the two Middlesex battalions occupied the villages of Athis and Fayt-le-Franc with practically no opposition. By nightfall outposts were covering Petit Moranfayt, Trieu Jean Sart, Ferlibray, and Richon.

The road situation was worse than ever. Railhead was at Aubigny-au-Bac, and supply lorries were unable to proceed any farther than the Honnelle River owing to the destruction of the bridges. Rain fell all the time, and cross-country tracts were impassable. All traffic was thrown on the main roads, which, to the west of the river, were now in such a state that all supplies were late. Arrangements were made for aeroplanes to drop food to the advance troops, but fortunately this was found unnecessary.

The enemy was now in full retreat on the whole of the British front. To the south the Guards Division entered Maubeuge, and to the north the Canadians were approaching Mons. The 56th Division marched forward through the villages of Coron, Rieu-de-Bury, Quevy-le-Grand, and Quevy-le-Petit, and by the evening were on the line of the Mons-Maubeuge road behind a line of outposts held by the 1st London Regt.

On the 10th November the 1st Londons continued the advance, preceded by cavalry. No serious opposition was encountered until the infantry had passed through Harvengt, when heavy machine-gun fire from both flanks held up the advance. A squadron of 16th Lancers attempted to get through, but failed. The infantry then attacked and cleared the ground, entered Harmignies, and held a line to the east.

Orders were received that night that the 63rd Division would carry on the advance as advance guard to the XXII Corps, and the necessary reliefs were carried out. The artillery of the 56th Division remained in action, and were just two miles south of the spot where Brig.-Gen. Elkington was in action on the 23rd August 1914, at the battle of Mons. Gen. Hull, on the other hand, had actually held an outpost line before Harmignies with his battalion on the 22nd August, and had moved to the north to hold a line from Obourg to Mons on the 23rd. After the battle the celebrated retreat had taken him through the village of Nouvelles due west of Harmignies, and so through Quevy to Bavai, Caudray, Ham, and so on. What memories this second visit to Harmignies must have brought back to him! From retreat to victory—from a battalion to a division— Harmignies 1914, Harmignies 1918.

Brig.-Gen. Coke also fought as company commander in August 1914 within five miles of the spot where he finished in 1918.

At 7.30 a.m. on the 11th November the XXII Corps issued orders that hostilities would cease at 11 a.m. on that day, and that all troops would stand fast.

Just before 11 o'clock all batteries opened fire. Each gunner was determined to be the last man to fire a shot at the Germans. And then, in the midst of the rolling thunder of rapid fire, teams straining every nerve to throw the last shell into the breach of their gun before the " cease fire " sounded, 11 o'clock struck, the first blast of the bugles pierced the air, and with the last note silence reigned.

" There was no cheering or excitement amongst the men," writes Brig.-Gen. Elkington. " They seemed too tired, and no one seemed able to realise that it was all over."

G. Q.G.A.
le 12 *Novembre,* 1918.

Officiers, Sous-officiers, Soldats des Armées Alliées,

Après avoir résolument arrêté l'enemi, vous l'avez pendant des mois, avec une foi et une énergie inlassables, attaqué sans répit.

Vous avez gagné le plus grande bataille de l'Histoire et sauvé la cause la plus sacrée : la Liberté du Monde.

Soyez Fiers !

D'une gloire immortelle vous avez paré vos drapeaux.

La Postérité vous garde sa reconnaissance.

Le Maréchal de France,
Commandant en Chef les Armées Alliées,
F. Foch.

The division did not move to the Rhine, but remained in this area, with headquarters at Harvengt. They mended the roads, they drilled, and they had sports. Towards the end of January 1919 demobilisation had reached a point which rendered the division ineffective as a fighting unit.

The London Scottish were moved to the 9th Division, in Germany, on the 16th January, and the 7th Middlesex to the 41st Division on the 25th February. On the 14th March Gen. Hull gave up command of the division.

But their work was done. Officially the 56th Division returned the first cadre on the 14th May, the last on the 10th June, 1919.

The total casualties of this division were :

Officers . . .		1,470
Other ranks . .		33,339
Total . .		34,809

APPENDIX

GENERAL OFFICERS COMMANDING

Rank.	Name.	Remarks.
Major-Gen. .	O. P. A. Hull, O.B.	Joined Royal Scots Fusilier Regt. 16/11/87. Middlesex Regt. 24/2/12. Brigade Major 11th Brigade 10/11/03 to 9/11/07. General Staff Officer, 2nd Grade, Staff College, 10/3/15 to 4/2/16. Commanded the 4th Bn. Middlesex Regt. at the battle of Mons. Brigadier commanding 10th Brigade 17/11/14. After his illness he commanded the 16th Division from the 23/2/18 until he resumed command of the 56th.
Major-Gen. .	W. Douglas Smith, O.B.	Royal Scots Fusilier Regt. Commanded 56th Division 24/7/17 to 9/8/17.
T/Major-Gen.	F. A. Dudgeon, O.B.	The South Lancashire Regt.

G.S.O.s 1

Rank.	Name.	Remarks.
Lieut-Col. .	J. E. S. Brind, O.M.G., D.S.O.	From Royal Artillery. Joined the 56th Division 6/2/16 and left 31/10/16.
Lieut.-Col. .	A. Bryant, D.S.O.	The Gloucestershire Regt. With the 56th Division 30/10/16 to 23/12/16.
Lieut.-Col. .	G. de la P. [B. Pakenham, O.M.G., D.S.O.	The Border Regt.

G.S.O.s2

Rank.	Name.	From.	To.	Regt.
Major .	A. E. G. Bayley, D.S.O.	5/2/16	1/10/16	Oxford and Bucks Light Infantry.
Major .	E. A. Beck, D.S.O.	28/9/16	17/2/17	The Royal Scots Fusiliers.
Major .	W. T. Brooks, M.O.	15/2/17	3/9/17	The D.O.L.I.
Major .	F. B. Hurndall, M.O.	4/9/17	9/7/18	The 20th Hussars.
Captain, T/Major	T. O. M. Buchan, M.O.	9/7/18	Demob.	The Queen's R.W. Surrey Regt.

G.S.O.s3

Rank.	Name.	From.	To.	Regt.
Captain .	T. W. Bullock	5/2/16	20/4/16	The Dorsetshire Regt.
Captain .	M. G. N. Stopford, M.O.	10/6/16	5/12/16	The Rifle Brigade.
Captain .	J. D. Crosthwaite, M.O.	7/12/16	7/7/17	The 1st London Regt.
Captain .	E. L. Rabone, M.O.	11/7/17	11/11/17	The Worcestershire Regt.
Captain .	O. W. Haydon, M.O.	11/11/17	11/5/18	The Middlesex Regt.
Captain .	T. L. O. Heald	14/5/18	4/2/19	The 5th Cheshire Regt.

A.A. & Q.M.G.s

Rank.	Name.	From.	To.	Regt.
Bt. Lieut.-Col.	H. W. Grubb, D.S.O.	5/2/16	4/12/17	The Border Regt.
Bt. Major T/Lieut.-Col.	W. M. Sutton, D.S.O., M.O.	4/12/17	Demob.	Somerset Light Infantry.

D.A.A.G.s

Rank.	Name.	From.	To.	Regt.
Captain .	W. M. Sutton, D.S.O., M.O.	5/2/16	4/12/17	Somerset Light Infantry.
Major .	A. O. Dundas	4/12/17	10/12/18	The Middlesex Regt.
Major .	A. Scott, D.S.O., M.O.	10/12/18	Demob.	A. & S. Highlanders.

D.A.Q.M.G.s

Rank.	Name.	From.	To.	Regt.
Major .	F. J. Lemon, D.S.O.	5/2/16	22/4/18	The West Yorkshire Regt.
Captain T/Major	T. F. Chipp, M.C.	23/4/18	2/2/19	The Middlesex Regt.

A.D.C.s

*Lieut. .	H. C. B. Way	10/2/16	Demob.	The 2nd London Regt.
2/Lieut. .	C. Burn-Callender	4/3/16	2/2/17	The Montgomeryshire Yeomanry.
Lieut. .	H. M. Woodhouse	10/4/17	30/4/17	The Notts Yeomanry.
2/Lieut. .	C. Y. Jones	26/5/17	23/7/17	The 13th London Regt.
Captain .	G. A. Greig	24/7/17	9/8/17	The Royal Scots Fusiliers.
Lieut. .	R. W. Broatch	10/8/17	Demob.	The 14th London Regt.

* NOTE.—Lieut. H. C. B. Way was away from 4/2/18 to 4/4/18 as A.D.C. to G.O.C. 16th (Irish) Division.

56TH DIVISIONAL ARTILLERY HEADQUARTERS
C.R.A.

Col., T/Brig.-Gen.	R. J. G. Elkington, C.M.G., D.S.O.	6/2/16	Demob.

BRIGADE MAJORS

Major .	W. J. McLay	6/2/16	4/6/16
Major .	J. A. Don	28/6/16	27/9/16
Major .	D. Thomson	277//16	21/1/18
Major .	H. D. Gale, M.C.	21/1/18	Demob.

STAFF CAPTAINS

Captain .	B. Macmin	6/2/16	22/1/17
Captain .	N. C. Lockhart	22/1/17	12/2/19
Captain .	J. D. Hendley Smith	12/2/19	Demob.

ARTILLERY

1/1st London Brigade R.F.A. (280th Brigade R.F.A.)

Commanded by :
Lieut.-Col. L. A. C. Southam until March 1918.
Lieut.-Col. Batt.

1916

April 16th. 93rd Battery joined and designated D/280th Brigade R.F.A.

May 6th. Designated 280th Brigade R.F.A.

„ 17th. B.A.C. posted to 56th D.A.C.

„ 28th. 93rd Battery ceased to be D/280th Bde. R.F.A., and was transferred to 283rd Bde. R.F.A., and the original 1/11th London Howitzer Battery became D/280.

Nov. 5th. Reorganised into four 6-gun batteries ; " A," 93rd, and " C," 18-pounders ; " D," howitzers.
93rd Battery and one section " R " Battery transferred from 283rd Bde. R.F.A. The original " B " Battery split up : one section to " A," and one section to " C."
" D " Battery only had 4 howitzers until 25/1/17, when one section 500th Howitzer Battery joined from 282nd Bde. R.F.A.

1/2nd London Brigade R.F.A. (281st Brigade R.F.A.)

Commanded by Lieut.-Col. C. C. Macdowell.

1916.

April 15th. 109th Battery joined.

May 12th. Designated 281st Bde. R.F.A.

„ 16th. B.A.C. posted to 56th D.A.C.

„ 28th. 10th (Howitzer) Battery transferred from 283rd Bde. R.F.A. and designated D/281st Battery R.F.A.
109th Battery transferred to 283rd Bde. R.F.A.

Nov. 5th. Reorganised into four 6-gun batteries.
" A," 109th, and " C " 18-pounders ; " D " howitzers.
109th Battery and one section " R " Battery transferred from 283rd Bde. R.F.A.
The original " C " Battery split up. One section to " A " Battery. One section to " B " Battery.
" D " Battery only had 4 howitzers till 23/1/17, when one section 500th Howitzer Battery joined from 282nd Bde. R.F.A.

1/3rd London Brigade R.F.A. (282nd Army Brigade R.F.A.)

Commanded by Lieut.-Col. A. F. Prechtel.

1916

April 16th. 109th Battery R.F.A. joined and designated " R " Battery. (Duplicate—see 281st Bde.)

May 6th. Designated 282nd London Bde. R.F.A.

„ 7th, 8th, and 9th Batteries designated " A," " B," and " C " Batteries.

May 17th. B.A.O. posted to 56th D.A.O.
„ 28th. " R " Battery posted to 283rd Bde. R.F.A.
            B/167th (Howitzer) Battery joined and designated D/282nd Battery R.F.A.
            Reorganised into four 6-gun batteries. " A," " B," and
Nov. 5th. " O," 18-pounders; " D " howitzers.
to 500th How. Bty. R.F.A. joined 4/12/16.
1917 One Section to D/280th Bde. R.F.A. One section to D/281st Bde. R.F.A.
Jan. 25th. B/126th Battery R.F.A. joined and designated A/282nd Battery.
            The original "A" Battery having been split up, one section each to " B " and " O."
            One section D/126th Battery R.F.A. joined 25/1/17.
Jan. 20th. Designated 282nd Army Bde. R.F.A.
„ 25th. One Section 56th D.A.O. joined and designated 282nd B.A.O.

1/4TH (LONDON) HOWITZER BRIGADE R.F.A. (283RD BRIGADE R.F.A.)

Commanded by Lieut.-Col. Wainwright.
1915
Nov. 19th. Half of the B.A.O. left for Salonica to join 10th Division.
1916
May 6th. Designated 283rd (Howitzer) Bde. R.F.A.
„ 17th. B.A.O. transferred to 56th D.A.O.
„ 28th. " R " Battery joined from 282nd Bde. R.F.A.
            109th Battery joined from 281st Bde. R.F.A.
            93rd Battery joined from 280th Bde. R.F.A. (all 18-pounders).
            10th (Howitzer) Battery transferred to 281st Bde. R.F.A.
            11th (Howitzer) Battery transferred to 280th Bde. R.F.A.
Nov. 5th. 93rd Battery and one section " R " Battery transferred to 280th Bde. R.F.A.
            109th Battery and one section " R " Battery transferred to 281st Bde. R.F.A.
            Brigade ceased to exist, but the new organisation was not completed until January 1917.

56TH DIVISIONAL AMMUNITION COLUMN

Commanded by Lieut.-Col. E. W. Griffith.
1916
May 17th. The B.A.C.s of 280th, 281st, 282nd, and 283rd Bdes. R.F.A. absorbed. Then consisted of " A " Echelon (H.Q., Nos. 1, 2, and 3 sections) and " B " Echelon.
1917
Jan. 25th. One Section (No. 2) became the 282nd Army Bde. Ammunition Column.
Sept. " B " Echelon reorganised as S.A.A. Section.
            Reorganised as H.Q., No. 1, 2, and S.A.A. Sections.

TRENCH MORTARS

1916

March 8th. "X" "Y," and "Z" 2-inch Medium Batteries formed. Four mortars each.

May. "V" Heavy Battery formed.

1917

Sept./Oct. Medium Batteries handed in 2-inch mortars and were armed with four 6-inch mortars each.

1918

Feb. 13th. Medium batteries reorganised into two batteries ("X" and "Y") of 6-inch mortars each.
Heavy battery taken over by Corps.

1919

Feb. 6th. Reduced to Cadre. Surplus personnel to Brigades and D.A.C.

ROYAL ENGINEERS
(See O.R.E.)
416th (Edinburgh) Field Coy. R.E.
512th (London) Field Coy. R.E.
513th (London) Field Coy. R.E.
56th Divisional Signal Coy.

PIONEER BATTALION
1/5th Bn. Cheshire Regt. (Earl of Chester's).
Commanded by:
Lieut.-Col. J. E. C. Groves, C.M.G., T.D., 14/2/15 to 21/2/18.
Major (T/Lieut.-Col.) W. A. V. Churton, D.S.O., T.D., 21/2/18 to end.

MACHINE GUN CORPS
56th Bn. Machine Gun Corps formed on 1/3/18.
(See Divisional M.G. Officers.)

R.A.S.C. UNITS
213th Coy. R.A.S.C.
214th „ „
215th „ „
216th „ „
Divisional Train commanded by:
Lieut.-Col. A. G. Galloway, D.S.O., to Sept. 1917.
Lieut.-Col. E. P. Blencowe, D.S.O., to May 1918.

R.A.M.C.
2/1st London Field Ambulance.
2/2nd „ „ „
2/3rd „ „ „

1/1st London Mobile Vet. Section.

247th Divisional Employment Coy. formed in May 1917.

A.D.sM.S.

Rank.	Name.	From.	To.	Regt.
Colonel .	E. G. Browne, C.B., A.M.S.	Feb. '16	Feb. '17	R.A.M.C.
Colonel .	G. A. Moore, C.M.G., D.S.O.	Feb. '17	Feb. '18	R.A.M.C.
Colonel .	E. O. Montgomery-Smith, D.S.O., A.M.S. (T.F.)	Feb. '18	Demob.	R.A.M.C.

D.A.D.sM.S.

Major .	L. M. Purser, D.S.O.	Feb. '16	Sept.'16	R.A.M.C.
Captain .	D. Jobson Scott, M.C.	Sept. '16	Feb. '18	R.A.M.C. (T.F.)
Major .	W. T. Hare, M.C.	Feb. '18	Demob.	R.A.M.C.

D.A.D.sV.S.

Major .	F. Hibbard	5/2/16	30/9/16	
Major .	W. Ascott, O.B.E.	1/10/16	Demob.	

D.A.D.sO.S.

Major .	J. Bishop	6/2/16	10/3/16	
Captain .	P. S. Tibbs	11/3/16	23/7/16	
Lieut. .	V. C. Ward	24/7/16	22/11/16	
Captain .	W. D. Harbinson	23/11/16	27/5/17	
Major .	J. W. Burbidge	28/5/17	Demob.	

C.sR.E.

Lieut.-Col.	H. W. Gordon, D.S.O.	6/2/16	Oct. '17	Royal Engineers.
Lieut.-Col.	E. N. Mozeley, D.S.O.	Oct. '17	Demob.	Royal Engineers.

DIVISIONAL MACHINE GUN OFFICERS

Major .	E. C. S. Jervis	Jan. '17	May '17	R. of O. 6th D.G.s
Major .	Roberts	May '17	Aug. '17	M.G.C.
Lieut.-Col.	E. C. S. Jervis	Aug. '17	Mar. '18	R. of O. 6th D.G.s.

167TH INFANTRY BRIGADE

BRIGADE COMMANDERS

Major (T/Brig.-Gen.)	F. H. Burnell-Nugent, D.S.O.	6/2/16	26/7/16	The Rifle Brigade.
Bt. Col. (T/Brig.-Gen.)	G. Freeth, C.M.G., D.S.O.	27/7/16	Demob.	Lancashire Fusiliers.

22

BRIGADE MAJORS

Rank.	Name.	From.	To.	Regt.
Bt. Major	G. Blewitt, D.S.O., M.C.	6/2/16	5/12/16	The Oxford and Bucks Light Infantry.
Captain .	M. Stopford, M.C.	5/12/16	25/3/18	The Rifle Brigade.
Captain .	C. E. Clouting	25/3/18	8/4/18	General List.
Captain .	C.W.Haydon, M.C.	25/4/18	Demob.	Middlesex Regt.

STAFF CAPTAINS

Captain .	O. H. Tidbury, M.C.	6/2/16	27/12/16	Middlesex Regt.
Captain .	T. F. Chipp, M.C.	27/12/16	23/4/18	Middlesex Regt.
Captain .	H. F. Prynn, M.C.	23/4/18	Demob.	13th London Regt. (Kensingtons).

168TH INFANTRY BRIGADE

BRIGADE COMMANDERS

Bt. Col. (T/Brig.-Gen.)	G. G. Loch, C.M.G., D.S.O.	5/2/16	Demob.	The Royal Scots.

BRIGADE MAJORS

Major .	P. Neame, V.C., D.S.O.	5/2/16	28/11/16	Royal Engineers.
Captain .	J. L. Willcocks, M.C.	28/11/16	3/7/18	The Black Watch.
Captain .	A. R. Abercrombie, D.S.O., M.C.	3/7/18	11/8/18	The Queen's Regt.
Captain .	R. C. Boyle	11/8/18	Demob.	West Somerset Yeomanry.

STAFF CAPTAINS

Major .	L. L. Wheatley, D.S.O.	5/2/16	7/3/16	A. & S. Highlanders.
Captain .	R. E. Otter, M.C.	7/4/16	20/4/17	London Rifle Brigade.
Captain .	J. C. Andrews, M.C.	26/4/17	7/3/18	Q.V.R.
Captain .	E. F. Coke, M.C.	7/3/18	Demob.	8th Canadian Infantry Battn.

169TH INFANTRY BRIGADE

BRIGADE COMMANDER

Brig.-Gen. (Bt. Col.)	E. S. D. E. Coke, C.M.G., D.S.O.	5/2/6	Demob.	K.O.S.B.

BRIGADE MAJORS

Rank.	Name.	From.	To.	Regt.
Captain .	L. A. Newnham	5/2/16	27/5/17	Middlesex Regt.
Captain .	W. Carden Roe, M.C.	27/5/17	24/3/18	Royal Irish Fusiliers.
Captain .	Chute	28/3/18	9/4/18	
Captain .	T. G. McCarthy	1/4/18	Demob.	2nd London Regt.

STAFF CAPTAINS

Captain .	E. R. Broadbent, M.C.	5/2/16	5/11/17	8th Hussars.
Captain .	F. Bishop	5/11/17	Demob.	1/5th Bn. Cheshire Regt.

INFANTRY BATTALIONS, 167TH BRIGADE

Battalion.	Commanding Officers.	Remarks.
1/7th Middlesex Regt.	Lieut.-Col. E. J. King, C.M.G., to 2/11/16, and from 4/2/17 to 14/5/17 Lieut-.Col. E. D. Jackson, D.S.O., from 2/11/16 to 4/2/17 A/Lieut.-Col. F. W. D. Bendall, from 15/5/17 to 17/8/17 A/Lieut.-Col. P. C. Kay, D.S.O., M.C., from 31/8/17 to 16/2/18. A/Lieut.-Col. M. Beevor, from 16/2/18.	The Battalion went to Gibraltar Sept. 1914. France to the 23rd Brigade, 8th Division, in Feb. 1915.
1/8th Middlesex Regt.	T/Lieut.-Col. E. D. W. Gregory, from 31/5/15 to Sept. 1915. Lieut.-Col. P. L. Inkpen, D.S.O., from Sept. 1915 to Oct. 1916, and Mar. 1917 to Aug. 1917. Lieut.-Col. F. D. W. Bendall, from Oct. 1916 to Mar. 1917. Lieut.-Col. C. H. Pank, C.M.G., D.S.O., Sept. 1917 to Mar. 1919. Lieut.-Col. M. B. Beevor, from Mar. 1918.	This Battalion went to Gibraltar in Sept. 1914. To the 88th Brigade, 3rd Division, in France during March 1915, and in April joined the 23rd Brigade, when it was amalgamated with the 1/7th Middlesex. Resumed independence on joining 56th Division.

Battalion.	Commanding Officers.	Remarks.
1/1st London Regt.(Royal Fusiliers)	Lieut.-Col. E. G. Mercer, C.M.G., T.D., from Jan. 1916 to June 1916. Lieut.-Col. D. V. Smith, D.S.O., V.D., from June 1916 to Oct. 1916 ; from Feb. 1917 to April 1917. Lieut.-Col. Kennard, from Oct. 1916 to Nov. 1916. Lieut.-Col. W. R. Glover, C.M.G., D.S.O., T.D., from Nov. 1916 to Mar. 1917 ; from April 1917.	Went to Malta in Sept. 1914. France Jan. 1915, joining the 25th Brigade, 8th Division, in March. To the 56th Division April 1916.
1/3rd London Regt.(Royal Fusiliers)	A/Lieut.-Col. A. E. Maitland, D.S.O., M.C., until Mar. 1917. Lieut.-Col. F. D. Samuel, D.S.O., T.D.	To Malta in Sept. 1914. France Jan. 1915 with G.H.Q. troops. Garhwal Brigade, Meerut Division, on 1/3/15. To 142nd Brigade, 47th Division, 1/1/16. Left 56th Division and joined 173rd Brigade, 58th Division, 2/2/18.

INFANTRY BATTALIONS, 168TH BRIGADE

Battalion.	Commanding Officers.	Remarks.
1/4th London Regt.(Royal Fusiliers)	Major W. J. Clark, until 23/3/16. Lieut.-Col. L. L. Wheatley, 8/4/16 to 11/10/16. Lieut.-Col. H. J. Duncan Teape, until 17/3/17. Lieut.-Col. A. E. Maitland, 17/3/17 to 20/4/17. Lieut.-Col. H. Campbell, 20/4/17 to 14/8/17. Lieut.-Col. A. F. Marchment, 14/8/17 to the end.	To Malta Sept. 1914. France Jan. 1915 as G.H.Q. troops. Joined Ferozepore Brigade, Lahore Division, on 1/3/15. To 140th Brigade, 47th Division, 1/1/16.

Battalion.	Commanding Officers.	Remarks.
1/12th London Regt. (Rangers)	Colonel A. D. Bayliffe, C.M.G., T.D.	To France 4/1/15 as G.H.Q. troops. Joined 84th Brigade, 28th Division, on 4/2/15. Brigade moved to 5th Division 19/2/15 and rejoined 28th Division 6/4/15. To G.H.Q. on 19/5/15. Left 56th Division 2/2/18, and joined 58th Division.
1/13th London Regt. (Kensingtons)	Lieut.-Col. H. Stafford until 28/6/16. A/Lieut.-Col. W. W. Young until 27/10/16. A/Lieut.-Col. J. C. R. King, until 13/6/17. A/Lieut.-Col. J. E. J. Higgins, M.C., until 5/8/17. A/Lieut.-Col. V. Flower, D.S.O., until 16/8/17. A/Lieut.-Col. R. E. F. Shaw, M.C., until 23/8/18. A/Lieut.-Col. M. A. Prismall, M.C., until 28/9/18. A/Lieut.-Col. J. Forbes Robertson, V.C., D.S.O., M.C., until 13/10/18. A/Lieut.-Col. F. S. B. Johnson, D.S.O.	To France on 13/11/14, and joined the 24th Brigade, 8th Division. To G.H.Q. on 19/5/15.
1/14th London Regt. (London Scottish)	Lieut.-Col. B. C. Green, C.M.G., T.D., until 2/8/16. Lieut.-Col. J. H. Lindsay, D.S.O., until 6/10/16. Lieut.-Col. James Paterson, M.C., until 6/3/17. Lieut.-Col. E. D. Jackson, D.S.O.	To France on lines of communication Sept. 1914. Joined 1st Brigade, 1st Division, on 7/11/14.

INFANTRY BATTALIONS, 169TH BRIGADE

Battalion.	Commanding Officers.	Remarks.
1/2nd London Regt. (Royal Fusiliers)	Lieut.-Col. James Attenborough, C.M.G., T.D., until Nov. 1916, and Feb. 1917 to April 1917. A/Lieut.-Col. J. P. Kellett, D.S.O., M.C., Nov. 1916 to Feb. 1917 ; May 1917 to Aug. 1917 ; Jan. 1918 to Oct. 1918 ; Jan. 1919. A/Lieut.-Col. R. E. F. Sneath, M.C., Aug. 1917 to Dec. 1917. A/Lieut.-Col.S.H.Stevens, M.C., Nov. 1918 to Jan. 1919.	To Malta Sept. 1914. France Jan. 1915 as G.H.Q. troops. Joined 17th Brigade, 6th Division, 1/3/15. The Brigade was transferred to 24th Division 1/1/16.
1/5th London Regt. (London Rifle Brigade)	Lieut.-Col. Bates, D.S.O., until 13/8/16. Lieut.-Col. R. H. Husey, D.S.O., 13/8/16 to 4/5/18. Lieut.-Col. C. D. Burnell, D.S.O., 4/5/18 to end. Also for one month, 22/4/17 to 20/5/17, during Lieut.-Col. Husey's absence. The latter C.O. was also absent from 26/3/17 to 22/4/17, and 12/8/17 to 3/12/17, when Major F. H. Wallis took command.	To France and joined 11th Brigade, 4th Division, 24/11/14. To G.H.Q. 19/5/15. To 8th Brigade, 3rd Division, 1/1/16.
1/9th London Regt. (Queen Victoria's Rifles)	Colonel J. W. F. Dickens, D.S.O., V.D. Lieut.-Col. F. B. Follett, D.S.O., M.C. Lieut.-Col. M. Beevor, D.S.O. Lieut.-Col. E. G. H. Towell	To France 24/11/14 and joined 13th Brigade, 5th Division. Brigade moved to 28th Division on 19/2/15, and back to 5th Division on 6/4/15. Left 56th Division and joined 58th Division 2/2/18.
1/16th London Regt. (Queen's Westminster Rifles)	Lieut.-Col. R. Shoolbred, C.M.G., T.D. Lieut.-Col. E. P. Harding, O.B.E., M.C. Lieut.-Col. P. M. Glazier, D.S.O. Lieut.-Col. S. R. Savill, D.S.O., M.C.	To France and joined 18th Brigade, 6th Division, 11/11/14.

INDEX

327

.

1333712R0

Printed in Great Britain by
Amazon.co.uk, Ltd.,
Marston Gate.